J O U R N A L S

Kurt Cobain filled dozens of notebooks with lyrics, drawings, and writings about his plans for Nirvana and his thoughts about fame, the state of music, and the people who bought and sold him and his music. More than twenty of these notebooks survived his many moves and travels, and have been locked in a safe since his death. His journals reveal an artist who loved music, who knew the history of rock, and who was determined to define his place in that history. Here is a mesmerizing, incomparable portrait of the most influential musician of his time.

Booze 30
Records/watch 50
food 20
ticket 100

200
100

KURT
COBAIN
JOURNALS

PENGUIN BOOKS

PENGUIN

Published by the Penguin Group
Penguin Books Ltd, 80 Strand, London WC2R ORL, England
Penguin Putnam Inc., 375 Hudson Street, New York, New York 10014, USA
Penguin Books Australia Ltd, 250 Camberwell Road, Camberwell, Victoria 3124, Australia
Penguin Books Canada Ltd, 10 Alcorn Avenue, Toronto, Ontario, Canada M4V 3B2
Penguin Books India (P) Ltd, 11 Community Centre, Panchsheel Park, New Delhi - 110 017, India
Penguin Books (NZ) Ltd, Cnr Rosedale and Airborne Roads, Albany, Auckland, New Zealand
Penguin Books (South Africa) (Pty) Ltd, 24 Sturdee Avenue, Rosebank 2196, South Africa

Penguin Books Ltd, Registered Offices: 80 Strand, London WC2R ORL, England

www.penguin.com

Published in the United States of America by Penguin Putnam 2002
Published in Great Britain by Viking 2002
Published in Penguin Books 2003
3

The moral right of the author has been asserted

Printed in China by South China Printing Co. Ltd

A CIP catalogue record for this book is available from the British Library

ISBN 978-0-141-01146-2

Don't read my diary when I'm gone

OK, I'm going to work now, when you wake up this morning, please read my diary. Look through my things, and figure me out.

JOURNALS

Dale, Count howmany times i use the word "FUCK".

Hello, it is me saying,

"everything is basically Raining, dull, and OK!"
fuck we were this close ⟶

to coming down to see the melvins play on the 29th but as History Repeats itself, shelli being the overbearing dominator of chris decided to not want to go at the last minute. and so gas money being split only two ways between Tracy and I would be too fucking expensive. are you coming to seattle Someday to play? YOU MOTHERFUCKERS BETTER STILL PLAY VILE VERMILLION VACANCY! or at least put it on the Next LP. any label interest yet? Alchemy seems to be in pretty sorry shape from what i hear. ever RAT Sub Core Dave Portnow? Dehumanizers? the reason i say this is because they must be hard up, for they signed DangerMouse! JESUSFUCKINGCHRISTALMighty

So within the last couple of months our demo has been Pirated, Recorded, and discussed between all the seattle SCENE luminaries. and the Dude Johnathan Poneman (Remember the guy who called me when you were over the last day?) MR Big-money inheritance, Right hand man of Bruce Pavitt. and also SUB POP Records financial investor, GOT us a show at the vogue on a Sub Pop sunday. Big Deal. but i guess hype and Regularly being played on KCMU probably helped, the amount of people who came to Judge us. NOT be at a BAR, get drunk, watch some bands & have fun. But just watch the ShowCase event. 1 hr. ~~We~~ ~~fel~~ there was a representative from every Seattle band there just watching ⟶

OH OUR LAST AND FINAL NAME IS **NIRVANA**

ooH eeerie mystical DOOM

We felt like they should have had score cards. And so after the set Bruce excitedly shakes our hands and says "wow Good job let's do a Record". [redacted] then flashes of cameras go off and this girl from BACKLASH says "Gee can we do an interview?" yeah sure why not. And then people say Good job you guys are great and now were expected to be total socialites. meeting people, introducing, etc.. **FUCK IM IN High SCHOOL AGAIN!** **I want to move back to Aberdeen.** NAH olympia is just as boring and I can proudly say ive only been in the Smithfield about 5 times this year. And so because of this Zoo-event weve at least gotten a contract for a 3 song single to be put out by end of August and an EP out in Sept or Oct. Were gonna try to talk them into an LP. NOW Johnathan is our manager, he gets us shows remotely in Oregon & Vancouver. He's paying for all recording & distribution costs & now we dont have to have outrageous phone bills. Dave is working out OK. Sometime next year sub pop is gonna have a caravan of 2 or 3 Seattle Bands go on tour. yeah well see. [redacted] Thru your past experiences Do you think it would be wise to demant receipts for recording, pressing costs?

enough about Records OH except this one night last month, Chris and I dropped acid and we were watching the late show (rip off of Johnny Carson) And Paul Revere and the Raiders were on there, they were so fucking stupid! Dancing around with moustaches, trying to act comical and Goofy. It really pissed us off and I asked Chris Do you have any paul Revere & the Raiders albums?

YeAH punctuAtioN, I WAS stoned Alot
when I WAS learning that stuff.

He sAid yeAh, so I looked thru his Big collection And found the Revere Records And Busted them. And he got mAd, then he lAughed And I searched three the rest of the Row And found EAgles, cArpenters, Yes, Joni Mitchell And sAid with frustration, "WhAt in the FUCK do you own these for? And so throughout the Rest of the night we busted About 250 shitty Chris Novoselic Records. not only did we clear more SPACE in the living room, chris declared that he feels Cleansed And revitalized.

I don't hang Around with RyAn or the other Aberdonians but when im in town I'll get your Sound GArden Record for you. We still make movies, the lAst one we did WAS in TAcomA At NeVER NEVER lAND. it's A surrealistic fantasy story book Place for Kids, And we mAde shelli weAr A mAsk of Cher's head cut out of An Album and dance Around by big mushrooms And butt fuck the wolf bending over to blow down the three little Pigs house. other stArs included Rick Derringer and John lennons Penis. NO comment on MAtts band MUDHONEY just to be on the sAfe side. SPEAKing of SAfe Sides my Girlfriend TrAcy now hAs A BrAnd New "88" ToyotA Turcell, A microwAve, food processor, Blender, And An espresso mAchine, I don't have A job until next month thru TYSS youth service in A printshop PArt time. I AM A TotAlly pAmpered spoiled BUM
NEXt letter will be less boring About Record deAls And more stupid drivel
GoodBye DAle write SOON.

The First song on the Dumb is no longer PlAyed
it is sickening And Dumb. Destroy it it is evil.
in the likes of whitesNAKE And Bon Jovi

The late 1980's.

This is a subliminal example of a society that has sucked & fucked itself into a Rehashing. value of greed.

Subliminal in a sense that there are no p-Rock collages of michael J fox Reaming Bruce Springsteen clinging to a missile.

instead you get the overall feeling that you paid way too much for literally Nothing stimulating

you may say Yeah but other than the xerox the layout has a sense of professionalism

Bull. the Jokes on you so kill yourself

No amount of effort can save you from oblivion.

power vomit magazine

No Address
No Editor
No Ad Rates

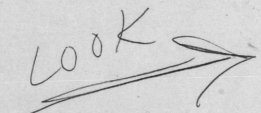

LOOK

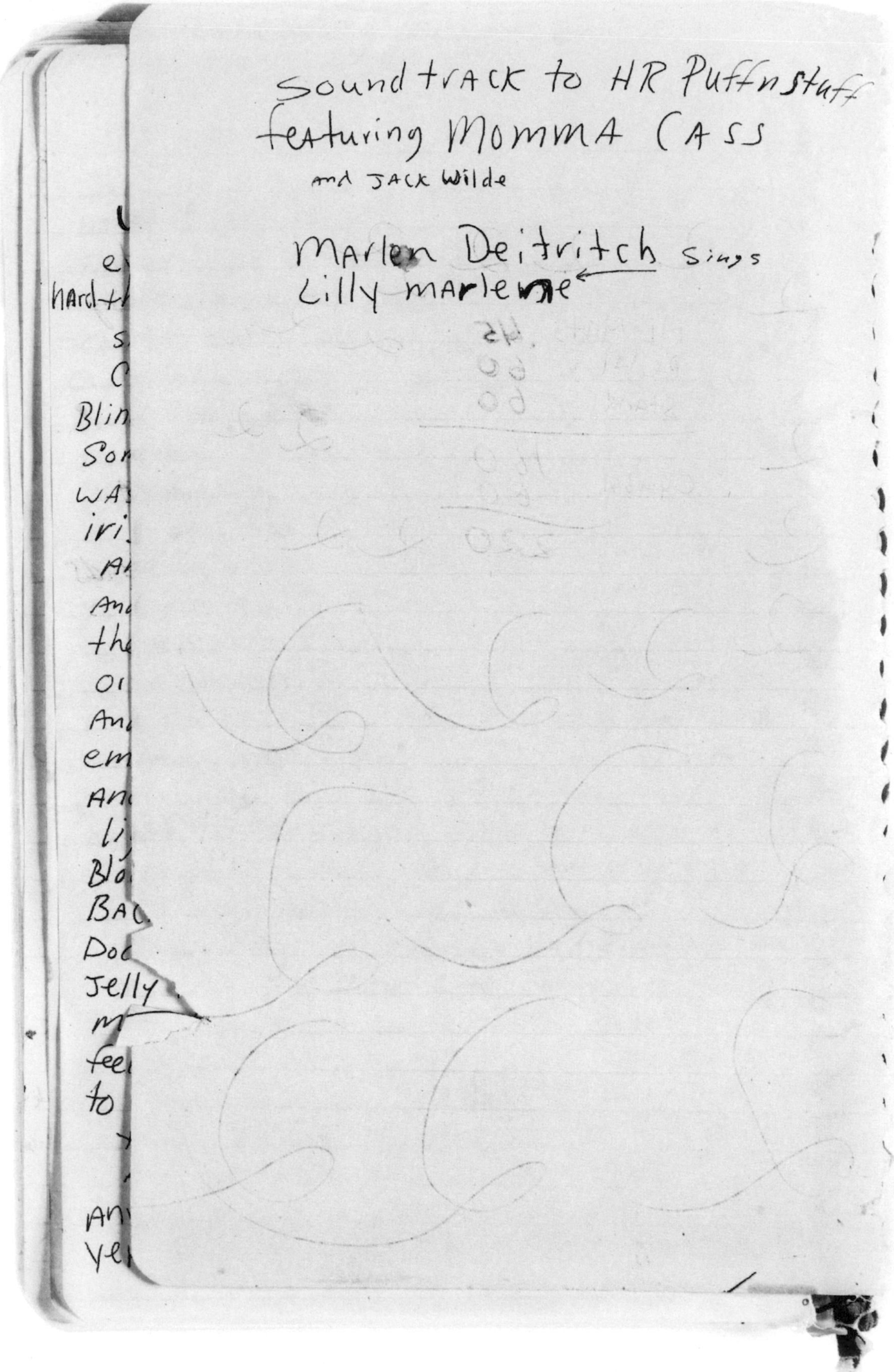
Soundtrack to HR Puffnstuff
featuring MOMMA CASS
and JACK Wilde

Marlen Deitritch sings
Lilly marlene

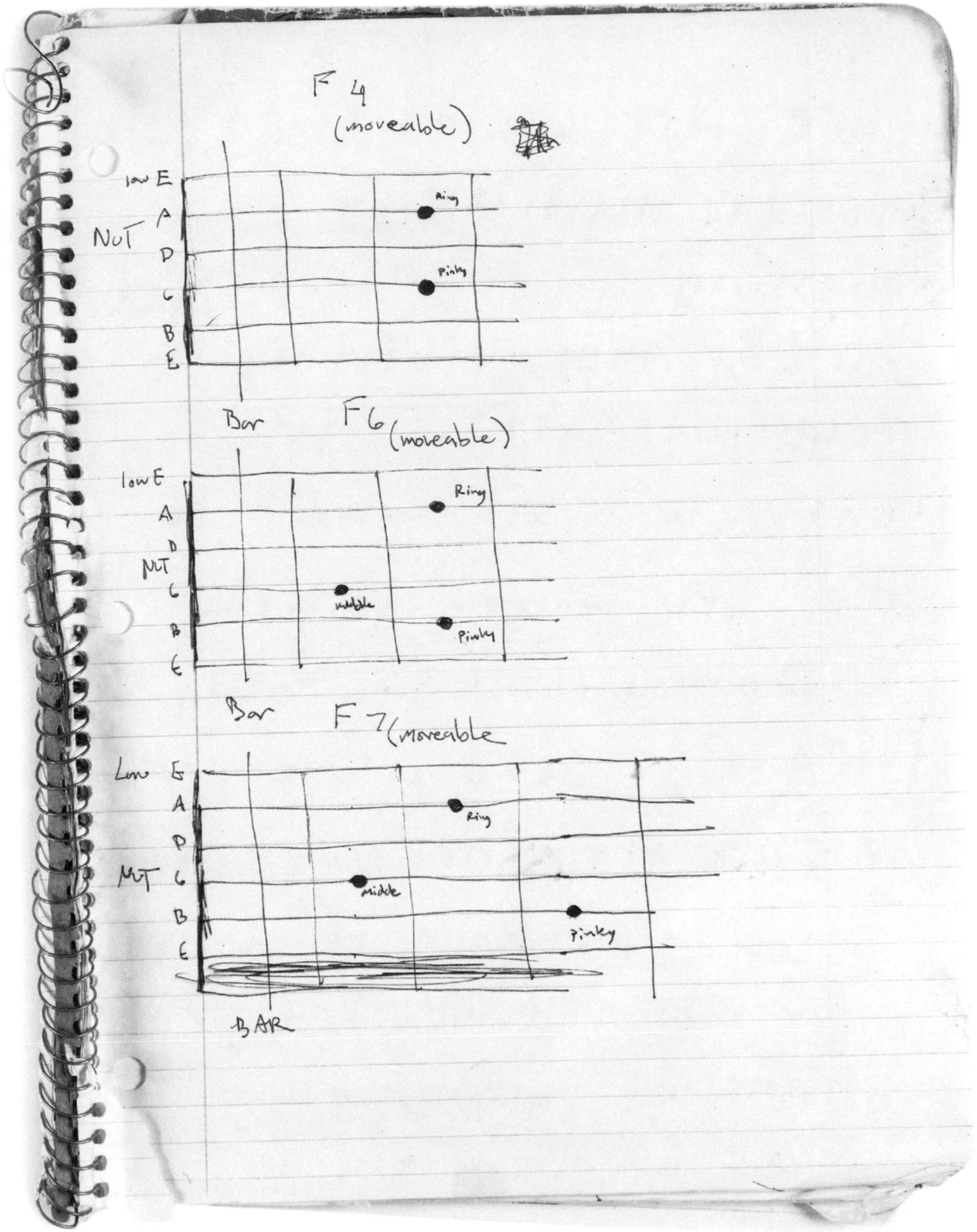
F 4
(moveable)
low E
A
NUT
D
G
B
E
Ring
Pinky
Bar
F 6 (moveable)
low E
A
D
NUT
G
B
E
Ring
middle
Pinky
Bar
F 7 (moveable
Low E
A
D
NUT G
B
E
Ring
middle
Pinky
BAR

We Are willing to pay for the majority of pressing of 1000 copies of our LP, And All of the recording costs. We basically just want to be on your label.

Do you think you could Please! send us a reply of Fuck off, or NOT interested so we don't have to waste more money sending more tapes? thanks. ~~N pear~~

NiRVANA.

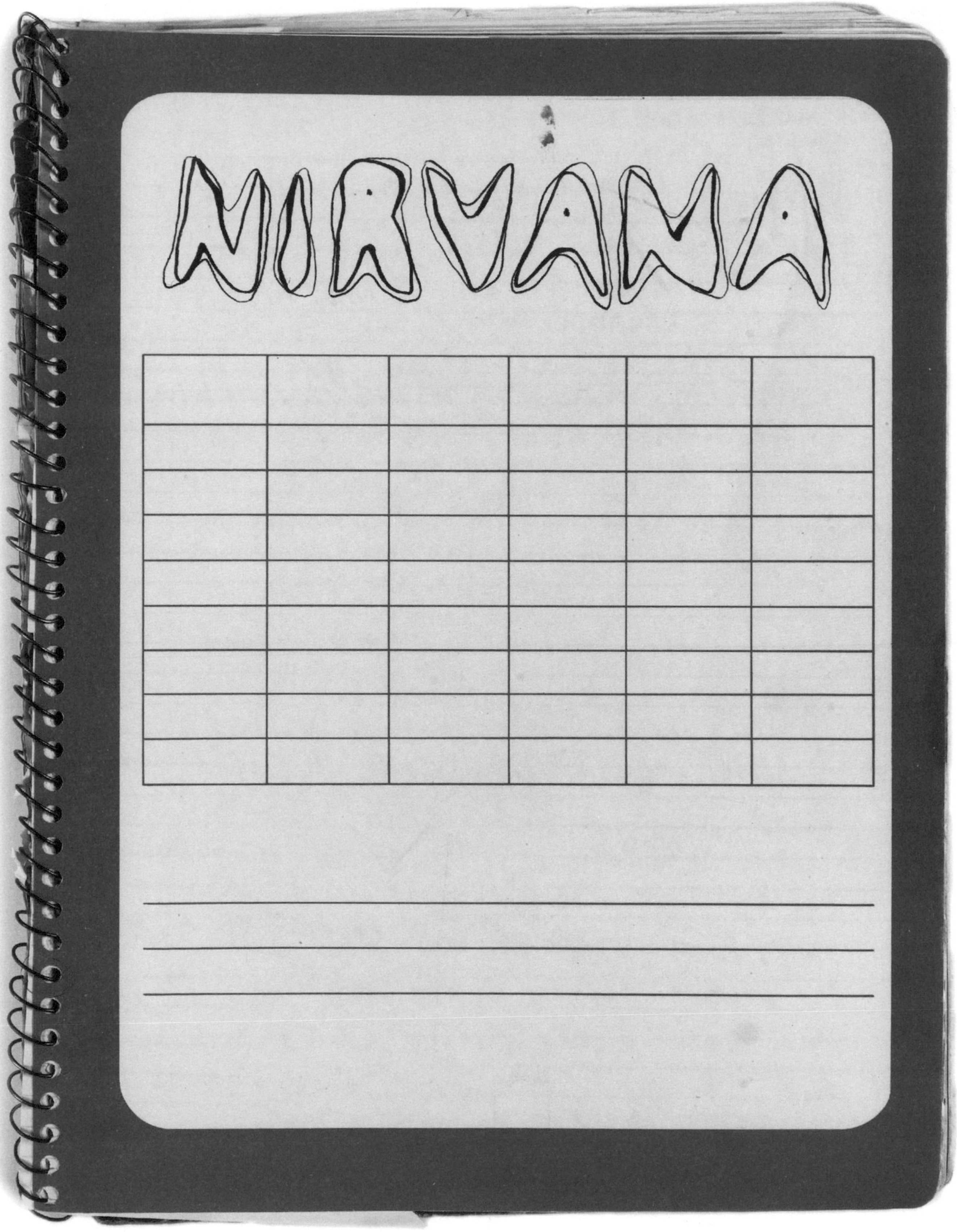
NIRVANA

they werent AS gross AS G.G. Allin but they Held their own to say the least. The tension grew because of A Delay with the P.A. which Helped the Release of tension when the first couple of notes of School were struck. people instantly Rocked back And forth with ~~w~~ eyes closed & beers clenched then spilt. 5 Roadie friends had to lock arms behind the P.A. CAbinets & Rock in back & forth in A wave pushing the crowd in hopes that the band wouldn't get hurt. But they did.

Kurdt the vocalist & Guitarist screamed his last scream to the 2nd song then BAM the crowd smacked the mike into his mouth. Blood oozed from his lip but they instantly started floyd the barber After wiping Kurts face. Chris the bass player Accidentally hit Kurt in the eye with His BASS Headstock it wasn't too ~~deep~~ At first until Kurt Rammed his Head into the wall next to him in protest. it opened more. So Kurdt took his guitar & hit Chris straight in the mouth causing A big cut lip. By now they were pretty Bloody, Chris looking worse And with only one wound. they were obviously becoming dizzy and were in PAin. but proceeded to play the set quite out of tune

Mead
If you read
you'll judge
the Spiral
notebook
11 In. x 8½ In. 70 Sheets
College Ruled
06540
The Mead Corporation, Dayton, Ohio 45463

20 School Zones
25 Streetof Cities & towns
50 County ROADS
55 HighwAy

PASS within 200 ft of Approaching car

Follow 20ft for Every 10. mph

TURN SIGNAL 100 Ft before

Lane use signals

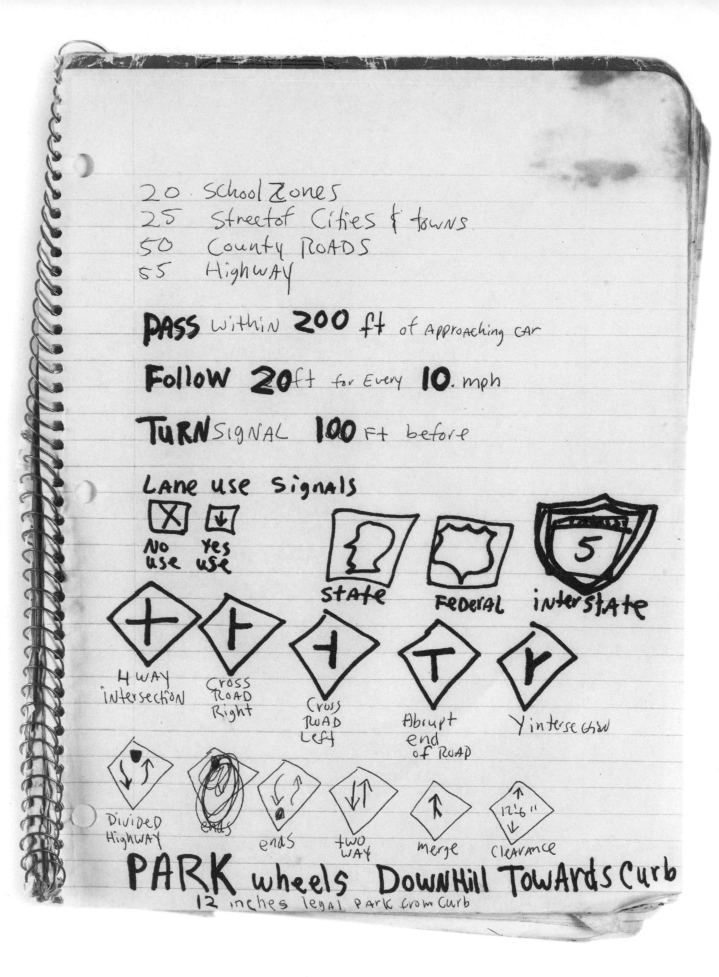

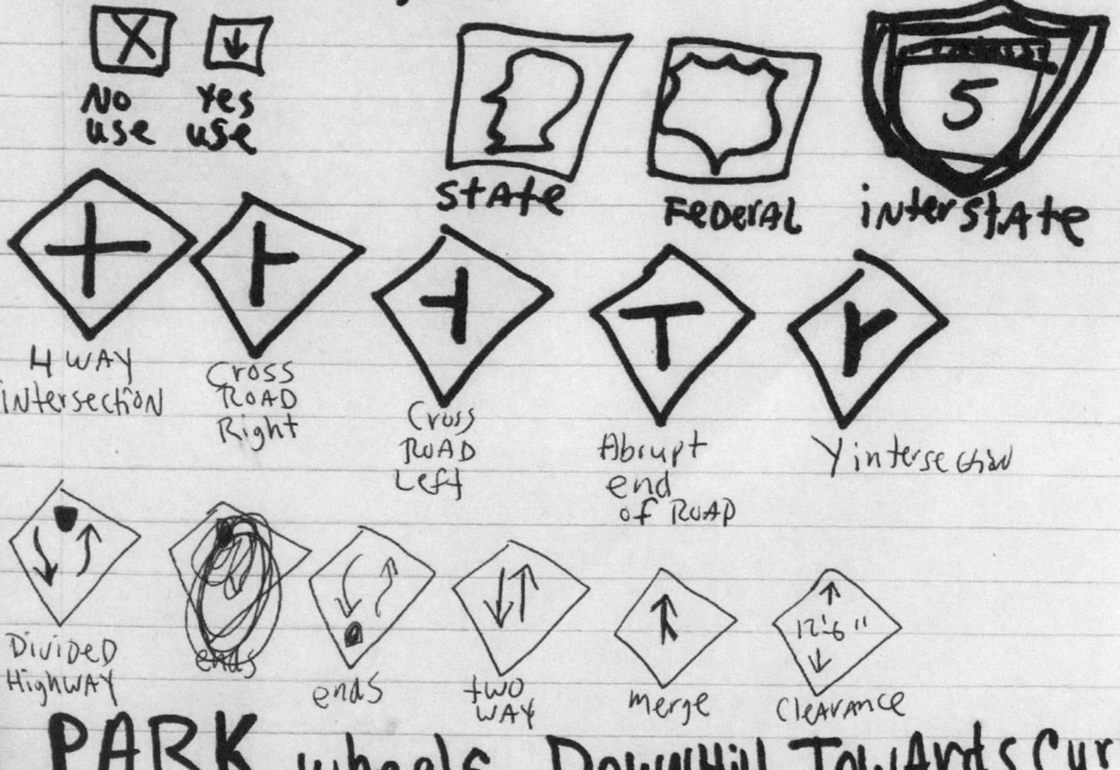

PARK wheels DownHill TowArds Curb
12 inches legal Park from Curb

speed

Highway 55
Cities Towns 25
School zones 20
County Roads 50

PASS within 200 ft of Approaching car

Turn Signal ON 100 ft before turning

Follow 20 ft for every 10 m.p.h.

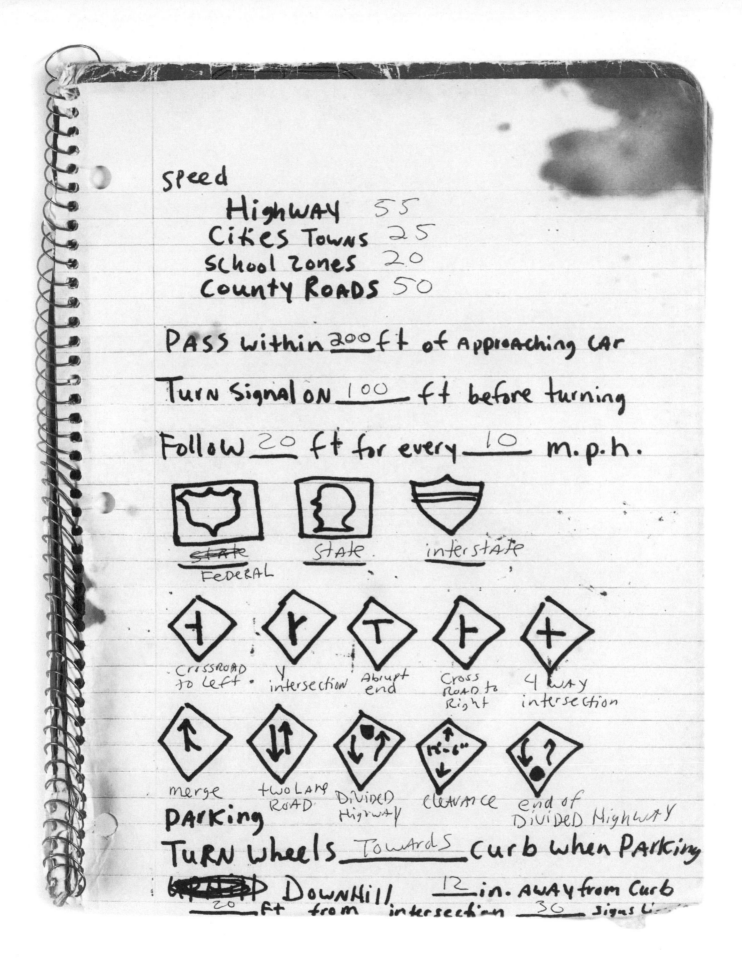

~~state~~ FEDERAL — state — interstate

Crossroad to Left — Y intersection — Abrupt end — Cross Road to Right — 4 way intersection

merge — two Lane Road — Divided Highway — clearance — end of Divided Highway

PARKING

TURN wheels Towards curb when Parking

[redacted] DownHill 12 in. AWAY from Curb

20 ft from intersection 30 signs li…

Dave, 5-29-88

A band needs to practice, in our opinion, at least 5 times a week if the band ever expects to accomplish anything.

We're tired of total uncertainty everytime we play a show, we think..."Are we going to suck"? "Are we tight yet"? We have shows and we don't practice! The two main reasons are, Chris and his work and you and your location. Chris can eventually alter his work schedule and at least practice every week night.

When we started with you, you claimed you could make it up 4 times a week and would move up here by July or August and it would be no problem for you. We were very hesitant to ever try this because of our experience with driving back and forth to Aberdeen and we knew it would eventually get on your nerves.

We don't blame you at all for being tired of driving, and we realize what a problem and hassle it is to get someone else to drive you up, but even if you could make it up every day we don't start until 8:30 or 9:00, which is not enough time to even go through the set. We know how long it takes to build a house and you won't move up here as soon as you have claimed, and in our morals and values, fixing up a race car isn't half as important as getting to practice or recording or touring.

→

We Also aren't convinced that you would get time off, or quit your job next winter to go on tour. The overall aspect of this situation is nothing more than Selfish. Getting a name on a record isn't shit. anybody can do it, but theres a big difference between Credentials & notoriety, and self respect through music.

Instead of lying to you by saying we're breaking up or letting this go any further we have to admit that we've got another drummer. His name is Chad, he's from Tacoma and he can make it to practice every night. Most importantly, we can relate to him. lets face it, you are from a totally different Culture.

Our hobbies and interests are different, and a band can't be a unit unless all the members are Compatible. We have really appreciated your loyalty and dedicated attempt at Keeping this band alive. You're a great drummer and we hope you pursue another band very soon. We expect you to be totally pissed off and hate our guts and we don't blame you, because this is very sudden and we have not tried to warn you that this was happening. This is not your fault. It's ours. We should have known it wouldn't work, but your enthusiasm and clear headed thinking made us want to try it. and we feel →

5-29-88

really shitty that we don't have the guts to tell you in person. But we don't know how mad you would get. All the luck to you and Laney and your drumming career. And if you wouldn't mind, we would like to suggest to other bands looking for drummers to check you out because your talent shouldn't go to waste.

please let us know when it is in your convenience for us to bring your drums & mic down. When you want to discurs this with us call. Sorry.

Kurt

Chris

P.S. Lani - Thanks for driving Dave up all the time - I know what an awful drive it is. Shelli & I enjoyed spending time with you while they were practicing. Call us sometime & we can get together and do something.

- Tracy & Shelli

J.F.K.: the lamest excuse ever. retrogression

transpose

revolve
reverted

Reversion relapse

botanical growing

such high expectations, so much support, every one wants it more than me. Almost feel like doing it for them, Such high Aspirations. infinity doesnt exist. mathematics are based on 10.

A ~~numbers of~~ ~~specific~~ numeral variations ~~eventually turn~~ are the synthesis of ~~a~~ retrogression, Such being: reactive, cause and effect, communicational, ~~and~~ scenario, ~~[illegible]~~ and social interplay with Situations ~~within~~ Amongst people, music, sports, ~~[illegible]~~ Herbacious WAR and regional determination of botanical & possibilities.

Hi, I dont have Dyslexia. An infared light will simulate the sun in times of winter.

A hypnotherapist will hold your hand and aid you into going back to bed. Downers & heroin make you itch. If you talk to a friend, the friend will offer you a list of remedies that youve already tried. The first seven years of my life were amazing, incredible, realistic and an absolute grateful joy.

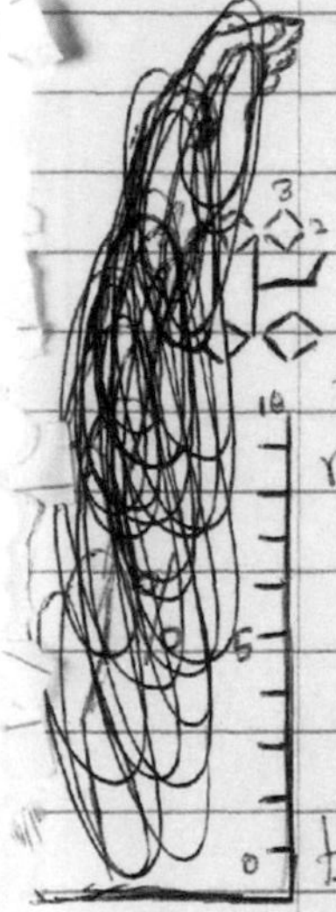

To be positive at all times is to ~~erase~~ ignore all ~~important~~ ~~and valuable~~ that is important, sacred or valuable.

To be negative at all times is to be threatened by ~~your~~ rediculousness and instant discredibility.

To translate opinions in an obvious search for proof of intellignce ~~(in the manor of~~ with abusive use ~~with~~ of obscure descriptive words is A desperational will to sincere, yet retarded expression.

rediculous

manner

expression

I ~~feel~~ there is a universal ~~feeling~~ sense ~~that~~ amongst our generation that everything has been said and done. True. but who cares it could still be fun to pretend.

This is the first decade since the early 1940s that two generations ~~[illegible]~~ ~~listen to~~ share the same music.
(the old school and new school)

Dear mark,

Hello. It sounds as if everything is working out [swell] with Donna. I can't wait to see & hear the results! Well i finally have heard almost all of your albums except all of the beathappening/Trees EP

I hope you don't mind but I recorded them on the dreadful cassette tape. which is something Im kind of against people doing, because it's not supporting the band. but I swear! If I ever get a job Im sure Ill buy all the records.

Well, on the back of the Clash's 1st LP it says: home taping is killing the music business oh! wow.

This stuff on the tape I sent is some 4 trk mello pretty, sleep music, I've been doing for the past couple of months.

It's obvious that it has been inspired from beathappening/young Marble giants music.

If you like some of it or if you have something of your own in which you thought I would be appropriate for the collaborating then Im willing.

~~hopefully~~ ~~we~~ NIRVANA is planning on Asking Calvin if he wants to put out A (K) Cassette of these songs & A couple obscure heavy songs too.

because ~~[illegible]~~ we feel like were not Accomplishing Anything by playing the seattle Club circuit & It turns out that our single will be out in Oct. (Love buzz - big cheese) but there isnt much hope for An EP within the near future, for Sub POP is having financial problems and the promise of An EP & LP within the year was just A bullshit excuse for Johnathan to keep us ~~[illegible]~~ from scouting other labels. & So here it is 8 months later & we finally put out A damn single. Weve sent the demo to A few labels. but no response.

So if you have any numbers or Addresses or if you meet someone & give them A demo It would be greatly Appreciated. We have About 30 bulk recording tapes & Any postage & handling will be gladly paid. We just feel like were becoming Stagnant in olympia with no record.

Just before I fall asleep and
when Im really bored I... Laydown and
think for awhile until I ~~subconciously go~~ fall
into a ~~[illegible]~~ semi hypnotic state of sub-
-conciousness, some call it daydreaming, some
call it just fucking spacing out. but i feel like
Im not here and it doesn't matter because Im
sick of putting myself in boring situations and
pre~~[illegible]~~tory conversations, just every day
basic sitcom happenings, some call it thinking
but when im ~~think I forget to think~~ in this
particular state of mind i forget to think and it
becomes strictly observatory. I notice things
very sensitively like if i focus really hard
I can see small transparent blotches of
~~dirt~~ debris on the outer shell of my eyes.
(or the conjunctiva). And can only follow it
as my eye moves downward. its like, watching
film footage of amoeba or jelly like
plankton under a microscope. and when
I close my eyes and look up to the sun
the Bright orange Redness radiates an
intense picture of Blood cells or what I
think are Blood cells. and they are moving
very rapidly and again I can only focus for
so long before my eyes strain and I have
to look away from the sun int a pillow, some call them stars
and Rub my eyes hard then I see
Tiny spheres of sparkling light which only
stay for a second then as my eyes focus →

Again ~~Admists~~ Amongst the water or Tears from rubbing I open then look up to the sky ^away from the sun^ And forget About stupid fucking little squiggly things moving on the outer layer of my eyes or the ~~B~~ close up Blood cells in my eye lids and I stare at the ~~clouds~~ ^sky^ with perrifial vision and not trying but just ~~to~~ happening to make out all kinds of faces objects statues in the clouds And I can do the same with the wood grain of the panelling on my walls. ~~And so what.~~

ONCE I SAW JESUS ON A Tortilla Shell.

UNCERTAINTY like opening your
eyes wide in the dark then closing them
hard then open and blinded by the sparkling
silver dots created from pressure on the
corneas, squint, roll, focus, then your
blind again but at least you saw light
somehow. maybe ~~it was tored~~ the light
was stored in the sockets or held in the
iris or clung to the tips of all the nerves
and veins. Then your eyes close again
and an artificial light appears before
the eyelids, probably just a light bulb
or a blowtorch! jesus its hot! my lashes
and brows are curling up and melting
emiting the worst smell of burnt hair
and thru the red transparency of the
light in my eyelids I can see a close up view of
blood cells move as I move my eyes
back and forth like footage of a
documentary of amoeba and plankton
jelly like see thru life forms moving
man they must be small I cant
feel them my eyes must be able
to see things MORE clearly
than ~~I had~~ expected it's like
a microscope but it doesn't matter
anymore cause they set me on fire now
yep Im sure of it Im on fire God damn
it

3 cups Quick oats
lArge Bowl

in SAuce pAn
2 sticks butter 1/2 cup milk
2 cups sugar 3 tbs cocoa
1/4 tsp salt 2 tsp vAnilla extract
rolling boil 2 minuts
pour over oAts stir
until they set

WAx paper

in which, I felt that she
One of many ways manipulated the circumstances and reversed the guilt onto me

I felt that when she would make an attempt to call a relative or friend for advice she would always choose these times when I was around in the house within hearing distance. to make it apparently clear that she is concerned "quote I don't know what to do with him, I care so much. He plays guitar and he plays it really good, but thats all he wants to do, He needs a dose of reality and to realize that he needs something to FALL BACK ON!

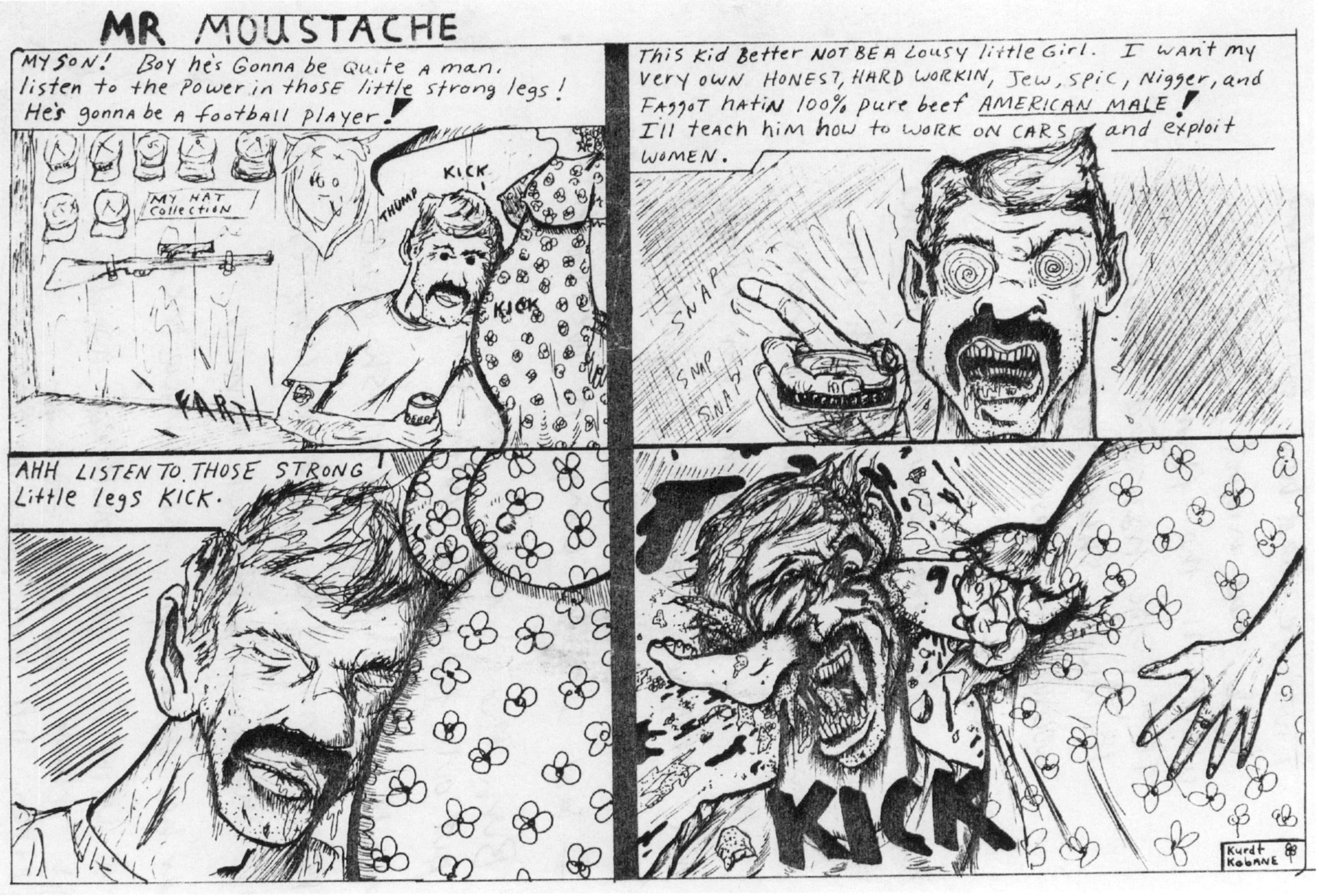
MR MOUSTACHE
MY SON! Boy he's Gonna be Quite A man. listen to the Power in those little strong legs! He's gonna be A football player!
MY HAT Collection
THUMP
KICK
KICK
FART
This kid Better NOT BE A Lousy little Girl. I want my very own HONEST, HARD WORKIN, Jew, Spic, Nigger, and Faggot hatin 100% pure beef AMERICAN MALE! I'll teach him how to work on CARS and exploit WOMEN.
SNAP
SNAP
SNAP
AHH LISTEN TO THOSE STRONG Little legs KICK.
KICK
Kurdt Kobane

In a last attempt to make it clear ~~here~~ that this girl did not have downs syndrome or a mongoloid, there is proof that Lakeside High school does not ~~have~~ or ever has had the facilities to teach those cronic retards, ~~and~~ in fact Darrin, Ace, and Trevor were also in one of her classes & she also had regular classes for normal people.

A lot of naive asshole kids just called her retarded because she never talked. ~~which you will find out later in the story how our association with her was badly labeled & mistaken.~~

The object of the guys who had been going there for the past month was to steal booze from the down stairs basement den.. while others distracted her by opening cupboard doors & pretending to eat all the food, one would go down & take a 5th & then exit out the downstairs.

It was basically a gift to Trevor the pot overlord who enjoyed pot not quite as much as booze, and to his helpers & I a reward of getting high in the woods near the school was always promised if we stold booze for him. Only being stoned within that week for the first few times was what I claimed as "something I will do for the rest of my life!" And I would practically do anything to ensure my supply of the fantastic weed ~~pot~~. So we did this routine every other day & got away with it for ~~quite a long~~ about a month →

And during that month happened to be the Epitomy of my mental abuse from my mother. ~~[illegible] before~~. It turned out that pot didnt help me escape my troubles too well any more And I was actually enjoying doing rebellious things like stealing this booze & busting store windows getting in fist fights etc.... & nothing even mattered. I decided within the next month I'll not sit on my roof and think about jumping: but ill actually kill myself And I wasnt going out of this world without actually knowing what it is like to get laid.

So one day after school I went to her house alone, and invited myself in and she offered me some twinkies and I sat on her lap and said "let's fuck" and I touched her tits and she went into her bedroom and got undressed in front of me with the door open and I watched & realized that it was actually happening so I tried to fuck her but didnt know how and asked her if she had ever done this before and she said a lot of times mainly with her cousin.

I got grossed out very heavily with how her vagina smelled & her sweat reaked so I left. My concience grew to where I couldnt go to school for a week and when i went back I got in-house suspetion in the office for skipping and that day the girls father came in screaming & accusing someone of taking advantage of his daughter

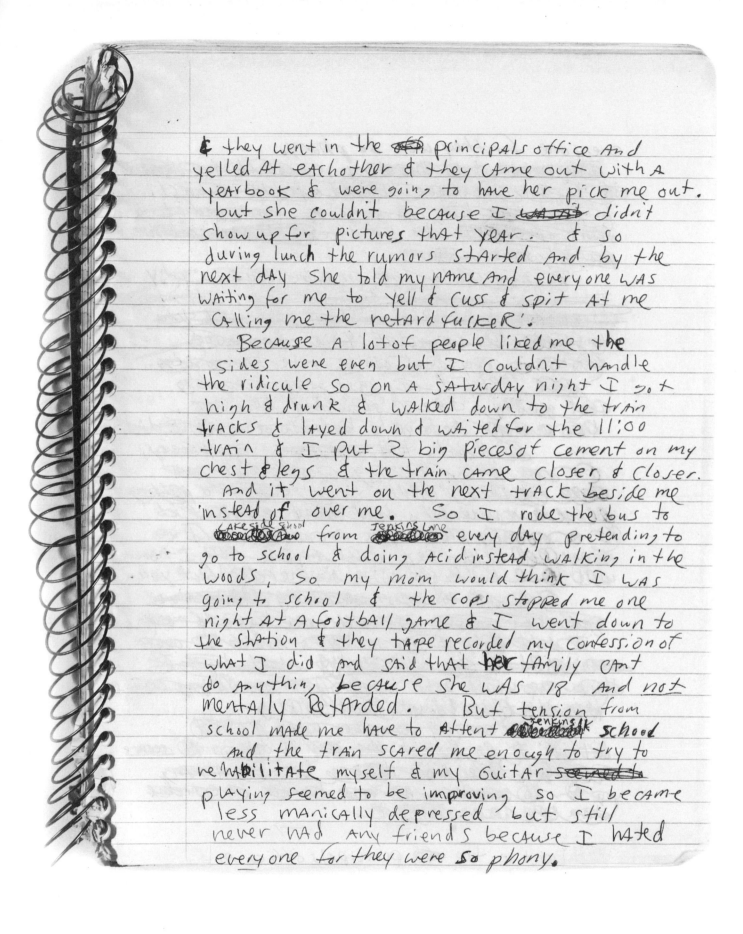

& they went in the principals office and yelled at eachother & they came out with a yearbook & were going to have her pick me out. but she couldn't because I didn't show up for pictures that year. & so during lunch the rumors started and by the next day she told my name and everyone was waiting for me to yell & cuss & spit at me calling me the retard fucker'.

Because a lot of people liked me the sides were even but I couldnt handle the ridicule so on a saturday night I got high & drunk & walked down to the train tracks & layed down & waited for the 11:00 train & I put 2 big pieces of cement on my chest & legs & the train came closer & closer. And it went on the next track beside me instead of over me. So I rode the bus to Lakeside School from Jenkins Lane every day pretending to go to school & doing acid instead walking in the woods, so my mom would think I was going to school & the cops stopped me one night at a football game & I went down to the station & they tape recorded my confession of what I did and said that her family cant do anything, because she was 18 and not mentally Retarded. But tension from school made me have to attend Jenkins school and the train scared me enough to try to rehabilitate myself & my guitar playing seemed to be improving so I became less manically depressed but still never had any friends because I hated everyone for they were so phony.

NIRVANA is from Olympia WA, 60 miles from Seattle. NIRVANAS Guitar/vocalist (Kurt Kobain) And Bass-(Chris Novoselic) lived in Aberdeen 190 miles from Seattle. Aberdeens population Consists of Highly bigoted Redneck-snoose chewing- deer shooting, faggot killing- logger types who "aint to partial to weirdo new wavers!" (chad) drums is from An island of Rich Kid-LSD Abusers. NIRVANA is A trio who play Heavy Rock with Punk overtones. They usually dont have jobs. So they can tour anytime. NIRVANA HAS never jammed on Gloria, or Louie Louie. Nor have they ever had to Re write these songs & call them their own.

NIRVANA is looking to put their music to Vinyl or accepting A loAn of About $2,000.00.

Kurdt

Lance Link

After Beat happening

Crybaby & Richard Simmons

Hot Dog eating contest

* Penis Balloon insertion for erection

* light bulb swallower

Rem

H Rollins

L Lunch

Tards

Bill murray lounge

Stairway to Heaven

* Davey & Goliath

Bros Quay

Spoons magnets Baby

* monster tard movie

Jesse Hello,
Believe me, I have purposely been delaying writing you for a while so when our single finally comes out I could send it to you as well as a letter. But God time flies and Sub Pop is broke and full of shit. And I didnt realize how long its been since I received your letter. So Im sorry!
Hey cheer up dude, your letter sounded like youre kinda bored.
I cant wait until you come down for Christmas, it will be the most exciting ~~$~~ event this year. We got our test pressings back for the single, Ive been waiting for so long that Im not even ~~excited about~~ looking forward to it coming out. Weve refused to do anything else with Sub Pop even though they really want us to put out an EP. Weve decided to put out our own LP. We found a record pressing plant that will press 1000 records for $1,600.00. So at $8.00. a piece we only have to sell about 250 records to get our money back, and the rest is pure profit, then all we have to do is find a distributor.
We played with the Butthole Surfers. And then D.O.A in Seattle. The Melvins are coming back to play a couple shows with us.
Chris and Shelli broke up. God am I relieved! She is still living in Tacoma

and Chris is temporarily staying in Aberdeen for free at his moms. I'm very content with the relationship Chris, Chad and I have, we get along great and have a lot of dedicated fun. We are becoming very well Received in seattle & other places in WASH. Promoters call us up to see if we want to play, instead of us having to Hound people for shows. Its now just a matter of time for labels to hunt us down, now that weve promoted ourselves pretty good by doing small Remote tours. OK. enough about the band.

Ive got a janitor job, working with this older guy cleaning 4 restaurants. Pays cash under the table part time.

Tracy and I get along just fine, as usual. Lately Ive found myself becoming lazy. I hardly write any stories and I dont work on songs quite as intently as in the past. You know why? ? ?

television Television is the most evil thing on our planet.

Go Right now to your tV and toss it out the window, or sell it and buy a better stereo. I have the flu Right now so I dont feel like conjuring up witty literature. my eyes burn & when I fart, hot bubble acid ooze squirts from my

Reed & Maloy
~~ADA~~ ADAM-12 Episode Hell.

Greetings,

NIRVANA is A three piece spawned from the bowels of A Redneck logger town called ~~of~~ Aberdeen WA. and ~~the~~ hippie commune from Bainbridge ~~Isl~~ Island. Only together for 7 months Kurdt—Guitar vocals — Chris bass & chad—Drums have acquired A single on Sub Pop Records (A song on Sub Pop 200 comp,) A Demo, success & fame & A following of millions, Selling their bottled sweat & locks of hair have proven to be the largest money maker so far, but in the future! dolls, peechees, lunch boxes & bed sheets are in the works. AN LP is due this April from the wonderful ~~head~~ offices of Sub Pop world headquarters. talent Agents bruce Pavitt (Alias Henry Mancini) and Johnathan Poneman (Alias fred flintstone) have "treated the boys good", the boys ~~and~~ hope to work on more projects with them in the future.

NIRVANA sounds like black sabbath — playing the KNACK, Black flag, led Zeppelin, & the stooges, with A pinch of bay City Rollers. their musical influences are: H.R. Puffnstuff, ~~[illegible]~~ Marine Boy, Divorces, DRugs, Sound effects Records, the Beatles, Young marble Giants, slayer, leadbelly, IGGY,

NIRVANA sees the underground music SEEN As becoming, stagnant And more Accessible towards commercial MAjor LAbel interests. Does NIRVANA want to change this? No way! We want to cash in & suck butt up to the big wigs in hopes that we too ~~can~~ get High & fuck wax figure-hot babes, who will be required to have A certified Aids test 2 weeks prior to the day of handing out back stage passes. Soon we will need chick spray Repellant. Soon we will be coming to your town & Asking if we can stay At your house & use your Stove. Soon we will do encores of Gloria & louie louie At benefit concerts with All our celebrity friends.

We Realize that there was once A 60's band called NIRVANA but dont get us ~~mixed up~~ confused with them because they totally Suck Big fucking Dick.

N pear olympia wa
98506

Good Bye.

GREETINGS,

NIRVANA is a three piece spawned from the bowels of a redneck - logger town called Aberdeen WA, and a hippie commune on Bainbridge island.

Although only together for seven months KurDt-guit-voc, Chris-bass and Chad-drums have acquired a single on Sub Pop records, one cut on the Sub Pop 200 compilation, a demo, an LP in April, success,fame and a following of millions.

Selling their bottled sweat and locks of hair have proven to be their biggest money makers so far, but in the future: dolls, pee chees, lunch boxes and bed sheets are in the works.

From the wonderful offices of Sub Pop world headquarters our talent agents Bruce Pavitt and Johnathan Poneman have treated the boys good.

NIRVANA hope to work on more projects with them in the future.

NIRVANA sounds like: Black Sabbath playing the Knack, Black Flag, Led ZEP, the Stooges and a pinch of Bay city Rollers.

Their personal musical influences include: H.R Puffnstuff, Marine boy, divorces, drugs, sound effect records, the Beatles, Young Marble Giants, Slayer, Leadbelly and Iggy.

NIRVANA sees the underground music SEEN as becoming stagnant and more accessible towards commercialized major label interests.

Does NIRVANA feel a moral duty to change this cancerous evil?

No way! We want to cash in and suck butt of the big wigs in hopes that we too can GET HIGH and FUCK. GET HIGH and FUCK. GET HIGH and FUCK.

Soon we will need chick repellant spray. Soon we will be coming to your town asking if we can stay over at your house and use your stove.

Soon we will do encores of Gloria and Louie Louie at benefit concerts with all our celebrity friends.

NIRVANA c/o SUB POP
1932 1st AVE..#1103. Seattle WA 98101
or

Thank you for your time.

FUCK NOW, SUFFER LATER

GREETINGS,

NIRVANA is a heavy-pop/punk/dirge-combo spawned from the bowels of Seattle Washington.

Although only together for seven months KURDT Guitar/voc, CHRIS-bass, CHAD- drums and JASON-guitar have acquired a single, an LP entitled "Bleach", one cut on the SUB POP 200 compilation, sucess, fame and a following of millions.

Selling their bottled sweat and lochs of hair have proven to be their biggest money makers so far, and in the future: dolls, pee-chees, lunch boxes and bed sheets are in store.

From the towering offices of SUB POP world headquarters our talent agents Johnathan Poneman and Bruce Pavitt have treated the boys swell.

NIRVANA hope to produce more projects with them in the future.

NIRVANA sounds like mid-tempo-Black Sabbath playing the Knack, Black Flag, the Stooges with a pinch of Bay City Rollers.

Their personal musical influences include: H.R. Puffnstuff, Speed Racer,DIVORCES, drugs, sound effects records, the beatles, rednecks, asorted hard rock, old punk rock, Leadbelly, Slayer and of course the Stooges.

NIRVANA sees the underground SeeN as becoming stagnant and more accessible towards commercialized major label interests.

Does NIRVANA feel a moral duty to change this cancerous evil?

NO way! We want to CASH IN and SucK UP to the big wigs in hopes that we too can GET HIGH AND FUCK GET HIGH AND FUCK.GET HIGH AND FUCK.

SOON we will need groupie repellant spray. SOON we will be coming to your town asking if we can stay over at your house and use the stove. SOON we will do encores of GLORIA and LOUIE LOUIE at benefit concerts with all our celebrity friends.

NIRVANA c/o SUB POP
1932 1st ave. # 1103. Seattle Wa 98101 or

Thank you for your time.

MARK,

WHOA! Polly Perreguin is
my favorite song as of this decade.
Ive been soaking up the sounds of
the Screaming Trees for a few
months and [redacted] I think its way
better than most, Although in the
pop Genre I like pixies &
Smithereens a bit better. But
Polly Perreguin, Jeezus GOD!
what a complete masterpiece.
Hey hows tour? oh. Donna Seems
to fit in just fine. I predict
the mighty Major label in the future
for you people. Heres some well,
fuck, I must Admit screaming Trees
influenced pop weve been experimenting
with. We played with the Butthole Surfers.
they wouldnt move their drums. Jeesus!
Got paid $75.00 whole dollars.

Sub Pop is Always broke. So were
openly looking for any other offer. They
mean well but we don't feel its fair
for mudhoney to be favored & catered
to A higher level than the otherbands.
Oh well. [redacted] we want
to tour in March. if you have any #'S
or suggestions, we would appreciate
any Help.

NIRVANA

Kenichewa
Dear ______________.

NIRVANA is A three piece from the outskirts of Seattle WA.
Kurdt-Guitar/voice and Chris-bass have Struggled with too many un dedicated drummers for the past 3 years, performing under such names as: Bliss, throat Oyster, Pen Capch Ted ed Fred ETC.. for the last 9 months we have had the pleasure to take Chad-drums under our wings and develop what we are now and always will be NIRVANA.

3 regularly broadcasted Carts on K.C.M.U (Seattle College Radio also KAOS olympia)
Played with: Leaving Trains, Whipping Boy, Hells Kitchen, Trecherous Jaywalkers & Countless local acts.

Looking for: EP or LP We have about 15 Songs Recorded on 8 Tracks at Reciprocal Studios in Seattle.
Willing to compromise on material (some of this shit is pretty old) Tour Any-time forever
hopefully the music will speak for itself
Please Reply THANK YOU Area code (206)
N PEAR olympia WA. 98506

Things the band needs to do

1) Send some fucking demo tapes
get chad to fucking fork over
Some money.

2) Press Kit
1) get ahold of charles and Alice
to get some pictures
2) have Tam write out a story line
3) then copy them off. ~~Simple!~~

3) Find a practice place

4) Call Nann Warsaw in chicago. Ask if
she has any connections with Touch-n-go
Also ask for ~~a list~~ her to send a list of
Prominent magazines & Record stores that
we could make contacts with.

5)

AT **EVERY** stop you must check:

1 OiL
2 wAter
3 Air pressur
4 transmission
5 Battery wAter
6 BrAke fluid
7. PACK Bearings
8. check lights
9. lug nuts
10. WASH VAN
11. Radiator Hose
12. Windows

*LOCK ALL DOORS

NO Guests, groupies, BAnd members etc.

NO use of Any GAS Corporation services Besides EXXON. NO exceptions

Every 400 miles there will be An inspection check of VAN cleAnliness And equipment Count.
Find A sAfe place to pull over And tAke every piece of musicAl equipment out: refer to ~~musicAl equip~~ electronic pAmphlet in glove compartment.

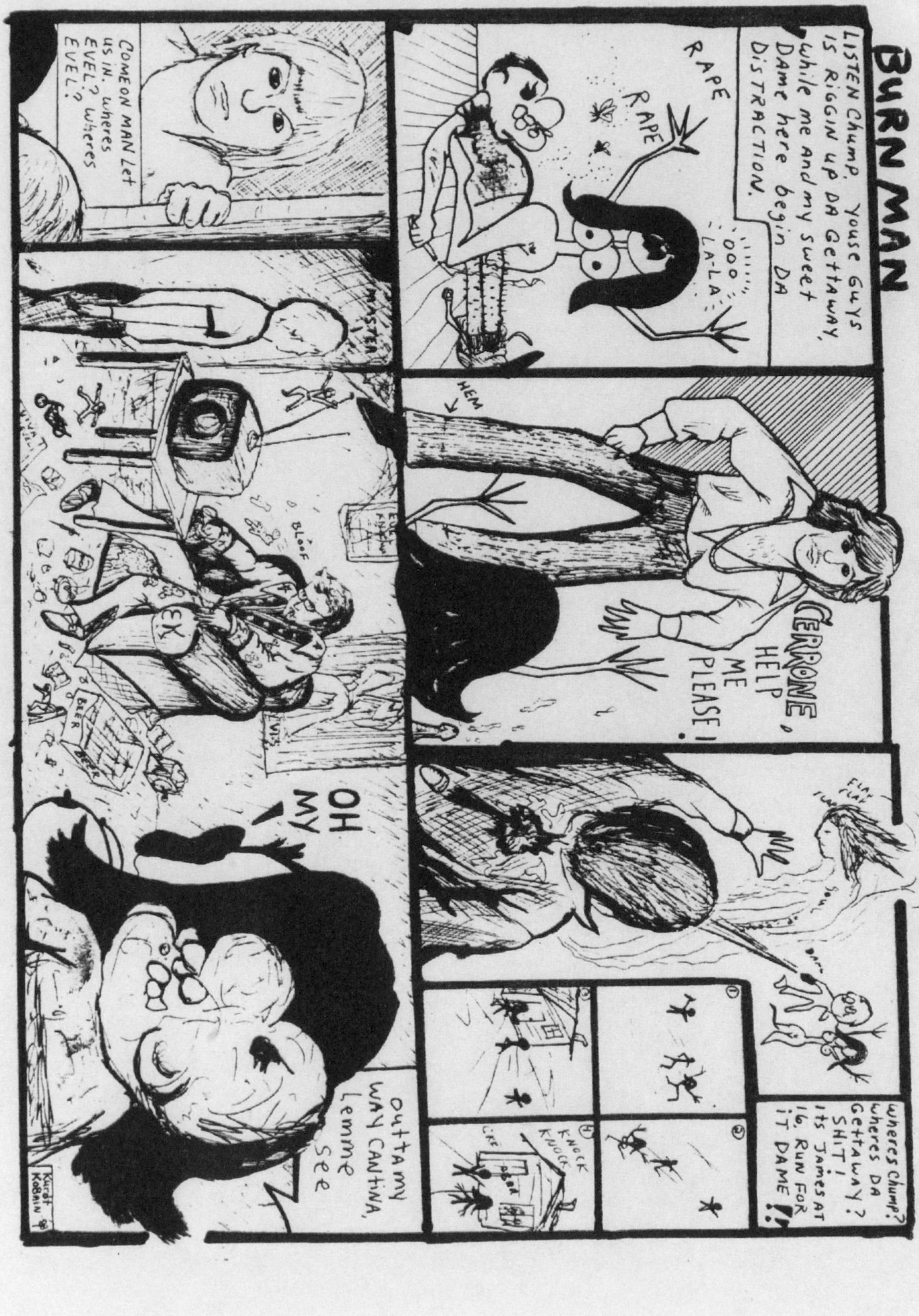
BURN MAN
LISTEN chump, youse guys is riggin up DA Gettaway, while me and my sweet Dame here begin DA DISTRACTION.
RAPE
RAPE
OOO LA-LA
HEM
CERRONE, HELP ME PLEASE!
FLAY FLAY
wheres chump? wheres DA Gettaway? SHIT! Its James at 16, Run for it Dame!!
KNOCK KNOCK
COMEON MAN Let us in. wheres EVEL? wheres EVEL?
MASTER
BLOOF
EK
BEER
ELVIS
OH MY!
outta my way cantina, Lemme see
Kurdt Kobain

Part time Janitorial position

in the olympian newspaper

7 months at lemons Janitorial
1 year at polynesian condominium resort
in Ocean Shores
2 summers work at Aberdeen YMCA
& Weatherwax High school

& 9 months at Lamplighter Restaurant
in Grayland WA.

13 4 6-10

5

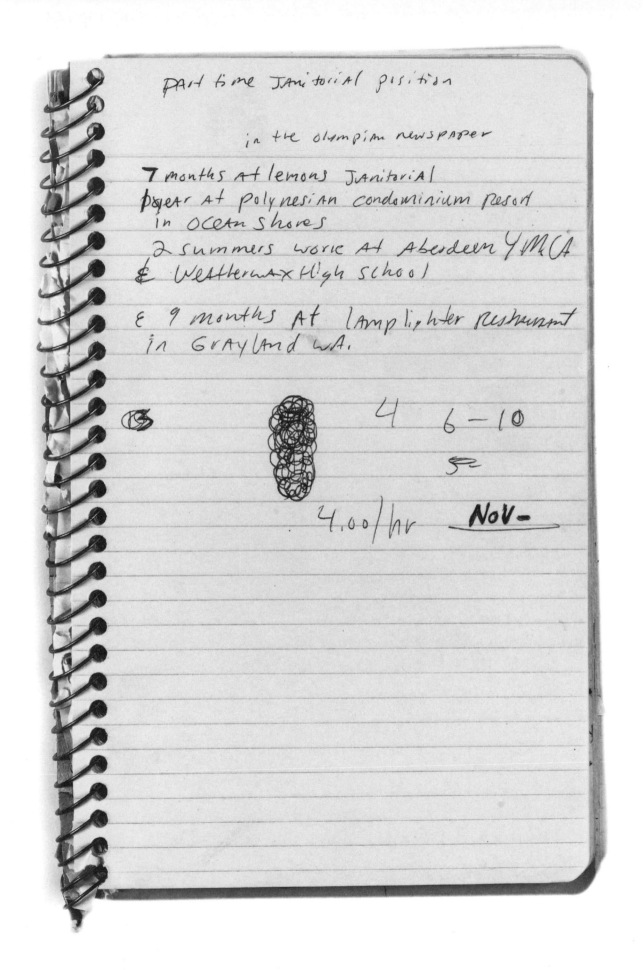

4.00/hr NOV-

2 1/2 yrs experience

Lemons Janitorial Sept 87 - feb 88
Basic Route cleaning buildings $4.50/hr

Polynesian Condominium hotel Resort ocean shores $5.00/hr
Sept-86 - June 87 C/o Betty Kaales (housekeeping)
maintenance basic odd jobs, windows
Carpet cleaning, moved to olympia

Aberdeen Y.M.C.A c/o Alfie Bensinger $3.35/hr
MAY 86 - Sept-86
lifeguard, preschool swimming instructor, day care
baseball coach, maintenance. summer temporary employment

Lamplighter Restaurant grayland WA $4.25/hr
Sept 85 - March 86 C/o Bud & Audrey Turley
dishwasher, prep, clean up, busperson

Coast building
10029 So TACOMA WAY
off exit behind
127 TACOMA Cody's Restaurant

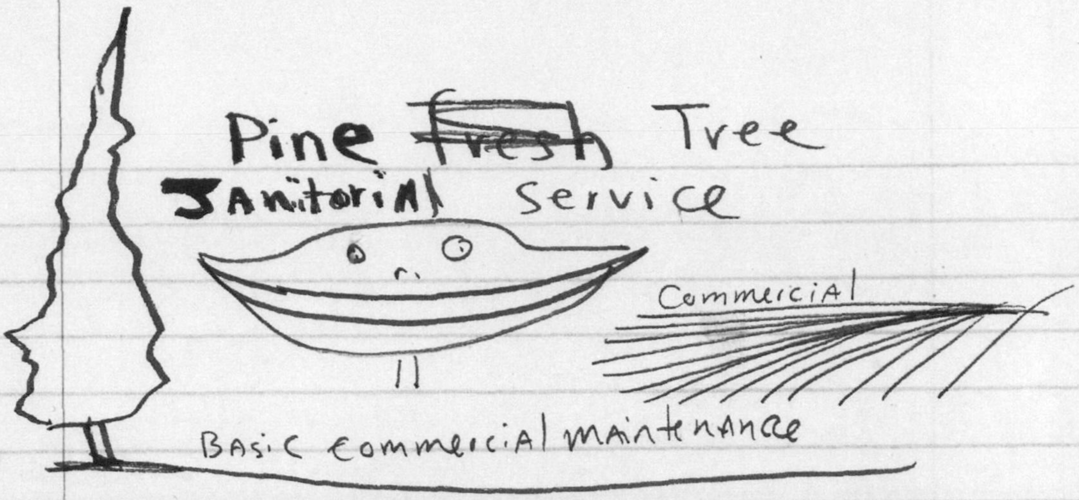

bathrooms - sink - toilet - mop - mirrors - Paper towel/ TP-supply. Office - Dust - vacuum - sweep - ashtrays - garbage - windows -

we purposely limit our number of commercial offices in order to ~~take time, and personally clean~~ personally clean while taking our time. we guarantee $50.00 lower rates, than your present Janitorial Service.

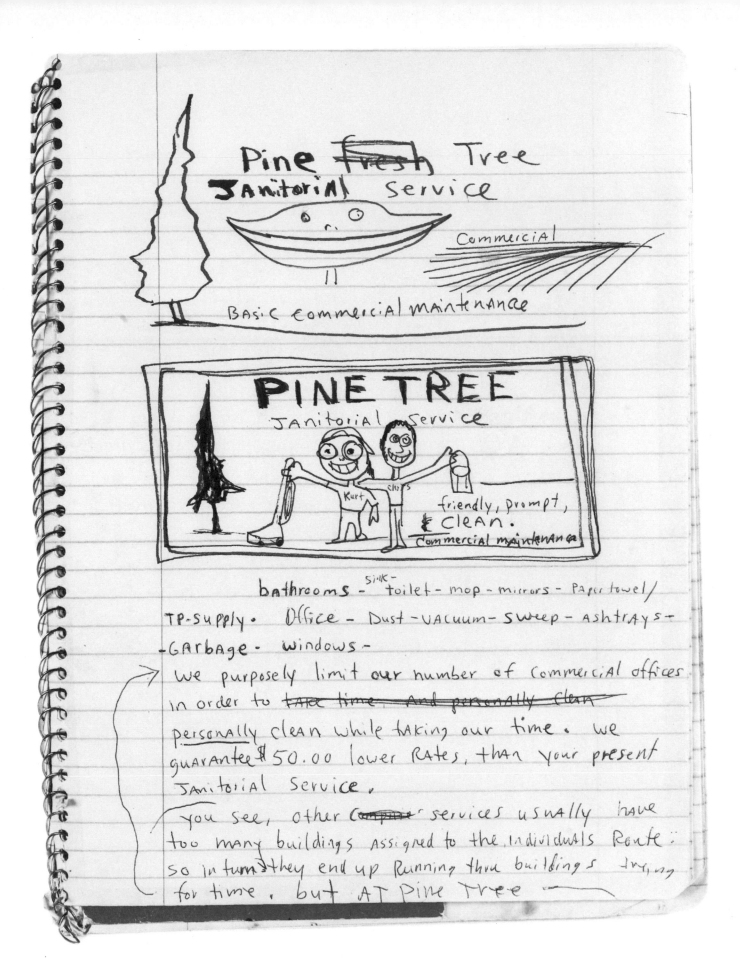

you see, other ~~compan~~ services usually have too many buildings assigned to the individuals Route: so in turn they end up Running thru buildings trying for time. but AT Pine Tree —

my lyrics are a big pile of contradictions. theyre split down the middle between very sincere opinions and feelings that I have and sarcastic and hopefully – humorous rebuttles towards cliché – bohemian ideals that have been exhausted for years.

I mean it seems like there are only two options for personalities ~~for~~ songwriters either theyre SAd, tragic visionaries like morrisey or michael Stipe or Robert smith. or theres the goofy, Nutty white boy, Hey, lets party and forget everything people like VAn HAlen or All that other ~~crap~~ Heavy metal crap

I mean I like to be passionate and Sincere, but I also like to have fun and act like a dork.

Geeks unite.

DOWNER

PORTRAY SINCERITY ACT out of Loyalty
Defend your free Country - wish AWAY PAIN
1 HAND OUT lobotomys to SAVE little familys
Surrealistic fantasy Bland Boring plain

Holy NOW IN Restitution - living out our DATE
2 with FUSION - IN our whole fleece shun iN
BAStard - don't feel guilty master writing

Somebody SAYS that their not much like I AM
3 I know I CAN - make enough up the words AS
you GO Along I SING then some .

SICKENING pesimist hypocrite master
Conservative Communist Apocalyptic Bastard
4 Thank you Dear GOD for putting me on this EArth
I feel very priviledged iN debt for my thirst

2 and 3

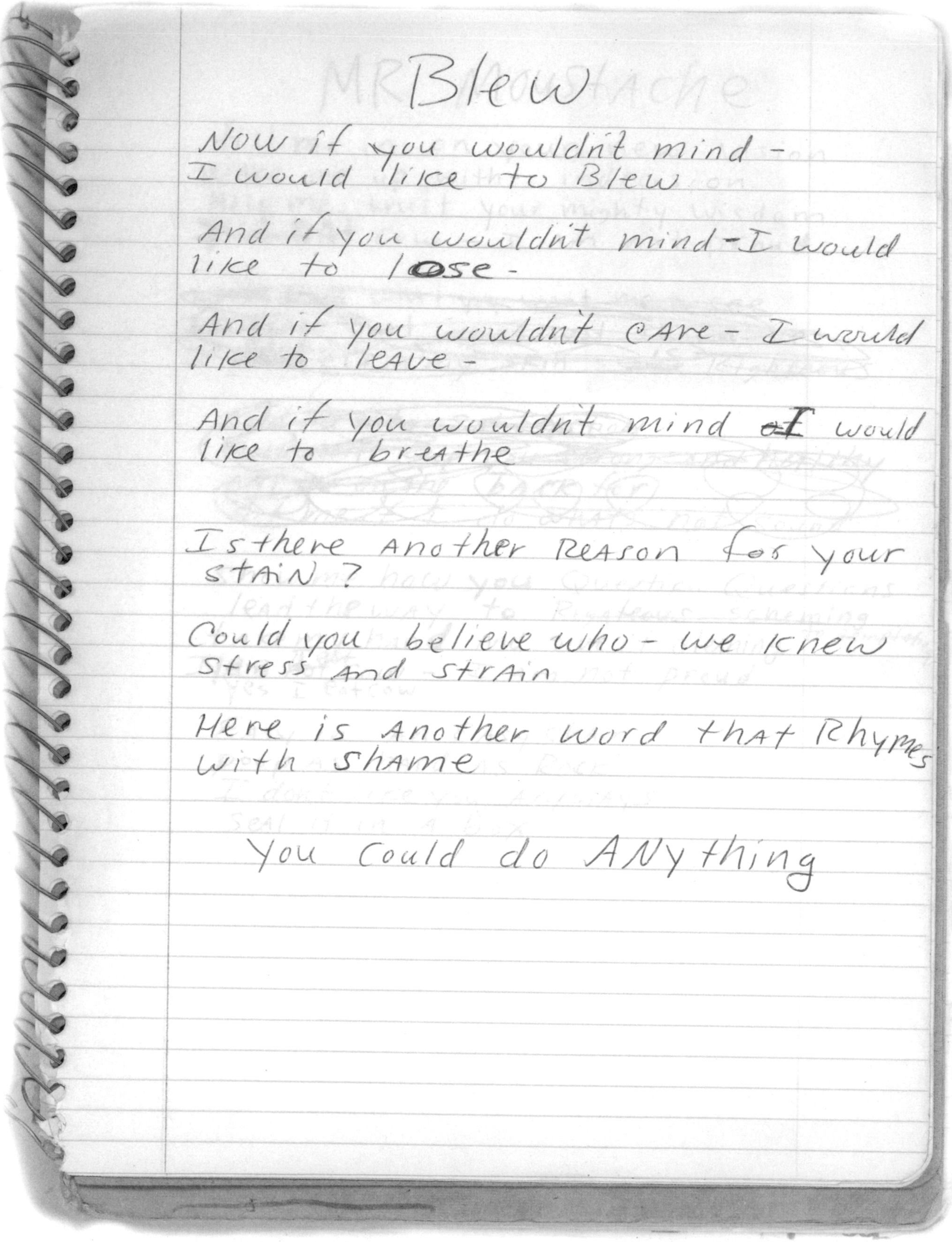

Blew

Now if you wouldn't mind -
I would like to Blew

And if you wouldn't mind - I would
like to lose -

And if you wouldn't care - I would
like to leave -

And if you wouldn't mind ~~of~~ I would
like to breathe

Is there another reason for your
stain ?

Could you believe who - we knew
stress and strain

Here is another word that rhymes
with shame

You could do Anything

MR Moustache

fill me in on your new vision
WAKE me up with- indecision
Help me trust your mighty wisdom
~~I Am not~~ Yes I EAt cow - I AM not proud

~~write down what you want me to see~~
~~I'll erase what youve just shown me~~
~~I don't~~ CANT ~~claim my skin~~ IS ~~Righteous~~

~~mold me into satisfaction~~
~~Milk will keep you strong and healthy~~
~~pat me on the back for~~ -
~~Hit me if I do whats not sound~~

Show me how you Question Questions
lead the WAY to ~~Righteous scheming~~ to temptation
take my hand And give it cleaning
~~I Am not~~ Yes I eat cow - I Am not proud
yes I eAt cow

EAsy in An EAsy chAir
poop AS hard AS Rock
I don't like you ANYWAYS
Seal it in A box

floyd the Barber

Bell ON Door ClAnks - Come ON IN
floyd observes my HAiry Chin
Sit down ChAir dont Be Afraid
SteAmed HOT Towel ON my fACe
I WAS shAved (3X's)
Barney Ties me to the chAir
I cAn't see Im Really scAred
floyd Breathes hard I hear A zip
Pee Pee pressed AGAinst my lips
I WAS ShAmed (3X's)
I sense others IN the Room
OPey Aunt Bee I PResume
they TAKe Turns iN cuT me up
I died smothered iN Andys Butt

I WAS shAved (3x's)

PAPER CUTS

when my feeding TiME
She push food thru the Door
I CRAWl towards the CRACKS of Light
Sometimes I CAn't find my WAY

~~[illegible]~~
newspapers spread Around
SOAKING All that they CAn
A Cleaning is due AGAIN
~~INCREASING CHANCE OF RAIN~~
A Good HOSING DOWN

The LAdy whom I feel A maternal Love for
CAnnot look me in the eyes. But I see
hers And they Are Blue And they Cock And
Twitch And masturbate

I SAID SO
~~Why - Because oh~~ - I SAID SO - I SAID SO

A REASON A REASON A REASON ~~Why~~ TRY AGAIN

BLACK windows Are PAINT
I SCRAtch with my NAILS
I See others just like me
why do they NOT Try escape?

They bring out the older ones
They point At my WAY
The older ones Come with lights
And TAKE my family AWAY

CONT. →

Paper Cuts
Continued

and very later I have learned to accept some friends of Ridicule - my whole existence was foryour Amusement and that is why Im Here with you

To Take you - with me To - your eyes are Blue
~~Believe~~ Relief to NIRVANA

NIRVANA NIRVANA NIRVANA

NIRVAN A NIRVANA NIRVANAAAH

HAirSPRAY Queen

I WAS your mind • you were my my ene me
(1) you were mine • I WAS WAS your ene me
you would mind • I WAS your your ene me
you were mine • I WAS WAS your enA

EArs RAnG 2x's

(1)

AT Night • the wishfull Goddess • AT Night
(2) Shell wish the HArdest • AT Night the Disco
Goddess • AT Night the witch ~~go gos~~h

(1)
(2)
Voice (1) DRoned

AT Night • the wishful Goddess • AT Night
Shell wish the HArdest • AT Night •
the Disco Goddess • AT Night •
the itch so modest • AT Night •
the crisco loch Ness • AT Right •
the mouthfull omelette • AT sight
the fishfull goblets • AT Night the witch go
GAAAAAAAAAAWD

Mexican Seafood

AH the itchy flAkes it is A flaming
All the Gels and cremes it is pertAining
to A fungus mold Cured by injection
Hope it's only AH A yeast infection

(2) OH well it burns when I - it hurts when
I pee - OH well it hurts when I - it hurts
when I see.

Now I Vomit cum And diahrrea
on the tile floor like OAtmeal pizza
fill my toilet bowl full of A cloudy puss
I feel the Blood becoming chowder rust

(2)

Roll into my Bed which does consist of
lice Bugs And fleas And yellow mucus
stAined dirt VASAline Toe JAm & Booger
stomAch Acid worms thAt DAnce in
SugAred sludge

NIRVANA

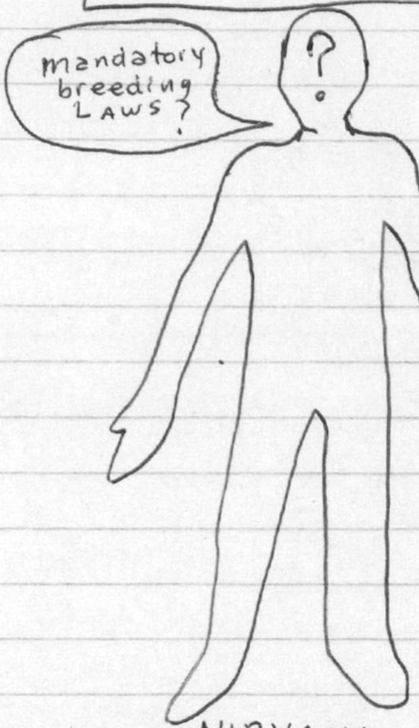

NIRVANA
CANT Decide whether they
want to be PUNK or R.E.M.
INDECISION CAN often
At times Kill A band, and
NIRVANA Are Suicidal.

~~R~~steal
SHEEP
At A Store
near
YOU

~~Because you want to not~~
~~because everyone else is~~

[redacted]

MANDATORY
~~Restrictions~~
BREEDING
LAWS
NOW

NIRVANA

The KKK Are the only NIGGers.

mAy women rule the world.

Abort Christ.

AssAsinate the Greater And lesser of two evils.

steal SHEEP At A store near you.

NIRVANA

Flowers
perfume
CAndy
puppies
Love
Generational Solidarity And Killing your Parents

SHEEP

NIRVANA

~~10 GrAmmy~~

3 time GrAnny award winners, NO. 1 on billbored top 100 for 36 consecutive weaks in A row. 2 times on the cover of Bowling Stoned, HAiled as the most original, thought provoking and important band of our decade by Thyme & Newsweak

Pen Cap Chew

OH Lesser God OH LoAthe me
OH lesser God OH your lonely
OH lesser God OH Bore me
OH lesser God OH OH

you get you get you get you get to me
Holy is the time it's such an easy way to go

you get you get you Get - You get to Be
Hide the struggle in the skin under A
finger nAil

OH lesser god OH loAthe me OH lesser god OH lonely
OH lesser god OH loAthe me OH lesser Dog OH lonely

WASte your time By SAving worthless Gullables
Kill A Pollitition And then wear His Clothes
this decade is the Age of Re-HAshing
Protest And then go to jAil for Tresspassing
GO Home (4x's)

CAn you see the Reason for my Entrope
is there something wrong without Society
Has your Concience got to you for Building
Trends - is that why unoticing you
EAt your pens?

GO HOME (8x's)

Aeroszeppelin

whats a season in a Right
If you can't have anything
whats the reason in a Rhyme
If a plan means anything
whats the meaning in a crime
it's a fan if anything
wheres a leaning in a line
it's A BRAND its A BRAND [redacted]

How a Culture comes again
it was all here yesterday
And you swear it's not a Trend
Doesn't matter anyways
theyre only here to talk to friends
Nothing new is every day
You[redacted] could shit upon the stage they'll be fans
if you Brand if you Brand if you BRAND

All the kids will EAT it up -
if its packaged properly
Steal a sound and Imitate
Keep a format equally
not an ODE
just the facts
where our world is nowadays
An idea is what we lack
it doesn't matter anyways

MELVINS

I remember painfully

you saucy upstart

Gyuto monks

if you need an explanation on what montsano is like, refer to any NIRVANA article of the past 3 years on the subject of Aberdeen, the two coastal logging slums are similar in the lack of cultural and good musical availability

I'm tired of people saying the melvins don't get the recognition they deserve

melvins when they finally get the recognition they deserve

they can look forward to un punk rock adoration from (late) fans waiting outside the venue waiting for autographs

the true adoration that matters is one they have already

by the small amount of fanatics who are into them already

I remember when the melvins played Jimi Hendrix & Cream songs

well they weren't the melvins then

them festival

I remember: when the melvins played lightning speed melodic, punk rock hard core with typewriter drumming.

then they started slowing down with a mix of stutters of melodic sabbath like abrasion

Black flag damage II

Buzz exitedly came over with Black flags my war claiming it was as important as their habit was financed by their earnings of pizza & bus boy Jobs

~~During the Summer month of the US~~ festival ~~in 84~~

I remember in the summer of 82 or 83 there was this extravaganza of a rock-like woodstock Concert held in some far away exotic land featuring all the contemporary Hard rock acts like ACDC or Van Halen. To the stoner world it was a big deal but for me it was something a joke I didnt pay much attention to it but I remember my friends staring up to the sky during the weeks prior to this Gathering with a fear of empty ~~unattainable~~ dreams that this festival is never to be apart of their hanging out of the smoker shed reality. in other words there wasnt a chance in hell that theyll save up enough pot money to make the long trek to the ~~fatherland~~ promise land of the US festival

I remember hanging out at montesano Washingtons thriftway when this short haired employee boxboy who kinda looked like the Guy in Air Supply handed me a flyer that reads: the Them festival. tomorrow night in the parking lot behind Thriftway free Live Rock music

Montesano Washington a place not accustomed to having live rock acts in their little village A population of a few thousand loggers and their subservient wives

~~I~~ showed up with stoner friends in a van we pulled into the parking lot behind the Thriftway other zombies slouch bobbed with combs in their BACK pockets ~~congregated~~ ~~in droves~~

~~we~~ There stood the AirSupply box boy ~~with~~ ~~a mechanic~~ holding a les Paul with A picture of Kool cigarettes laminated on it from A magazine a mechanic redheaded biker boy and that tall talkin guy, the first to ever wear skin tight levis, a bold and brave change from stickin finger or sanfrancisco riding Gear.

They played faster than I had ever imagined music could be played and with more energy than my iron Maiden records could provide, this was what I was looking for, AH punk ROCK The other stoners were Bored and ~~kept~~ ~~asking them~~ kept shouting, play some Def Leppard. God I hated those fucks more than ever I came to the promise land of A Grocery store ~~I~~, I found my special purpose the next day I spiked ~~up~~ the upper part of my head but I couldnt quite part with my stoner roots and the long hair in the back, thus developing the first Bi level hair cut in montesano history, I walked around for a week looking like rod stewart. I started following the melvins around. I was the Quiet tag along. one day they even let me try out for the band but I was

So I sat in the corner at hundreds of melvins practices

way too nervous ~~and~~ during the next few

years As I watched buzz transform from

typewriter drumming, speed core to

the constepation blues stemmed from the

influence of Black flags my war,

ST Vitus and a short lived stint with

various metal Blade recording artists. something

new was H ——— much transforming Buss do this

thru a few years of ~~[illegible]~~ internally personal

developments of strict morals and opinions niche like

sincere devotion to the celebration of energy and the appreciation

of spirituality ~~and sincere~~ Buzz stays true

to his school. giving off an air of if you even

think of me compromising I'll Kill you attitude

rolling his ~~[illegible]~~ eyes to the back of the head NArcoleptic epileptic little Boy ~~rolling~~ back n forth disease?

pissing sweat in a ritually ~~[illegible]~~ Autistic sway

downstroking muffled lowest notes possible chunk

Chopping block, Guttural bowel drones.

harmonic satanic and uh heavy. low

Deep Cool man Cool Goddamn the pusher man!

A lot of Mohawks said I used to like the melvins

until they became Black Sabbath Jeez ~~[illegible]~~ A typically

clever observation

The MeLVINS Are Alive

WORDS suck. I mean, every thing has been said. I cant remember the last real interesting conversation ive had in a long time. WORDS arent as important as the energy derived from music, especially live. I dont think ive ever gotten any good descriptions from lyric sheets, except WHITE ZOMBIE whos lyrics remind me that theres only so many words in the English language, and most good imagery has been used, as well as good band names, LP titles and not to mention the bloody music itself. GEE, I dont want to sound so negative but were dealing with the MELVINS. IN one live MELVINS performance you wont be able to understand very many words, as is with any band) but you will FEEL the negative ENERGY. Music is ENERGY. A mood, atmosphere. FEELING. The MELVINS have and always will be the king pins of EMOTION. Im not talking about fucking stupid human compassion, this is one of the only real istic reminders that every day we live amongst VIOLENCE.

There is a time and place for this music. So if you want to shake your groove thang to simple primal rock, then go see a fucking bar band! The MELVINS aint for you. And they probably dont want ya.

Like I said im not too hip on lyrics, so I didnt ask them about lyrics. Aparently their lyrics are almost equally important as the music. In their case I have to agree, even though I can hardly decipher any of the words, I can sense they display as much emotion as the music and therefore I hypocritically plead to you "BUZZ", On the next record have a lyric sheet, and if you need, have an explanation for every line. Im shure a lot of kids would dig it. man.

Speaking of BUZZ, he looks better in an afro than that guy in the movie CAR WASH. Im thinking he should take advantage of this blessing and be the first to go beyond the hip hops shaved symbols and architectured genious of scalp artistry and SCULPt a wacky far out cactus or Bull Winkle antlers.

He writes the songs, riffs first, lyrics second and goddamn is they good! Hes an all around nice guy.

DALE lost weight, bleached and chopped his hair. He plays even harder and an all around NICE GUY.

LORI kicks John Entwistles butt, and is all around nice guy.

They enjoy the GYUTO MONKS , Tibetan Tantric choir.

One of the only forms of religious communication in which I have been emotionally affected by along with the MELVINS and uh maybe the STOOGES or SWANS raping a slave EP'. The only good thing MICKEY HART ever did was to bring this sacred group of monks on a tour in which ive heard from many, seemed like an impersonal circus or freak show. Oh well they needed money to build a new monestary. They probably didnt notice the yochie dead heads hanging out in the audience. yuk!

The special technique in the monks vocalization is a long study of producing three notes or a full chord in the form of long droning chants. It makes for a soothing eerie feeling.

This is an interview that was written several months After matt left the Band in ~~se~~ oct.

are you satisfied with the new line up of the melvins and where you live?

are you ~~tired~~ sick and tired of people asking about the recent breakup with matt and A rumored wedding?

what do you see in this picture? → 

where do you work?

is pizza your favorite food?

is it possible to drive A stick shift in S.F?

Are you experimenting with electronic drums?

to hell with your influences, what's A list of stuff your're listening to lately?

Whos your favorite band?

Who?

NO. Really?

what do you think of the "Seattle sound"?

HAVE you heard the new Die Kreuzen Album?

Are you planning on coming to seattle or its surroundings areas to play a few show?

How many shows have you played in S.F. or its surrounding areas?
Whats the crowd response?

Do you think that the Album Gluey porch Treatments Actually exists or maybe there were only 15 Printed up?

I think the Album would sound even heavier on A dance club Sub woofer Sound system in A Euro Disco fag bar.
what do you think?

What really cool toys do you have?

do you think born Again is A good BLACK SABBATH Album?

did you know that C/Z is collaborating with Toxic shock & then have an add in some fanzines and amongst others names your 7" inch is listed?

wouldnt it be nice to walk into A store and Find A Melvins Record?

Are your song writing styles changing in any WAY.? or CAn we expect the same product forever from the melvins?

I didn't think so.

Tell me A story:

Now you Ask me A question And I will Respond with this

Thanks for the interview
We hope to see you sometime
Cheeri-O

Dale,

Kenichewah,

OKAY, I have not lost my soulful, imbeded roots as an honorary punk Rock, hard, heavy, GUNKA GUNKA GUNKA music slut. Nor have I been sucking up the cute, innocent and clean image Olympia has to offer either. but I have learned to appreciate some of this Calvin/simplistic stuff enough to do my own rendition, which is actually something Ive been planning on doing for years, so it's not really a rip off or a ~~[scribbled out]~~ borrowed influence. Im making up excuses because I dont think you'll like it, but I sent you it anyhow just to fill up space, ~~[scribbled out]~~ for I dont have much new music to let you hear. So anyways.. "How the Hell ARE you doing dale crover "master of DRUMS?"

Send me boom box stuff NOW! I dont think too many people will think you guys will suck, like you said the legworshipping whores might", but B.F.D!

Chris and I were wandering around the campus one saturday evening, and we came across this band playing. Inside we found 3 greeners jamming on bad psychedellic blues, because thats what Greeners do on Saturday evenings. They showed us their new $200.00 worthless whammy pieces of shit KRAMERS & New Laney amps, I wasn't impressed. And then over in the corner I noticed a left handed late 60's fender mustang. After swallowing my puke I calmly asked if they wanted to sell it and they said... "Oh that old piece of shit?" "I dont care, 50 bucks".

Chris entered the conversation and said. "I don't know man it's pretty junky." "OK twenty bucks. it's only pawn shop material anyways. It's nothing compared to our new Kramers.

So chris and I Ran blindly through a ~~b~~ thick forest towards the light and to the van and to a bank machine and bought the pre CBS "65" left handed fender mustang. The END

My amp blew up. I got 2 more evel knievel motorcycles. Rapeman. RAPEMAN! RAPEMAN! I don't have any of their stuff on tape yet. probably because they don't have anything out. but Rapeman are Steve Albini on Guitar/Vocals (from Big Black) & the drummer & bassplayer from Scratch Acid. I saw them last weekend and I think they are one of my favorite bands. I'll have to wait until I hear them on Record. but god damn they were fucking cool live!

I defrosted the icebox with a hammer.

hours later Tracy noticed an awfully powerful fume & so we thought it was Free-on so we got the animals outside & the fumes became so bad that we couldn't go in the apt at all. it started to burn our skin & so we stayed next door for 1 night & in Tacoma the 2nd night & turns out it wasn't free on but even more of a deadly gas called sulfer dioxide. Its like if you were to fill a bucket of Bleach & Ammonia & tie someones face to it. I left a butterscotch swiss miss pudding out over night & it turned Bright flourescent green. So dont beat on your ice box with a hammer.

I talked to Jesse again. he's not getting a divorce anymore, instead he's buying more credit cards.

Touch N Go

Demo

floyd the barber
Spank Thru
Hairspray Queen
~~Aerozeppelin~~
Mexican Seafood
Beeswax
Beans
paper cuts

Big Cheese
Love Buzz
Aeroszeppelin
~~paper cuts~~
pen cap chew
montage of heck

Scratch acid
side of
NIRVANA

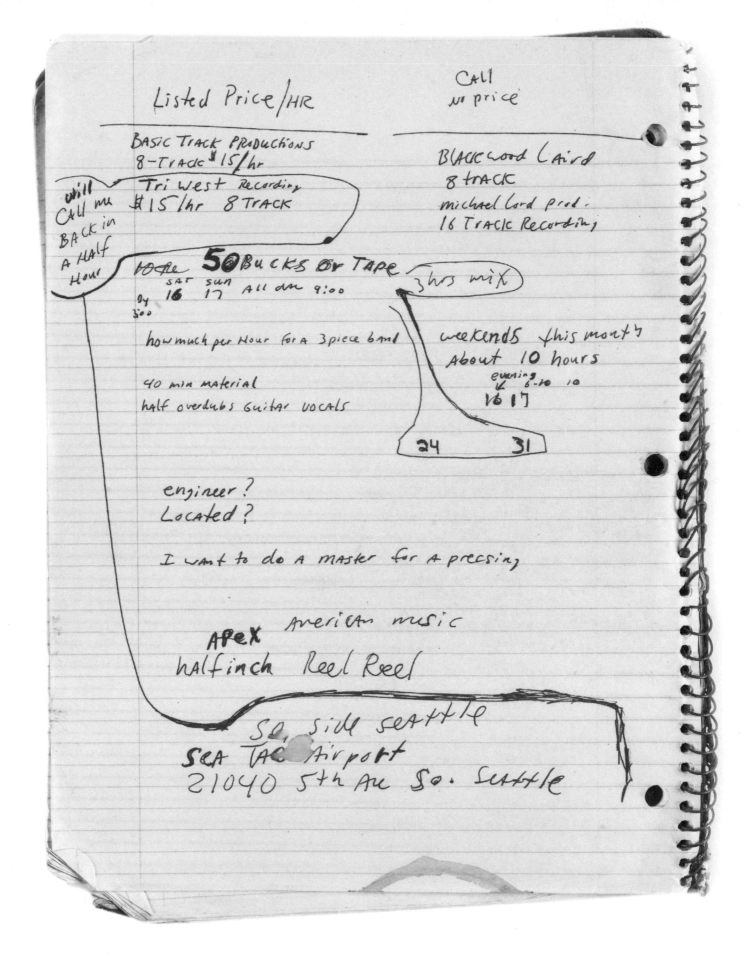

Listed Price/HR

Call
no price

BASIC TRACK PRODUCTIONS
8-Track $15/hr

Tri west Recording
$15/hr 8 TRACK

will Call me BACK in A Half Hour

Blackwood Laird
8 track
michael Lord prod.
16 Track Recording

~~Hope~~ 50 BUCKS Or TAPE

3hrs mix

SAT 16, SUN 17 All day 9:00

by 5:00

how much per Hour for A 3 piece band

weekends this month
About 10 hours

evening 6-10 10
16 17

24 31

40 min material
half overdubs Guitar vocals

engineer?
Located?

I want to do A master for A pressing

American music
APeX
halfinch Reel Reel

So. side seattle
SeA TAC Airport
21040 5th Av So. Seattle

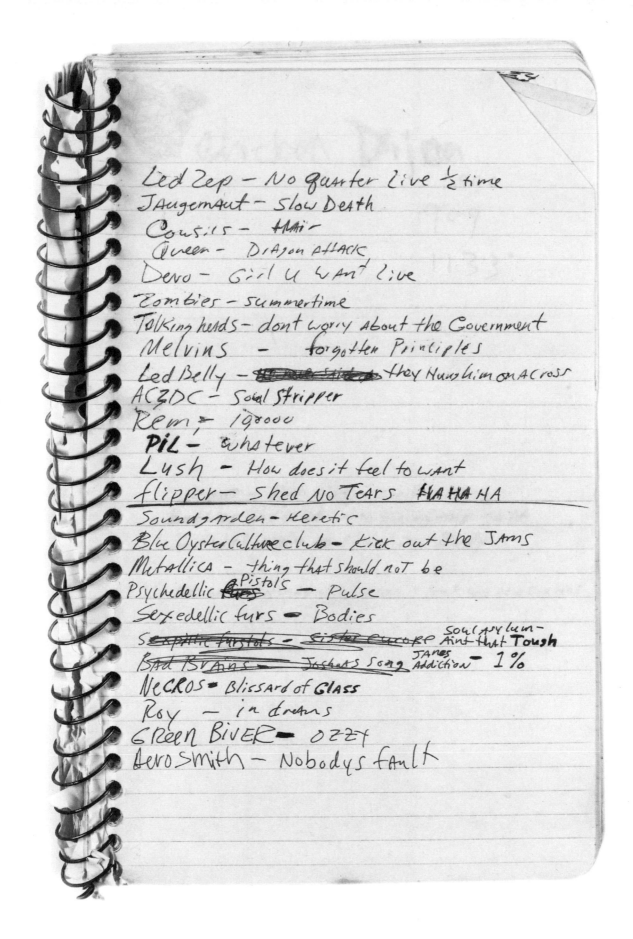

Led Zep – No quarter live ½ time
Jaugernaut – Slow Death
Cowsils – ~~Hair~~
Queen – Dragon Attack
Devo – Girl U want live
Zombies – summertime
Talking heads – dont worry about the Government
Melvins – forgotten Principles
Led Belly – ~~[illegible]~~ they hung him on a cross
AC/DC – Soul Stripper
Rem – 1,000,000
PiL – whatever
Lush – How does it feel to want
flipper – Shed No Tears HA HA HA

Soundgarden – Heretic
Blue Oyster Culture club – Kick out the Jams
Metallica – thing that should not be
Psychedellic ~~furs~~ Pistols – Pulse
Sexedellic furs – Bodies
~~Sexpillic furstols – Sister Europe~~ Soul Asylum – Aint that Tough
~~Bad Brains – Joshuas Song~~ Janes Addiction – 1%
Necros – Blissard of Glass
Roy – in dreams
Green River – Ozzy
Aerosmith – Nobodys fault

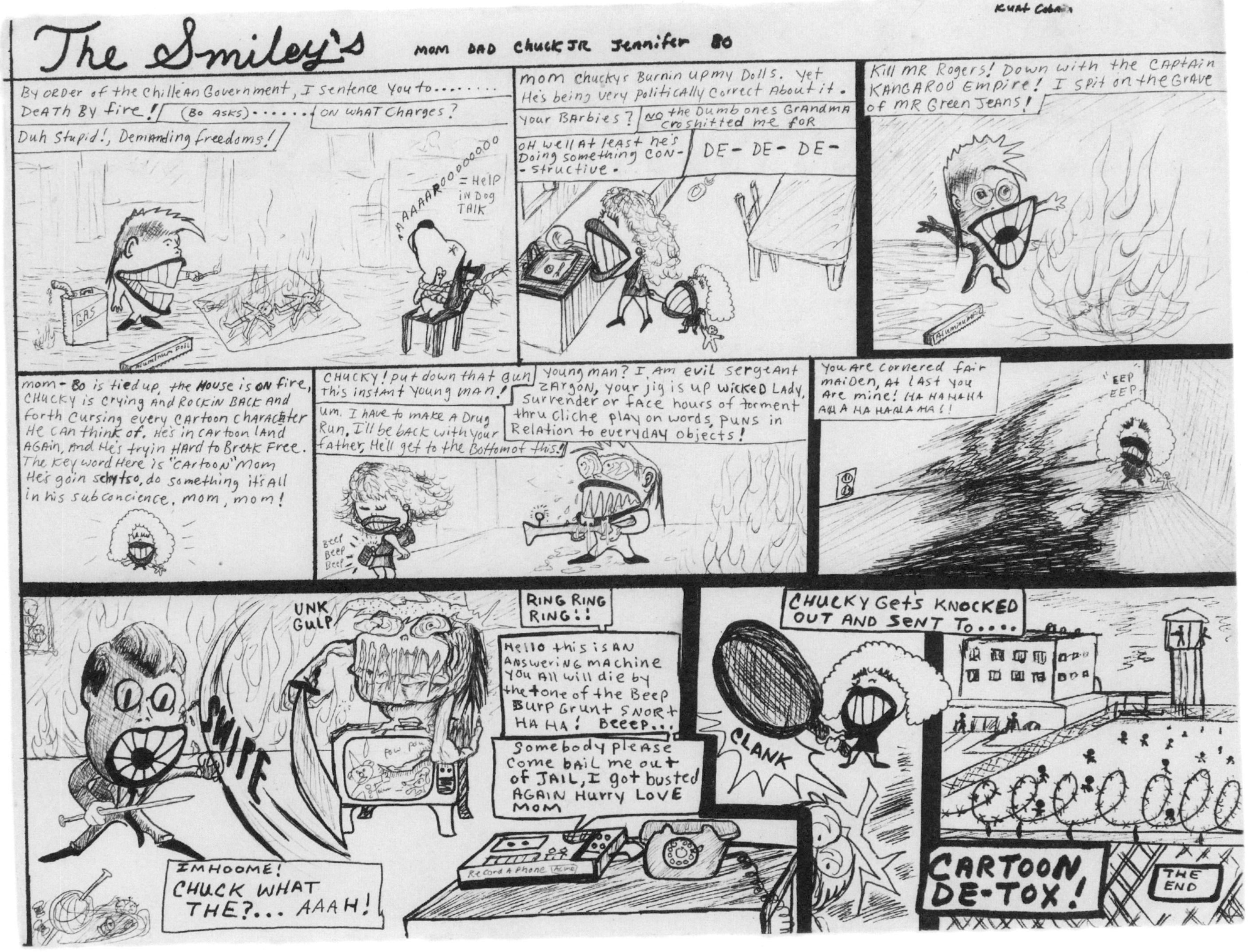
Kurt Cobain
The Smiley's
MOM DAD CHUCK JR Jennifer BO
By ORDER of the Chillean Government, I Sentence You to........
DEATH By fire!
(BO ASKS).......
ON WHAT Charges?
Duh Stupid!, Demanding freedoms!
AAAAARROOOOOOOO
= Help in Dog TALK
GAS
Aluminum Foil
mom Chuckys Burnin upmy Dolls. Yet He's being very politically Correct About it.
Your Barbies?
NO the Dumb ones Grandma croshitted me for
OH well At least he's Doing something CON--structive.
DE-DE-DE-
Kill MR Rogers! Down with the CAPTAIN KANGAROO Empire! I Spit on the Grave of MR Green Jeans!
mom-BO is tied up, the HOUSE is ON fire, CHUCKY is crying And ROCKIN BACK And forth Cursing every CARtoon CHARACter He CAN think of. He's in CARtoon LAnd AGAin, And He's tryin HARd to BreAK Free. The Key word Here is "CARtoon" Mom He's goin schytso, do something it's All in his subconcience, mom, mom!
CHUCKY! put down that gun this instant Young man!
Um. I have to make A Drug Run, I'll be back with your father, He'll get to the Bottom of this!
Beep Beep Beep
Young man? I Am evil sergeant ZARGON, your jig is up WICKED Lady, Surrender or face hours of torment thru cliche play on words, puns in Relation to everyDAY objects!
You Are Cornered fair maiden, At LAST You Are mine! HA HA HA HA AHA HA HAHA HA!!
EEP EEP
UNK GULP
SWIPE
IMHOOME! CHUCK WHAT THE?... AAAH!
RING RING RING!!
Hello this is AN Answering machine You All will die by the tone of the Beep Burp Grunt SNORT HA HA! BEEEP...
Somebody please come bail me out of JAIL, I got busted AGAIN Hurry LOVE MOM
Record A Phone Acme
CLANK
CHUCKY Get's KNOCKED OUT AND SENT TO....
CARTOON DE-TOX!
THE END

Bitching About PROG-ROCK

~~God I Fucking hate prog Rock~~
~~(And this time Bitching about?)~~

~~Ing Bing~~ Ing lots of Ings. Descriptive words end IN ING. like masturbating, over exagerating ~~& Explanding~~. munching, chewing hot stacked-earth momma sitting in the open woods of Nottingham early in the mornings fog. listening to STAIRWAY to Heaven while stringing beads. Not applying makeup. In tune, AquA man circles emulating from A forehead. Bouncing off of A crustal necklace. A neck strangled by piano wire. "I have friends both on land and in the sky." But the Sea mr French? "I dog paddle for I am now a teeny little goblin-dancing-pixie--zamphire master of the pan flute."

Sold over A zillion archery dummies in Europe Alone! The dummys are sex dolls stuffed with leaches & A substance of Ginger Root, penny Royal tea, Ginseng, B-vitamins, sweet cut-grass and A spoiled pound of ground baby veal (Lamb.)

Doctor Bronner claims! Apply the archery Dummy-substance naked in the forest. Dilute! Dilute! MR Merlin. Dilute! Dilute! sprinkling minute metal shavings into the eyes of A praised cult ~~statue figure~~ figurine. A male. Here now in the woods. Getting back to nature. The breath is visible as he exhales from the bull-like nostrils. scraping back leg into the ground. mounting the earth momma. no matter how hard you try, sex will always resurface.

Buffy and Jody get it on. Rick Wakeman does the soundtrack.

Hi first of all I enjoy your show.

Jesse Helms is A dirty homosexual.
The Imperial wizard of the KKK is a nigger.
~~Oooh! thee harsh words of a sweet or sour~~
~~Bitter-beer-batter grease splatter scatter.~~
~~MAD Hatter.~~
~~Do you like the shaggs?~~
Am I guilty of such hipness?
NO longer is there hipness or such Tom foolery
for this boy whos NAME is [redacted]. Hi that is my
name. I WAS thinking thee other day.
of my name and thought I would write you
<u>NOT</u> in regards to my name regardless of thee
sentence which MAY have thrown you off.
~~or get you off~~. I could only be such a
fool to modestly think ~~such a lord could~~
~~think~~ How could one such suck winding-force
of so many celebs colors in hopes of
~~Celebrating~~ celebrating the Calibre of
such hipness. MAY I throw out my hip?
I had A bAd fAll. I limped.
I limped with the best of them.
I have now come to the conclusion
that I have been [redacted] confused for many
days and I now love many days and
many many of those I love whom I have
So wrongly Accused of being hip.
Those who come to celebrate with one
Another only for the reasons of
companionship in which they so
Rightly share. They share the
same things. They seek out
others. So fuck.
AT peace AM I. [redacted] youre A good one.

"MONTE VISTA" SO TACOMA WAY

The name even reakes of suburban subdivision Hell. I walked into the place to buy a patch cord. After I bought it I noticied a bunch of amps behind a sliding glass door. There were new Peavy's marshalls Fenders. After Gawking at the list price I checked out the used amps. I noticed an old Fender. It's the kind thats about four Feet tall and has SIX tens in it. It's basically a twin reverb. So I closed the door, plugged in the ~~old~~ cheap Peavey tryout gee-tar And Fucked around with the reverb & tremolo. It sounded pretty cool kind of like the cramps. SHit it was only $200.00, ~~It~~ kind of beat, so I was interested. ~~So~~ Fuck it, I cranked it up way loud to see what kind of balls it had. Right then mr. Suavo Coolo ~~Friend~~ Friendly yo store dude walked in and turned it down. ~~_~~ He had a shit eating grin on and said "Jams eh". I said "yeah man".

"Can I put this on Lay-a-way"
He said "Sure $20 bucks down
15 bucks a week for ninety
days." "Far out" He went away
so I cranked it again, so he
walks back in with his diaharreha
smile and turns it down.
what a dick I should have
thrown it threw the godamn
sliding glass door. I said
Sheeeatt! I left. That old
Fuckin Fender would a blew any
way.

Globe trotters theme
Lucy in the Sky - William Shatner
The sensitive little boy - pro GAY Record
Pusherman - superfly sndtrk
Shes got you - PAtsy Cline
frustrated - chipmunk punk (CRACK)
Keep yor hands off her - leadbelly
JAVA - Floyd Cramer
IN Love / HONEY > Marine Girls
mollys lips - VASelines
BAllad of Evel Knievel
Somethin like that - NWA
TV Girl - Beat HAppening
Scratch it out > Go team (Tam sings)
Bikini twilight me & CAlvin & Toby
He never SAid A mumblin WORD - Leadbelly

Telly SAVALAS Greasing up his head And Ramming it in And out! IN And out of Another TV personalities ASS. who's ASS? who cares. either way it's A cheap way to get an immediate laugh.

________ ← ~~put the stars name here.~~

~~It would be even more Affective if it is A male. Homosexual scandals Amongst celebrities are always A shure fire chuckle getter.~~

~~How About Goober And Gomer givin it to eachother.~~
OR ~~Gary Coleman (Arnold on Different Strokes) And Emmanuelle Lewis (Webster) reesus monkey love in the 69 tongue butt position.~~ ~~Why Am I So Sexually conscious? Why can I not be clean? Have I read too many poems? or Charles Bukowski?~~ Is this the easy way out?
NO. Sex is dirty. It is over rated.
"I don't want to be touched After its over."
"It wasn't worth it to cheat on my partner."
It took him 3 days to realize why he was depressed. After All, his male friends approved with smurks and trumpeting farts. Besides tellys stubble scratched the inner walls of my colon. Do not be fooled by shiny, waxy baldness. His neck was A Jackhammer. Very talented. Shecky Greene Joined in. We ran up A Huge gold card Bill. That's Alright, I'm A High Roller. All my celebrity friends are Here with me. Here in LAS Vegas. Naked, shaved And Greased. These life size card board cut-outs store away easily in my closet. Lolli pop up you know where.
Lolli lolli lolli pop.

OH Im so damn proud of you.

A Triumphant victory for mandkind. maybe there is Hope. It brought A tear to my eye & A lump in my throat. Staring out the window in A traffic JAM for 3 hours watching the little LAwnmower cars zoom past hundreds of happy westerners receiving them with A compassionate, full contact smile and stare. Youve made it. Have some fruit. Now you too can purchase pastel bed sheets, Electronics and toilet paper of your wildest dreams. You have so much to learn. Thousands of Grown infants, Rosy red cheeks fully dressed in Acid wash pants & JAckets, males with moustache, Ladies with permanent hair. Look over there! it's my mom. She is so many years more advanced in the Art of shopping & matching outfits from the luxury of selection. you have so much to learn. Rock and Roll has now just begun. Don't hide the products you have bought under your seats. prepare yourself for A full search as you enter back through the border. Take note of the leaflets and flyers on your windshield informing you where to acquire credit And legal representation. I'm happy for you. please Reproduce. were doing All we can over here As well.

groon

APly
APPly

Stewie glzdly and rightensly
WAlk you
through the
mysterious
world of
fashion

LAydown your WARM bAbies on my cold feet
At the end of my Bed
I Apologize for Apologizing
TASte buds SOAK Absorbant sponge water and
my tongue Runs Across the roof of my mouth
and it feels like A SMAll Rib CAge
Giant Nose HAir Booger Hinge

I don't mind my captivity, but the pelt
and habitat description
next to the cage is a bit distasteful,
Fucking Bull HAd A Vision, He would write A
punk Rock operA

THE STORY

his nAmeis forest And he is the one
who put's CAlcium in the TAb soft drinks.
and his followers wAve their Arms in unison
with his. Clenching, crimping irons And
MAscArA (blAck), "We must mAke the Woods
Pretty AGAin)), shouted the steAm engine inventor.
Yes but what About the Piles of MAsses?
the HeApiny mounds of sponge, Severed Pore,
And TAste bud Chunks, nervously bitten And
SPAT out of the mouth from the ChiwAwA
HeAd, Johnny MAthis monster? asked Chowder.)
It is sucking dry All the resin from the
Bong WAter River. I sAy we destroy the filter
WAlls! (shouted Helium Boy.) And then (fucking Bull) spoke..

Skip 2 pages
And go on →

He spat ~~chew~~ Dark brown bubbling snoose from the dried veins of New Age believers. it soaked into the ground instantly which reminded him that the woods are in greater need of emergency than he thought. he said "look my friends, spit and see the Quickness of the Soil.

And as all 5 beings spat and observed. Tony Defranco crabs surfaced and gobbled what little moisture they could before being stepped on and crushed and quickly ~~gobbled up~~ consumed by our hero's. the feast was celebrated with an offering of ~~spam~~ fresh squeezed grease pockets of spam and pepperoni chunks filled to the Rim of an ancient 1990's ~~[illegible]~~ Teenage unwanted baby skull.

But this does not explain our misfortune grunted Buttchowder. Please, please tell us more Fucking Bull and so fucking Bull spoke again.

It was in my vision that I saw stoners destroy a church with No Roof and only 3 walls. and there were candles, many candles and the Virgin Mary Hooked ~~on~~ thru her back on a meat hook, and one of the male stoners said "Dude Hooker headers!" then stopped dead in his tracks with his hand just softly touching her firm breast and noticed how painfully Beautiful she was, how pure and white, how peaceful wrapped in chicken and barbed wire with a not yet

ON All drums - get rid of Hi HAT Hiss.

Downner - Re-Do All vocals & get someone with A Deep voice to repeat solo vocals in monotone

[illegible] Re-Do All Guitar & bass

Floyd - Re-Do bass - Dub extra Guitar

Paper Cuts - Dub Guitar - Dub Singing Harmony

[illegible] Re-Do-Bass

Spank thru - Re-Do Bass

~~[illegible]~~

Hairspray Queen - Re-Do everything

Pen Cap chew - Re-Do everything

Mexican Seafood - Re-Do Guitar Drums Voc.
(Dales drums)

ERECTUM

Love Buzz Big cheese ERECTUM weirdo
Beeswax Aeroszeppelin vendetagainst
Annoyeyourcist

A finished anarchy sign spray painted on her Robe. Then his head turned slowly to his mates, ~~and~~ ~~cried~~ A trickle of Teardrop Rolled down his ugly fucking zitted out face and cried: "This is WRONG! We MUST STOP This"! and so one of the girl stoners kind of put all her weight on one foot and stuck her acid wash ASS out, ~~held a cigarette~~ took a big drag off of a lucky STRIKE cigarette, gave a very cool blank/stoned expression under those heavily eye shadow (Blue) thicker than snot lashed eyes, exhaled and in a groggy dry wheezing, charred lung voice said, "So what we're bored." And the others immediately Ran around screaming. Wooo Hooo (in that tone of voice that says "I'm very drunk, excited and a TOTAL idiot"!) they smashed and Burned and SPRAYed Black flag, DRI ~~[illegible]~~ as well as Dokken and Whitesnake. Then Guess what? asked fucking Bull, ~~they after a while they got Bored and went away~~ what? what happened said Butt Chowder? fucking Bull said: ~~[illegible]~~ After awhile they became bored with vandalizing the church and went ~~[illegible]~~ away to buy a gram. So I suggest we all just connect our vitals to this ancient cow milking Hookah and Relax, because the River will never dry up for it is fed by the mountains which will always be addicted to boredom.

The END

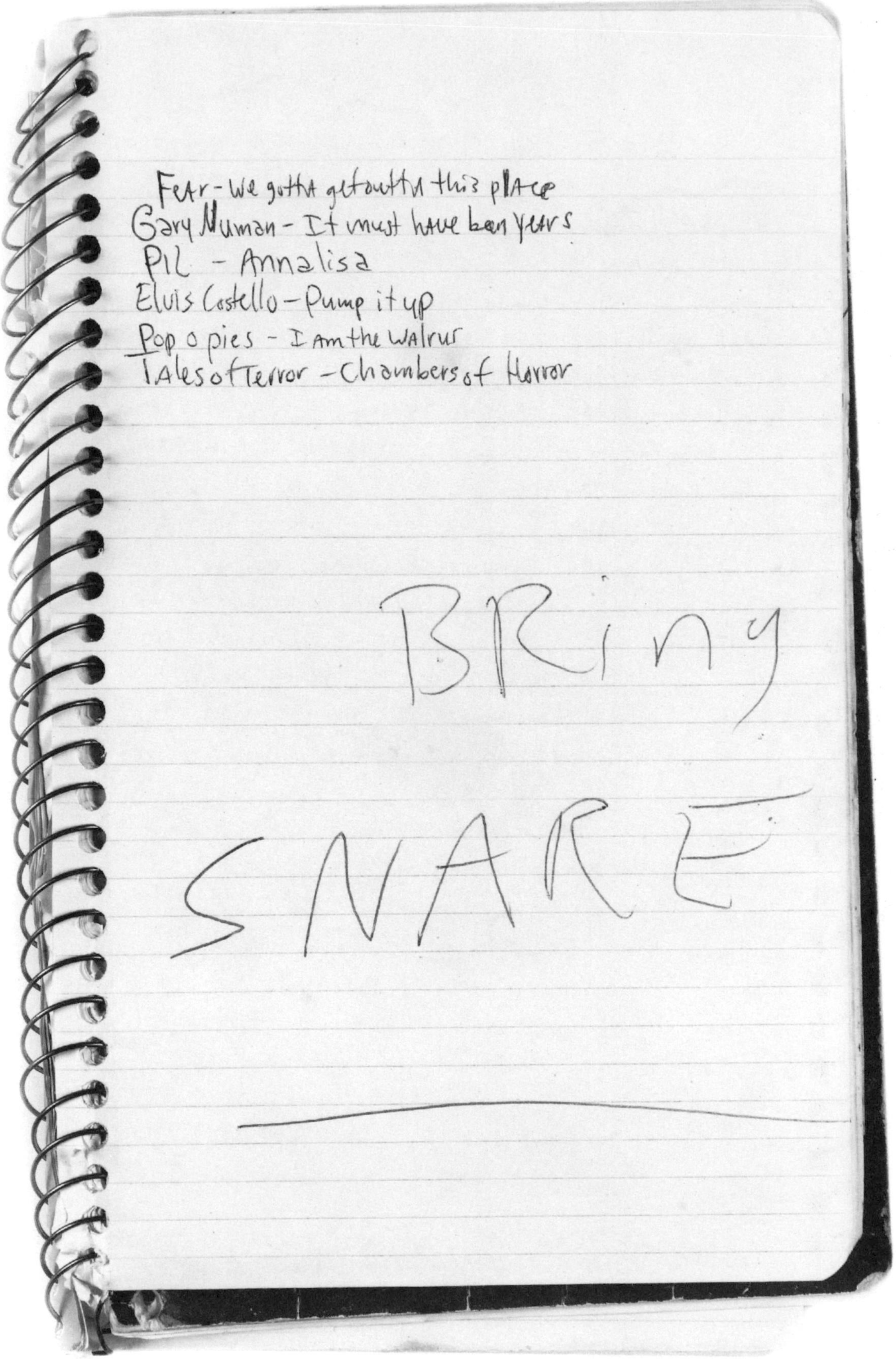
Fear - We gotta getoutta this place
Gary Numan - It must have been years
PiL - Annalisa
Elvis Costello - Pump it up
Pop o pies - I am the walrus
Tales of Terror - Chambers of Horror
BRing
SNARE

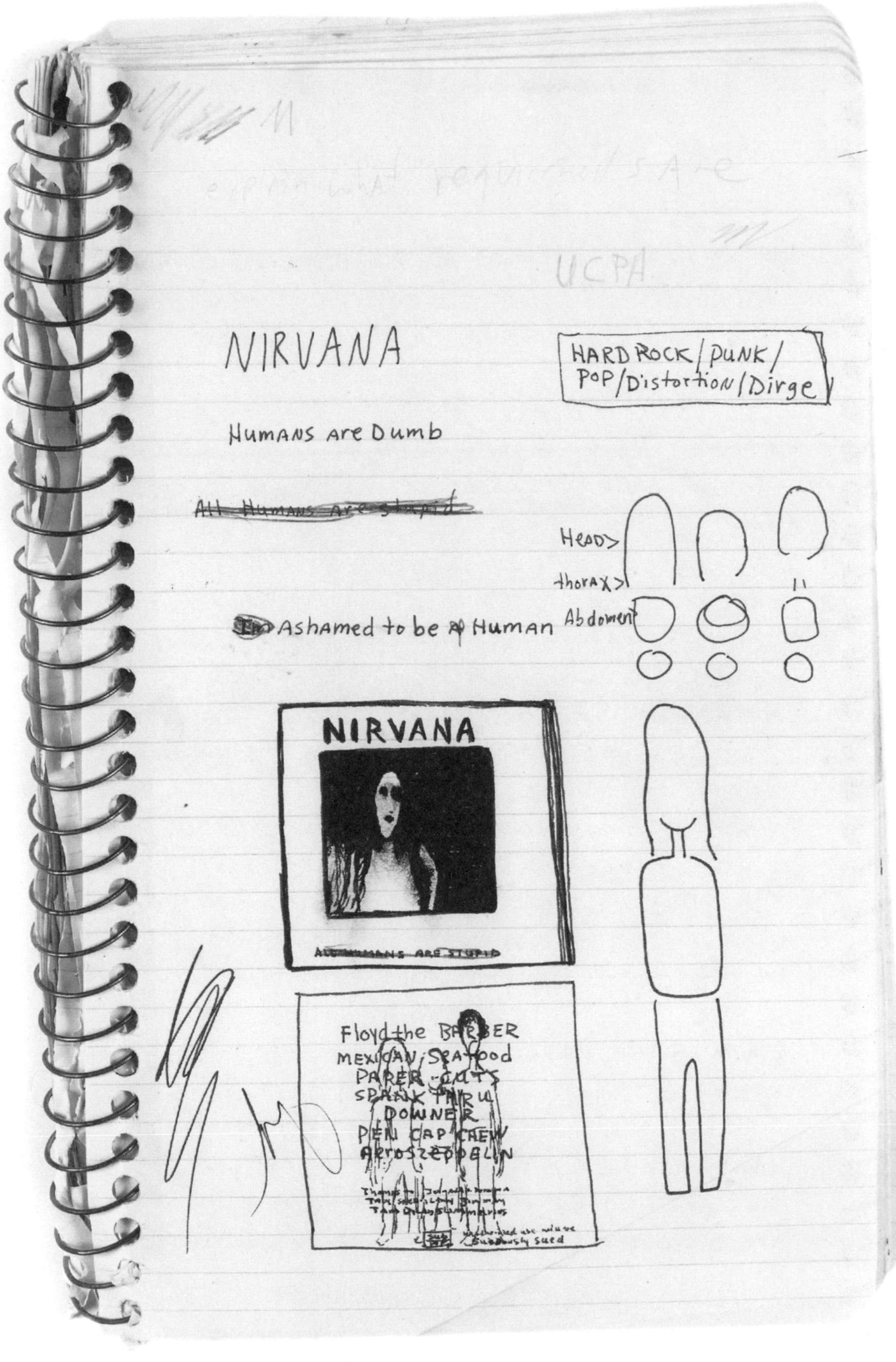

UCPH

NIRVANA

HARD ROCK / PUNK / POP / Distortion / Dirge

Humans are Dumb

~~All Humans are stupid~~

Head>

thorax>

Abdomen

Ashamed to be Human

NIRVANA

~~ALL HUMANS ARE STUPID~~

Floyd the BARBER
MEXICAN SEAFood
PAPER CUTS
SPANK THRU
DOWNER
PEN CAP CHEW
AEROSZEPPELIN

Critic goes GOD

The first thing i did WAS burn All my Charles Bukowski books. I got the tinfoil out and spreadit on the floor, Ripped the ~~books~~ filthy innards of plankton-literature into small pieces, and struck A match. I Turned out the lights and watched the flames along with some home Super 8 movies I had made while under the influence of this life I've decided to change. The movies were typical Gore slash shit along with puppets fucking, oh And the psychic TV-~~[illegible]~~-like effect of Arty subjects turning and floating ~~[illegible]~~ in A meaningful surrealistic sense. bullshit, it was like watching A Real estate seminar, but it set A nice background for my MTV Direction towards god. God. God. God. Im Crosslegged, Rosary to ~~my Right, Bible to my left.~~ the left of me, Bible to the Right, here I Am stuck in the middle with you". stuck in the middle with you.' who sang that song? Atlanta Rhythm Section? steve miller, UM, God. 'Atlanta Rhythm Section has the dorkiest looking members, that one Guy with Greasy pig fat hair, and Black Rimmed Glasses. But the

Stupidest looking 70's Rock star has to be that one Guy in Slade, the fucker cut his bangs so high up on his forehead. "He looks like Woody from the bay City Rollers". I know this kid in Aberdeen who looks <u>exactly</u> like woody. Jesus you wouldn't believe it, the same teeth and Nose, ~~it's not sad it's just funny.~~ I would love to look like Woody, then I could start my band and were Play Saturday Night. "Was kiss on Saturday Night live? Naw ~~they~~ they couldn't have, ~~people~~ fans would have trashed the studio & beat up Don Pardo, ~~and Raped Lorraine Newman.~~ I would love to be those kids on the back of Kiss Alive, the ones holding the banner. Kiss. I don't even like Kiss.

Rock Trivia. God im so sick of Rock Trivia, big deal it's like what am i gonna do when I'm old, if i already know everything About Rock-n-Roll by the time im 19? God only knows ~~now adays~~ there's No facts to be learned About All these worthless Ripoff Nostalgic bands of the 80's. OH yeah i decided to eventually become an H addict and slowly decay on the streets of Idaho. or some middle of the road state like that. Ill be so bored that ill just read About what I lived thru And purposely stayed NAive, because you mR Rock Critic Are gonna be Bored when your old. Bored Bored Bored. So Am I so Are old People today. I don't WAnt A GrAnd daughter of mine changing my soiled Rubber underwear ~~And~~ while I sucking on Ry-Krisp, Clinging to existence just so I cAn reminice About my life As A professional Remeniscent. Besides, my memory is Already shot, from too much PoT smoking A few years back. I SAW these Hippies on the merve Griffin show claiming they had NASAl SPRAYS wich would increase youre memory, I Also SAW this couple who swore, with the proper trAining, "you cAn have up to 10 orgAsms before ejAculAting, sure if you tie A rubber bAnd to the end.

All this wonderfully important deep thought hindered me from REAlizing that the entire House WAS filled with smoke from the Charles Bukowski Books, And A very nice sized flame had spread to the curtAins, which AlArmed me I had only A few minutes to Get out of the House, So much for God.

Sexually Transmitted Diseases
in the espresso at the Smithfield

Green River - Aint Nothin to do
Dead Boys - Dead River Boys
Dicks - Police force
Clown Alley - on the way up
Vox Pop - Production
SKIN DIVER - AD NO. 7
Shockin Blue - HOT SAND
Bangles - Hazy shade of Winter
the eyes - Don't talk to me
Saccharine Trust - Peace frog
~~youre n~~ Big Dipper - youre NOT PATSY
Big BLACK - CRACK UP
Big Boys - A Political
Alice Cooper - Muscle of Love
GReg Sage - StRAight AHEAD
MAl Funkshun - Stars and You
SMelvins - SMell My Finger
DeVO - TURN AROUND
White Zombie - RATMOUTH
Zombies - Time of the Season
DICKS - off Duty Sailor
A PART of the Tape that will be Fast forwarded every time it's played
The Tonsil Song HA HA HA HA HA HA HA HA HA HA HA

Throughout the periods of 1976 to 1983, a man by the name of Chuck Taylor brutally sexually ~~an~~ Tortured 9 women, one man and one 13 yr old boy, within the area of Greater Los Angeles.

In Comparison to other so called "Celebrity" murderers one wouldn't think of Chucks Case as a Record setting toll of victims, in mathematical sense, (no". yet in Ritualistic Highly detailed, well planned taste for the bizarre (yes". Chucks story hasnt become the most well know folk tale as had ED Geine, simply because facts havent been revealed as in depth until now, where ED Geine may have wore his victims skin and ate their flesh, Chuck did that and far exceeded Ed's descriptiveness for his own so called Ceremony. Chuck recorded every day of his waking life.

suicide note found with Chuck Taylors body feb. 17. 1983

To whom it may concern,

Please excuse Chucks absence from life. ~~I~~ ~~cant~~ I do not expect anyones sorrow for my death maybe relief if anything. I can't describe what mental illness is, Ive tried and tried with writings And doctors and my only conclusion is satan has taken over my soul and mind, please use my brain as an example and try to find out whats wrong, like the guy in texas who shot those people in the tower. to all the relatives & friends of my victims Im deeply sorry Im ~~Im~~ very sorry Ha HA HA Im not sorry HA HA HAHA HA you motherfuckers cunt! Chuck Taylor (not a basketball star.)

Born Sept 1st 1958 in SANTA CLARA California Chuck Joseph Taylor, son of Fred and mary Taylor was a perfectly normal Healthy, Happy baby, full of sunshine and Joy. A first Grandson and nephew for both sides of the family, Chuck was the center of attention, often hearing harmless quarrels over "who gets to hold him" between several young teenage Aunts. Fred and Mary just married out of Highschool, were immature, just starting out, already used to their white trash homestyle. Depression hadn't set in yet so they were pretty much Happy. Fred had a short temper and worked two jobs while mary with another baby on the way stayed at home giving young chuck now 5yrs old more than enough loving attention and encouragement. He loved monsters. All kinds, they were more interesting than Super heroes and often against his parents wishes he would plead with his baby sitter to let him watch the friday night Horror movies, and very consistently would end up crying or wetting his pajamas in fear within minutes of the beginning. Yet he still insisted, "monsters are the best" he had drawings, comic books, posters, models and masks Truly an obsession, but most of his influences were cheesy old space invader or Dracula movies. wich has baffled doctors on his case of wich, why or how he possibly could think up such vulgar re-enactments of horror while playing with his sisters dolls. arranging nativity scenes of murder with Jesus mary and Joseph figurines along with, G-I Joes and barbie's, cautiously cutting holes in them filling them up with moms red nail polish, finding him in a trance like state rocking back and forth screaming fuck you bad peoples fuck you

He was usually veri clean about his seizures, He always made sure there were newspapers down and a wash rag handy and the knives and matches were on an old cigarbox the lights dim, curtains closed, wearing the same old football jersey that was way too small, no pants and most important to make sure dad wasnt home.

Recalling many painful instances. his younger sister Jenny was often unable to defend for herself against Chucks agressive abuse, he was always holding her down and sat on her face and farting, talking her into A ~~tasting~~ Guessing game, tied to a chair and blind folded tickled till she peed her pants and then forced to taste A Collected sample and regularly sexually explored her,

"He wouldnt do the usual tortures like other older brothers, like a simple peeled grape and being told it's A cats eyeball, Chuck would always give me tobasco sauce or his soiled finger that had been up his Anus, call it relative blood or whatever I still couldnt help but feel sorry for him, because he's the one that witnessed dad's abuse towards mom."

Almost every night Fred Taylor came home from a degrading laymens job intoxicated, hungry and very angry. as if it were a routine at 7:30 each nite Chuck would be greeted by his dad standing in ~~the~~ his bedroom doorway swaying back and forth with a transfixed hateful expression. "Git in here boah its time to see how bad yer momma's been today, come on Goddamnit! Git yer fucking little wimpy ass in here! grabbing him by the neck Chuck would be pushed into his parents bedroom. the door slamming shut and mom already naked huddled on a

Corner of the bed in a natural crying plead
knowing that she might as well get it over with before
dinner gets too cold. Taking off his belt, loosening his
trousers fred would beat mary Rape and Sodomize
her ~~just hard enough to be classified as S&M~~
during the intercourse Chuck was commanded to
watch while Fred stared at his son and Repeated the
same speech every night. Your Gonna Grow up to
be a man Chucky a man! you see this winch?
theyre good for nothin but cookin and fuckin! your
Gonna go to school and yer gonna be a doctor Chuck
Goddamnit your not Gonna be like me you hear? ugly
A Good Boy that's my Boy you fuckin Bitch! ugly! ugly
turning to mary you had to have kids, well these
kids is Gonna be fine people not Bad like you
Ugly Fucking Bitch! Chucky? what you gonna do Boah?
A winner I can't hear you! A winner dad OK now go
on git, Jenny was never asked to witness this probably
because dad thought when she gets older she could
leech off of a rich Boy and Support Daddy and momma
Chuck would never talk about it when I questioned
him i felt so sorry for him that i must have felt this
self destructive need to put up with his abuse and
Chuck had a very clever and sly way of mixing laughing
playing and having fun with abuse. one minute
we would be playing & the next he would Hit me
and go into a jekyll and Hyde personality, then when his
tension was relieved he would comfort me to stop my
crying begging me not to tell mom and Hell never do it
again. Bribes of candy or toys were always a good pay off
for a 4 yr old little Girl, and if bribes didn't work
threats usually would.

With good intentions and noticing traces of
Abnormal hyperactive behavior and numerous complaints from
school Mary Taylor devoted A lot of time in helping Chuck
become more relaxed. after All if "VAlium helped her nerves,
then why not chucks!! the long talks and reading time
special Attention seemed to help some, but the long term
affect of downers seemed to counteract to his nerves
A bit too strong, wich bore the many trips to the doctors
for Treatment of hypertension and involuntary nervous seizures,
chuck now 9 yrs old by this time is very used to medications.

School WAS fine in kindergarten, he seemed
to have A few good friends and willing to learn gave him the
everpopular standard mark by his teacher as "A pleasure to have
in class" but gradually thru 1st And second grades Chucks
over bearing personality gave him quite A few enemies
especially with girls, the pretty ones were Afraid of
him and the ugly ones got beat up by him. Condemning
unatractive people At such an early Age proved to be A key
relation to his Antics later on in life. As A few
psychologists on chucks case Agreed it started when chuck
now proclaimed "A future responsible man". by his father
WAS Asked to dispose of A retarded [illegible] kitten one of seven
wich All eventually dissapeared [illegible] in A litter of his sisters
momma CAT SNO white. A Gunny SACK in the river WAS
expected not ~~cutting of~~ decappatation, cutting it's
stomach out, spreading the innards on his face And
Repeatedly running his tongue on it's rib cage. When
Questioned of this by one of the psychologists
Chuck Replied

"I wanted to see if the roof of my mouth felt the same as a rib cage, and you know what? it does! every body ~~has~~ in the world has rib cages in the roof of their mouths - cool huh? He also insisted that peas have mashed potatoes in them". His mother remembers "He seemed to have a different pet each month it wasn't until years after he moved out that we found all the animal bones in the basement!!"

Over looking his serious hyperactivity ~~people~~ kids that knew him couldn't help but admit that Chuck had a very bizarre yet funny sense of humor, this humor crowned him the class cut up and falsely gave him friends who took advantage of him just to see the next gag which was always directed towards hurting, scaring or humiliating an individual, and by the 6th grade at age 12 ~~he~~ experienced his first expell from school by defacating in a paper towel and hurling it into the face of an unpopular teacher.

and when he was let back to school it was well worth it for he had even more attention from his peers."

Elvis
Cooper

Aneurysm

Come on over & do the twist
over do it & have a fit
Come on over & shoot the shit
I love you so much it makes me
sick

she keeps it pumpin straight to my heart

SAPPY

And if you SAVE yourself
you will - think your happy
He'll keep you in A JAR
then you'll - think your happy
He'll give you breather Holes
then you'll - think your happy
He'll cover you in grass
then you'll - think your happy now
(Your in A Laundry Room)
Conclusion came to you AM

And if you HEAL yourself
you will MAKE Him happy
you'll wallow in your shit

And if you cure yourself

Verse Chorus Verse

Neither side is sacred ~~theres no room~~ no one wants to win
feeling so sedated think I'll just give in
TAKin medication till our stomachs full
wouldnt wanna fake it - if I had A soul

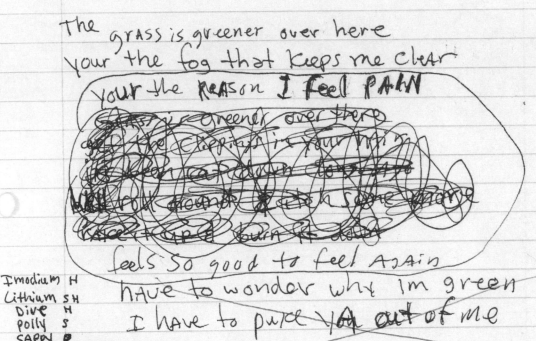

The grass is greener over here
your the fog that keeps me clear
your the REASON I feel PAIN
~~grass is greener over there~~
[illegible]
feels so good to feel Again
~~have to wonder why Im green~~
~~I have to puke ya out of me~~

Imodium H
Lithium SH
Dive H
polly S
SAPPY P
token Eastern song H
Verse chorus verse P
IN Bloom H
PAY to PLAY H
~~Not like them~~ S I think is dumb
Been A son P

maybe when Im ~~younger~~ I'll refuse to Grow
injecting ~~Nutrition~~ progress moves too slow
maybe when im older I'll hold and stomach in
maybe when IM ready we could try again

CRYBABY JERKINS fouls it up AGAIN
GANGLIA
shake it off Soy Boy
BIG DUMP
FWUMP
BENNY HANNAS Restaurant
DINNER COOKED Right at your TABLE. by Professional Chinese master chef. Fudge
SPECIAL TODAY :
fry BABYS ON TOAST with JUICE
THUNDER CHICKEN
CRACK
sizzle
pop
BENNY HANNAS COOKED AT YOUR TABLE
Thunder CHICKEN 90¢ A Bottle
AAAA Fudge! Ize Be gittin my Busted chops Butcher cover profit from GLANDULAR tubesteak LARVA, NO FUN! NO FUN! NO FUN!
sellin them DAMN Porcelin Ash trays SHAPED AS lungs fancys my NARDS
SHISTE! Now that the warehouse is completed, Sheet Rock copper wire & Round shiny slugs of metal from electrical outlets need to Be Picked up. the Molds of Porcelain were
soon to Be Whittled, But Just in the Nick of Time CRY Baby JERKINS APPEARS AND will soon:
FOUL IT UP AGAIN
Disguised AS CORN-POOP
SATAN SATAN SATAN SATAN SATAN SATAN SATAN SATAN

Dive

Pick me - Pick me yeah
Let a low long signal
At ease at least yeah
everyone is Hollow
Pick me - Pick me yeah
everyone is waiting
Pick me - Pick me yeah
~~you we~~ even pay them
you can

Hey
Dive Dive Dive Dive in me

Kiss this kiss that yeah
let a low long signal
At ease at ease yeah
You can be my Hero
Pick me pick me yeah
everyone is ~~Waiting Hollow~~ waiting
Hit me Hit me yeah
~~I can even swallow~~
Im real good at Hating

Hi Eugene,
Im staying at a friends house here in Olympia listening to a crappy college radio show. Ive realized that its not because there are no good bands but because the DJs have Bloody awful taste in music. OH yes, and to prove my point, right now theyre playing a NIRVANA song from an old demo.

Hows Captain America? I hear were playing some shows together when we go over to England. I cant wait! were really looking forward to it. all our friends will be there at Redding. mudhoney Babes in Toyland Sonic Youth, Iggy etc. Ashure blow out!

Well, we won the WAR.

Patriotic propaganda is in full effect.

We have the privilege of purchasing Desert Storm trading cards, flags, bumperstickers and many video versions of our triumphant victory, When I walk down the street I feel like Im at a Nurenburg rally.

Hey, maybe Nirvana & Captain America could go on tour together in the States and burn American flags on stage. well be going out again in Sept If youre interested, Ill keep you posted. well, heres the live mollys lips 7" I find it embarrasing because its just simply a bad version but it was a great privilege to play one of your songs and to play together at a show and to meet you all. It was easily the GREATEST moment of my life

The Vaselines have been my favorite #1 band for a long while now and and Geez. I cant wait to see you all soon and thanks for writing.

I got evicted from my apt., I'm living in my car so I have no address but here's chris's phone number for messages

your Pal Kurdt

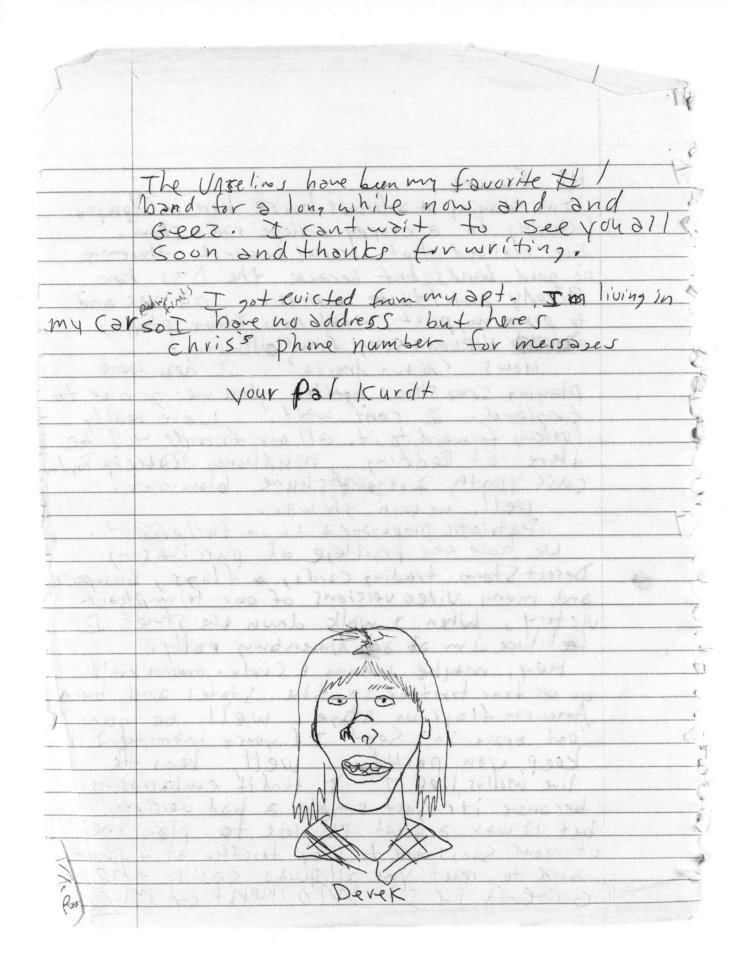

Derek

1 Stooges - Raw power
2 Beatles - ~~meet the Beatles~~ Something new
3. Lead bellys last sessions
4 Scratch Acid - 1st EP
5. Butthole surfers - 1st EP
6. Vaselines - 1st EP
7. Fang - Land Shark
8 Smithereens - especially for you
9 Tales of terror - tales of terror
10. Pixies - Surfer Rosa
11. mudhoney - Superfuzz Bigmuff
12. Flipper - Generic flipper
13. Black flag - my war
14 Black Sabbath - master of Reality
15. credence Clearwater - Bayou
16 Blue Cheer - Vincebus eruptum
17. The Knack - Get the Knack
18. Saccharin trust - 1st EP
19. Roy Orbison - Greatest hits
20 Gang of four - Entertainment
21. Wipers - ~~Youth of America~~ is this real
22. Shocking Blue - Shocking Blue
23. Bad brains - Rock for light
24. Beat Happening - Jamboree
25. Aerosmith - Rocks
26. Shonen Knife - ~~K cassette~~ burning farm
27. young marble Giants - YMG
28. velvet underground - white light white heat
29. Sex pistols - never mind the Bollocks

- I am threatened by ridicule
- I am overly concience of the sincerity my voice.
- I like to have sex with people
- I love my parents yet I disagree with merely everything they stand for.
- I understand and appreciate the religion for others.
- my emotions are affected by music.
- punk rock means freedom
- I use bits and pieces of others personalities to form my own.

Hi, I like punk rock more than anything in the whole wide world. and so I thought I'd would xerox words on paper & staple them together and sell them to punk Rockers & others who dont know much about punk Rock and for those who dont care or who dont deserve the privilege and also to those who are Bored with it.

I Also dont know very much about punk Rock

As far As the History is concerned But I do have An opinion on what punk Rock means to me it means freedom from:

Well, me too. I'm bored or just uninspired. maybe were just taking a break, a rest or recovery from Hardcore. I never really liked hardcore, mainly because it was too macho and there were so many intimidating rules. I remember when I first started hanging out with friends who were a few months more advanced in proper punk rock lingo & ettiquette, I said, "hey lets listen to some punk," and this guy said "man its not called punk anymore its called HARD CORE!" Gee, I felt like a heel. HARD CORE was an obvious mutation of 77 punk because punk popularity reached the suburbs and then all of a sudden Jocks who already had short hair from the wrestling team got involved because it was supposedly an easy energy release and an excuse to fight. I could probably explain why I never liked hardcore in a million different ways but lets just say it wasn't my cup of TEA, All you have to do is read ~~AP~~ the letter section from MAXIMUM ROCK-N-ROLL from the PAST 6 years and you may understand what I mean.

Dispensable as recycled toilet tissue, they breed like rabbits and their hands will be sent back attached to key chains. If Jimmi Hendrix were alive he would more than likely have a long back (bi level) hair cut and slick, sequin threads sporting a new Aero dynamic-90's guitar with zebra stripes and a pointy headstock. Iggy pop at a recent gig in L.A. Jammed with slash from Guns-n-roses on a 20 minute rendition of louie louie.

The journalist left a red circle, imprint from the camera lens on the forehead of a mother who has 5 sons in the persian gulf. She was asked to describe just ~~exactly~~ how she feels of this situation while holding her sons military portraits in her lap. A student listening to old R.E.M watches the mother on T.V. and becomes exited by the idea that has just burst from his environmentally & socially de[illegible] mind: "maybe there will be reason now for A REVOLUTION!

I like following the rise of entertainers careers while they struggle to make it, ~~while in their early to late twenties~~. I like to know everything about them, and if enough information isn't available, then tabloids will be sufficcent. I like punk rock. I like girls with weird eyes. I like drugs. I like passion. I like things that are built well. I like innocence. I like and am grateful for the blue collar worker whos existence allows Artists to not have to work at menial jobs. I like killing gluttony. I like playing my cards wrong.

But my Body And mind wont Allow me to TAKE them

I like various styles of music. I like making fun of musicians whom I feel pladgerise or offend music as art by exploiting pushing their embarrasingly, pathetic versions of their work onto ~~people.~~ the public. I like to write poetry. I like to ignore other's poetry. I like vinyl. I like nature and animals. I like to swim. I like to be with my friends. I like to be by myself. I like to feel guilty for being a white, American male.

I love to sleep. I like to fill my mouth with seeds and spit them out at random as I walk. I like to taunt small, barking dogs in parked cars. I like to make people feel happy and superior in their reaction towards my appearance. I like to feel predjudice towards people who are predjudice. I like to make incisions into the belly of infants then fuck the incisions until the child dies.

I like to dream that someday we will have a sense of Generational Solidarity amongst the youth of the world. I like to make insidious efforts to avoid conflict. I like to have strong opinions with nothing to back them up with besides ~~MY PRIMAL~~ sincerity.

I like sincerity. I LACK sincerity. these are not opinions. these are not words of wisdom, this is a disclaimer, a disclaimer for my lack of education, for my loss of inspiration, for my unnerving quest for affection and my perfunctory shamefullnes ~~or~~ towards many who are of my relative age. It's not even A poem. it's JUST A Big pile of shit like ME.

I like to complain and do nothing to make things better. I like to blame my parents generation for coming so close to social change then giving up after a few successful efforts by the media & Government to deface the movement by using the mansons and other Hippie representatives as propaganda examples on how they were nothing but unpatriotic, communist, satanic, unhuman diseases. and in turn the baby boomers become the ultimate, conforming, yuppie hypocrites a generation HAS ever produced.

I like to calmly and rationally discuss my views in a conformist manor even though I consider myself to the extreme left.

I like to infiltrate the mechanics of a system by posing as one of them, then slowly start the rot from the inside of the empire.

I like to ASSASINATE the lesser & Greater of two evils.

I like to impeach God.

I like to Abort christ.

natural less violent

I like to fuck sheep.

I like the comfort in knowing that women are Generally superior, and naturally less violent than men.

I like the comfort in knowing that women are the only future in rock and roll.

I like the comfort in knowing that the Afro American invented Rock and roll yet has only been rewarded or awarded for their accomplishments when conforming to the white mans standards.
I like the comfort in knowing that the Afro American has once again been the only race that has brought a new form of original music to this decade: i.e. hip hop/rap.

censorship is VERY American.

I have met many minds able to store and translate a pregnantly large amount of information, yet they havent an ounce of talent for wisdom or the appreciation of passion.

The conspiracy towards success in America (ugh) is immediacy. To expose great repetition to the minds of small attention spans. fast, speedy, now with even more nacho cheese flavor! here today, gone tomorrow because yesterdays following was nothing more than a tool in every individuals need for self importance, entertainment and social rituals. Art that has long lasting value cannot be appreciated by majorities. only the same, small percent will value Arts patience as they always have. this is good. the ones who are unaware do not deserve false suggestions in their purchasing duties.

tips

~~music has absolutely nothing to do with a musicians personal beliefs, it is not an~~ extention of ~~personality or a story~~ [illegible] ~~feelings~~ [illegible]

Scenarios revolve. Verbal communication is exhausted. sit coms are scenarios and so is our conversation. ~~To gather for a party to gather to~~

our party gathers ~~to congregate in~~ out of boredom. role playing for affection & acceptance and to disinfect nagging germs ending in silence, and accomplishment-produced violations on those who werent here to play. they were invited, maybe in a museum far from now.

I am now in my sad stage, before it was naive hate. I want to be the first to discover and discard before its popularity. Tomorrow the I wont care stage is predicted, and im not looking forward to it. maybe vegetables will diffuse the chemicals ~~which produces~~ i produce inside me, an easy excuse, (these chemicals.) I rarely use my instrument. it used to be so exciting. working on music is not a chore. Its now a waste of time to practice. Every other month I buy the results from the Air.

Ask not what you can do to your rock star.

NIRVANA

Order Sheet

↑ stickers ↑
2.00
whole
Dollars

T-shurts

L or XL

if you send $15.00 A peace

you'll recieve A
FREE T-shirt

Dont Buy this one

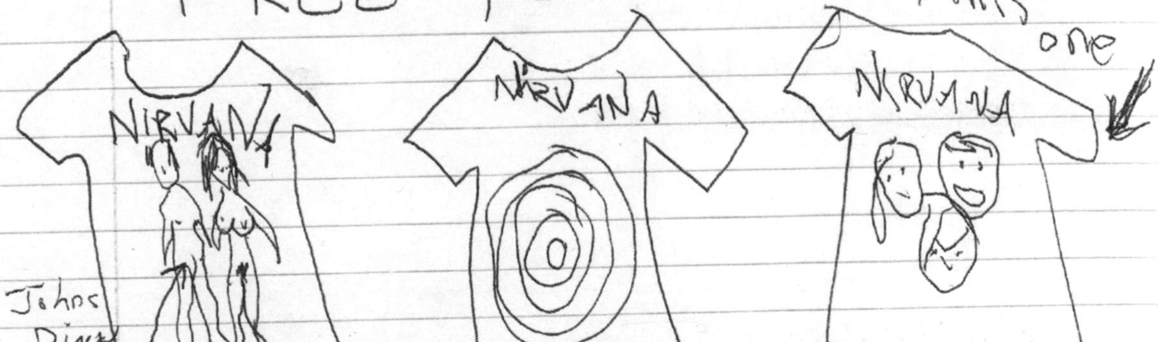

John-N-Bruce-o

Rings-o-Hell
Fudge PACKin

Backs say
sub-pop

Dumb,
stupid,
ugly Faces
of us.

A manic depressive on smack floating in A WArm depreVAtion tank, singing leonard cohen, masturbating, watching golfers fish while dreaming of A stamp collection.

the King of words is: EVERYthing

I can only fuck and Sing.

Have you ever felt like you cared so much that you wanted to kill your Germs?

who will be the King and Queen of the outcasts?

Ive lost my MIND many times, and my wallet many more.

IN the simplest terms:

1 Dont RAPE
2 Dont be predjudice
3 Dont be Sexist
4 Love your children
5 Love your Neighbor
6 Love yourself

Dont let your opinions obstruct the Aforementioned list

I was about 13 and going through the common ~~pre puberty~~ pre pubescent, hate your parents, wish you could still play with dolls but instead, feel unusually weird around girls-syndrome.

I was a rodent-like, underdeveloped, hyperactive spaz who could fit his entire torsoe in one leg of his bell bottomed jeans, and I was frustrated, I needed to let off some steam.

I went to the movies with my friends. we saw "Over the Edge."

Over the edge is a ~~movie~~ story of troubled youth, vandalism, parental negligence, and most importantly ~~[illegible]~~ realestate development dysfunctional families

Its fine in A sense that you can make A comfortable living At it - ~~but other than that it's not too apealing too apealing of A profession.~~ But besides financial security it really isnt that wise of a profession. one of the main problems I have is that ~~because~~ I feel like im being evaluated 24 hrs A day, being in A Band is hard work and the acclaim itself just isnt worth it unless you still like playing And I do god how I do love playing live, it's the most primal form of energy release you can share with other people besides having sex or taking drugs. So if you see A good live show on drugs and then later that evening have sex, youve basically covered All the bases of energy release, And we All need to let off steam, it's easier and safer than protesting Abortion clinics ~~or~~ praising God or wanting to hurt your Brother so go to A show dance around A Bit and copulate

Primary

The second time we broke it off
I lost a voice sincerity was washed
I love myself better than you - I know its
wrong so what should I do?

Im on a plaine - I cant complain

The 18th time we broke it off
I heard a noise so we burnt a cross
we walked hand in hand in our parade
took off our robes and began rape

you stole things from me - All Apologies
I stole things from you - I will stand accused
what else can i do - I belong to you
what else can there be - All Apologies

what else can I say - All my words are grey
what else should I write? - I dont want to fight
how else could I feel? - All our lips are sealed
what do you expect? - Im a nervous wreck

in the sun in the sun i feel as one
in the sun in the sun Im married
marriage
yeah yeah yeah yeah

NOT Finished

I Think ~~I~~ Im Dumb

mollys lips
Slushy - VAselines

Im not like them - but I can pretend
the sun is Gone - but I have A light
the dAy is done - but im having fun
I think im dumb - or maybe just happy

my heart is broke but I have some Glue
Help me inhale & mend it with you
well float Around & hang out on clouds
then well come down & have a hangover

Skin the Sun & fall asleep
breathe ~~[illegible]~~ AWAY - ~~your~~ the soul ~~[illegible]~~ ~~cheap~~ is weak
lesson learned - ~~[illegible]~~ ~~roll & tuck~~ wish me luck
Soothe the burn - WAKE me up

I've been told that an artist is in need of
constant tragedy to fully express their work,
but I'm not an artist and when I say I
in a song, that doesnt neccesarily mean
that person is me and it doesn't mean
im just a story teller, it means whoever
or whatever you want because everyone
has their own definition of specific words
and when your dealing in the context of
music you cant expect ~~universal~~ words ~~meanings~~ *
to ~~have~~ the same meaning as ~~in~~ everyday
use of our vocabulary because I consider music
art and when I say "that song is art"
I dont mean in comparison to A painting
because I feel the visual arts are not nearly
as sacred as the transcribed or Audio communications, but it is art and
~~ever was a more tragic loss this~~
~~society has~~ I feel this society ~~and other~~
somewhere has lost its ~~most valuable~~ sense
of what art is, Art is expression.
in expression you need 100% full freedom
and our freedom to express our
Art is seriously being fucked
with. FUCK, the word fuck has
as many connotations as does the
word Art and ~~I'm~~ far beyond
the point of sitting down and casually
~~explaining~~ complaining about this problem to the
Right wing control freaks who Are
the main ~~objectors~~ offenders ~~of~~ destroying

Art. I ~~[illegible]~~ wont calmly and literally complain to ~~you~~! I'm going to fucking kill. I'm going to fucking Destroy your MACHO, SAdistic, Sick Right wing, religiously Abusive opinions on how we As A whole should operate According to YOUR conditions. before I die many will die with me and they will deserve it. see you IN Hell

love kurdt
kobain

thanks for the TRAgedy I need it for my Art.

punk Rock is Art ~~the problem~~

punk Rock to me means freedom. the only problem ive had with the situationists ~~[illegible]~~ punk rock ethic is that absolute denial of anything ~~is~~ sacred, I find a ~~lot~~ few things sacred ~~[illegible] like~~ such as the superiority ~~of~~ women and the negro ~~and the things theyve had~~ contributed to ~~on~~ Art. I guess what im Saying is that Art is Sacred.

punk rock is freedom

expression and right to express is vital

Anyone CAN be artistic...

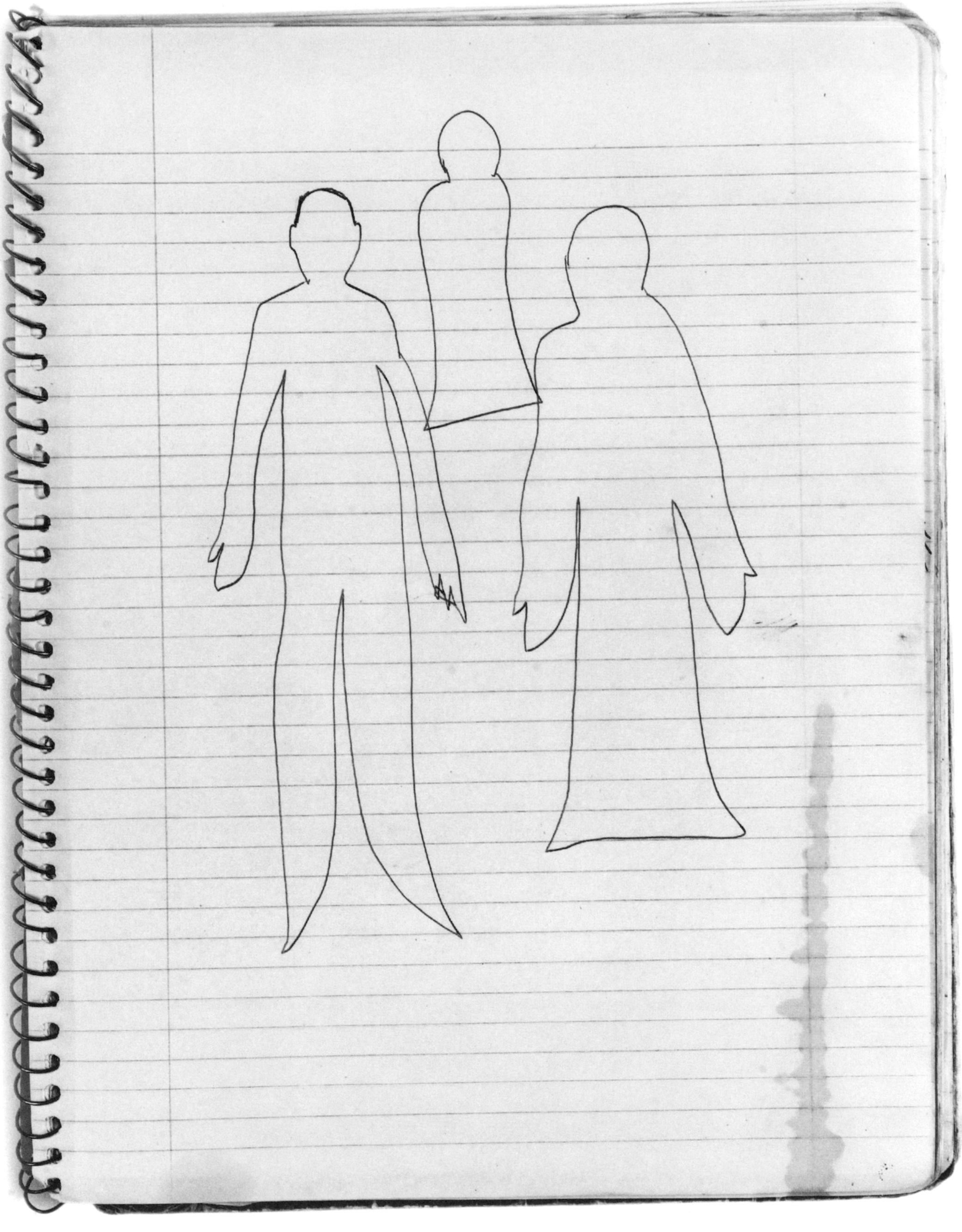

disparagement – Belittlement

I have a lot to say, but ill leave that to you, I'll leave that to those who have the ability to expound their whines better than I. The facts to back up the complaints and the patience to debate, the impossible deprogramming of the plantation owners, ~~and~~ their workers and their slaves. The slaves born into their world ~~are~~ un-questioning, ~~at~~ unaware through their generations acceptance of "thats just the way it is," stripped of culture in the pen, bred in a pen and losing ink, but refilling ~~to~~ prey of disposable goods and pray of the dispensable through the faith given by the feudal Lords, "take it or leave it."

impulse "like it or lump it." "I brought you into this world and ill take you out." "I'll be the judge of that." No instinct to escape, crawling over eachother in an overly populated tank, just lying there waiting to be fed eating more than you need and wanting more cause you never know if its ever going to come again. Breeding & eating & waiting & complaining & praying, ~~[illegible]~~

~~[illegible]~~

Rooms
22 Chis
15 Dave

~~like butter, he being old stoutly, did
he solidify into a pedophile.
sweat like butter melts and flows
through the valleys of ripe-old skin of
pink prunes~~

starting from the arm pit of an old man, ~~and down~~
in a rush of slow motion-flood gates,
blown wide-open. sweat [redacted] butter melts downward
through the valleys of ripe, pink-prune skin,
wrapped loosely around his ~~skeletal~~ marble Brittle arm.
congregating at the tips of uncut,
Jaundiced fingernails, beads meet and
~~and mix~~ Breed, then jump to their death,
they land as a ~~beads~~ ~~land~~ Splash on smoothe thighs
of infants Lying limp on beds of ~~angels hair~~ mo-hair
dirty books made him solidify into a pedophile.
Coalate Corelate Corralate Coralate Corilate Solidiphile into A Pedofile

I'm not well read, but when I do
read, I read well.

I dont have the time to translate
what I understand in the form of conversation,
I had exhausted most conversation ~~this~~ at age nine.
I only feel with grunts screams and tones and with
hand gestures and my body. im deaf in spirit.

V

~~I keep myself~~

I purposely keep myself naive and away from earthly information because its the only way to avoid a jaded attitude.

everything i do is internally subronciouse because you cant rationalize spirituality

we dont deserve this privilege

~~I can only feel.~~

I cant [redacted] or speak, I can only feel.

maybe someday Ill turn myself into Hellen Keller by puncturing my ears with a knife, then cutting my voice box out.

If you want to know what the after life feels like, then put on A parachute go up in a plane, Shoot a good amount of heroine into your veins and immediately follow that with a hit of nitrous oxide then jump.

or, set yourself on fire.

youre

✓ IN Bloom
✓ Polly
✓ SAPPY
✓ Imodium
✓ PAY to plAY
✓ Somethings in the WAY
✓ Verse chorus Verse
✓ Sliver
✓ P-Rock
✓ Lithium

Give the Gift of music

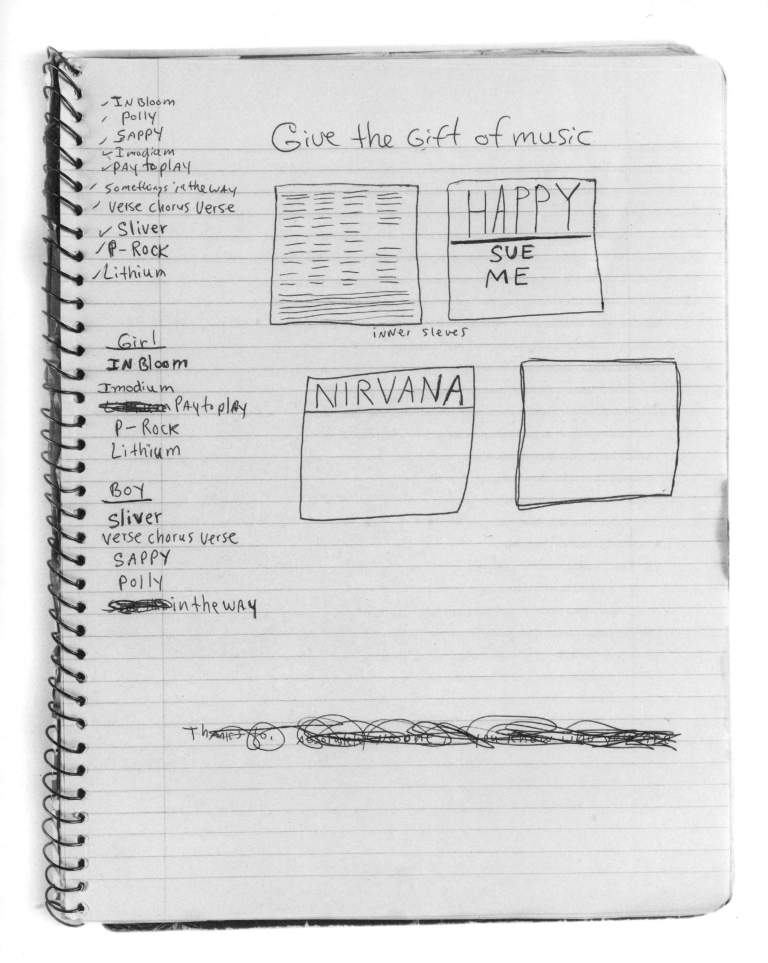

inner sleves

Girl

IN Bloom
Imodium
~~Something~~ PAY to plAY
P-Rock
Lithium

BOY

Sliver
Verse chorus Verse
SAPPY
Polly
~~Something~~ in the WAY

~~Thanks to: absolutely noone, you know who you are~~

NIRVANA
NIRVANA
NIRVANA

Please Send me All Daniel Johnston Cassettes

H ~~Blew~~
H ~~School~~
S ~~About A Girl~~
H ~~IN Bloom~~
H ~~PAY to PlAY~~
S ~~Polly~~
H ~~Imodium~~
H ~~Dive~~
SH ~~Lithium~~
S ~~SAPPY Buy Bye~~

To fellow punk Rockers

~~Neg~~ Crepe
IN Bloom
Lithium
About A Girl
~~Imodium~~ PAY ~~to~~ to PlAY
School

~~Blew~~ polly
Dive
SAPPY
Imodium
Neg crepe
Blew

~~for those of you who have been familiar with us since the last Album, we apologize for putting old songs on this LP. you may consider it a rip off or greatest hits Album, but to those who haven't heard our other LP and the ones who aren't as fortunate or at liberty to be subject to this kind of stuff. due to the limitability of an independent label, in other words you have to break in the sheep with tender loving care. use protection & gels.~~

NIRVANA SAYS

Thanks to Sonic Youth, mudhoney, Babes in Toyland, SUBPOP, TAD, Fluid, Vaselines, pixies, melvins, Young Marble Giants, STP, Beat Happening, K records, Scratch Acid, flipper, Black flag, Black Sabbath, Marine girls, Stooges, Butthole Surfers, Beatles, the who, the shaggs, velvet underground, Jandek, Daniel Johnston, the knack, Swans, Go team, Huddie leadbetter, Sonics, screaming trees, Dead moon, wipers, fang, Gang of four, patsy Cline, marlene Dietrich, killdozer, Saccharin trust, Alice Cooper, DEVO, B-52s, Blue cheer, shocking Blue, lee Hazlewood, half Japanese, Neil Young, Dinosaur Jr, Isaac Hayes, leonard cohen, ventures, monkees, CCR, Aerosmith, led zep, Big Black, Gyuto monks, sex pistols, MDC, Queen, Die kreuzen, Husker Du, Bad Brains, Jimi Hendrix, Ramones, Saints, Blondie, Sgt Barry Sadler, Billie Holiday, Shonen Knife, Red Cross, Johnny Cash,

inside sleeve cardboard stencil of visible man
to encourage promotion & vandalism

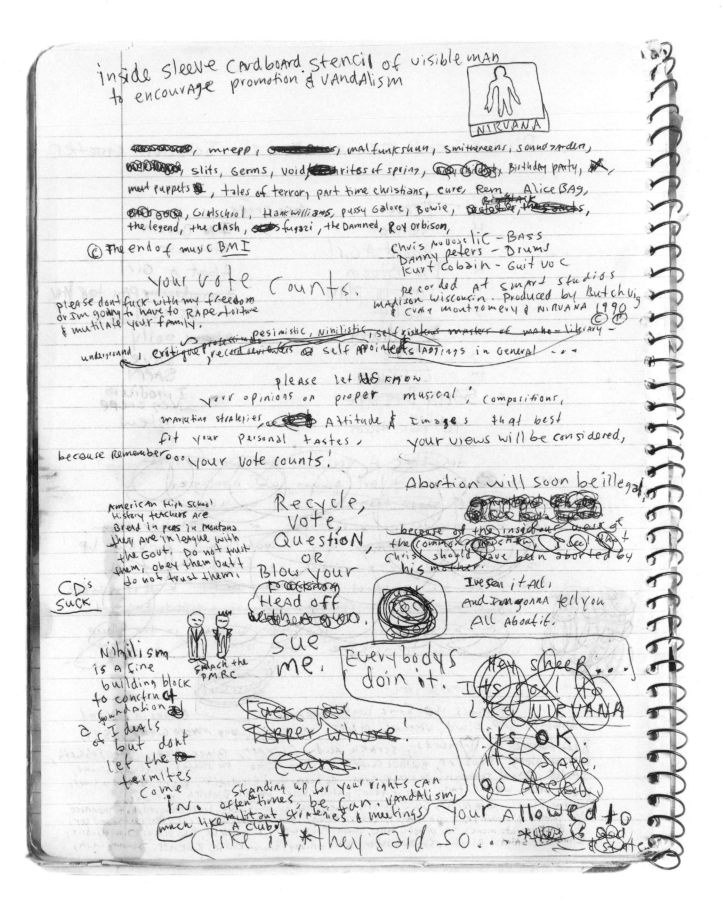

, mrepp, , malfunkshun, smithereens, soundgarden,
, slits, Germs, void, rites of spring, , Birthday party, ,
meat puppets , tales of terror, part time christians, cure, Rem, Alice BAG,
, Girlschool, Hank williams, pussy Galore, Bowie, , ,
the legend, the clash, fugazi, the Damned, Roy orbison,

© The end of music BMI

Chris Novoselic - Bass
Danny peters - Drums
Kurt Cobain - Guit voc
recorded at smart studios
madison wisconsin. Produced by Butch vig
& Craig montgomery & NIRVANA 1990 © ℗

your vote counts.

please dont fuck with my freedom
or Im going to have to RAPE, torture
& mutilate your family.

underground, critique, professionals, record reviewers, self appointed pesimistic, nihilistic, self existent masters of mako-library – ists, & artists in General ...

please let us know
your opinions on proper musical, compositions,
marketing strategies, , Attitude & Images that best
fit your personal tastes. your views will be considered,

because remember ... your vote counts!

Abortion will soon be illegal,
because of the insiduous views of
the common christian, I feel that
christ should have been aborted by
his mother.

American High School
History teachers are
Bred in pens in montana
they are in league with
the Govt. Do not trust
them, obey them but
do not trust them.

Recycle,
Vote,
Question,
OR
Blow your
Head off

CD's
SUCK

Ive seen it All,
And Im gonna tell you
All About it.

Nihilism
is A fine
building block
to construct
a foundation
of Ideals
but dont
let the
termites
come
in.

Sue
me.

Everybodys
doin it.

Hey sheep...
Its cool to
Like NIRVANA
its OK.
Its safe.
go Ahead.

Fuck you
Tipper whore.
Cunt.

Standing up for your rights can
often times, be fun. vandalism,
militant strategies & meetings
much like A club.

Your Allowed to
like it * they said so. * & state.

I started it first
I started it first
It was me
me
Im the one
I was the Originator
Ill take the blame
me
it was me
I was the instigator
the grandfather
the first and foremost
I was doin it long
Before anyone
It was me
Ill take all the blame
Ill take full responsibility
my fault
I started it all
I started it first
me
Im the one
Blame me
point the finger at me
Heres my receipt
where do I sign?
give me whats owed to me
give me whats rightfully mine
give me what I deserve

2

I DeAS for Video

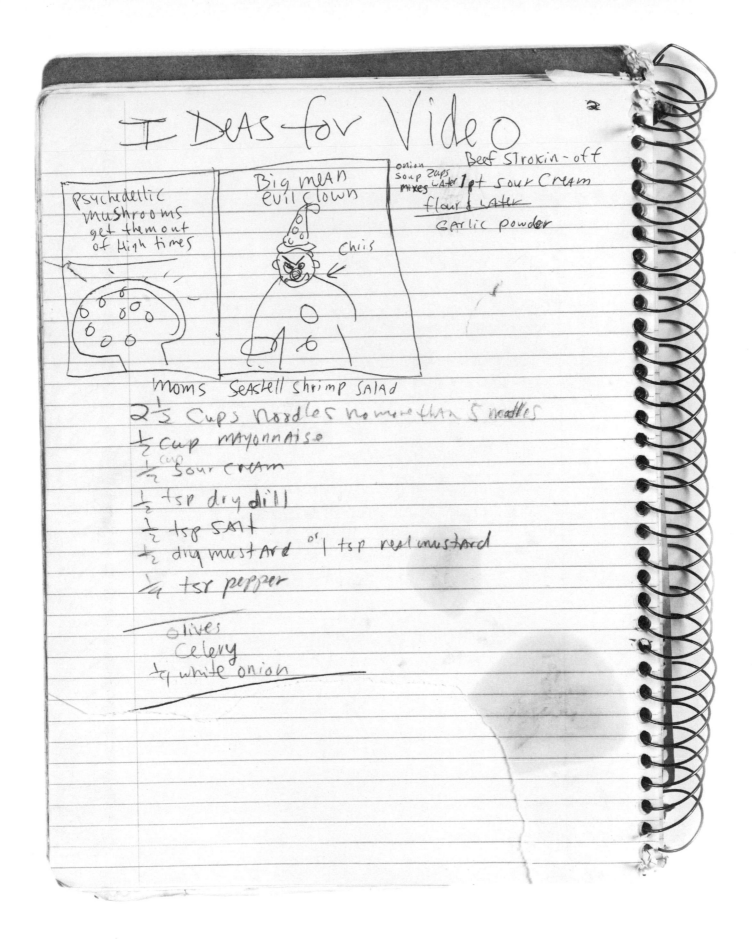

onion soup mixes
2cups water
Beef Strokin-off
1pt sour Cream
~~flour & water~~
Garlic powder

moms Seashell shrimp salad

2 1/2 Cups noodles no more than 5 noodles
1/2 cup mayonnaise
1/2 cup sour cream
1/2 tsp dry dill
1/2 tsp salt
1/2 dry mustard or 1 tsp real mustard
1/4 tsp pepper

olives
Celery
1/4 white onion

K

1 ms 2 Henke 3 stinky Bitch 4 Reynolds montesano patti flake legs kissing game 5 6 7 Junior High

8 Chuck & Jim summer monte grandpa Cobain grandma 9 uncle Jim 10 mom greasy embers 11 12

It is time now for all the 'fortunate' ones, the cheerleaders and the football jocks to strip down naked in front of the entire school at an assembly and plead with every ounce of their souls for mercy and forgiveness, to admit that they are wrong. They are representatives of Gluttony and selfish ~~animalistic~~ values and to say that they are sorry for condoning these things will not be enough, they must mean it, they must have guns pointed to their heads, they must be petrified to ever think of being the stuck up, self righteous, segregating, guilt spreading, ass kissing, white, right wing republicans of the future.

Kill the Rockefellers

IN Bloom
Lithium
polly
☆ P Rock
Imodium

Pay to play
sliver
Been A son
sappy
☆ Verse Chorus Verse
☆ Somethin, in the way

gotta find A WAY, A better wAy
to find A way

what I need
Someday
memoria
SPANK Thru
☆ Lounge Act
Second time
I dont have the Right
Dumb
Libido
mommA

~~P-ROCK~~

just because your paranoid
doesn't mean theyre not after you

US out of ~~America~~ CANAdA
~~US out of~~

God is Gay and so Am I

God is love love is blind and So Am I

I have no opinions
because I agree with everyone

Rubbing Alcohol

HERE I AM! inspired to write only because i'm pissed off.

I dont feel As bitter AS I want to be.

I need to re learn the english language.

I am insincere because I cant choose or decide fast enough.

my penmanship seems scatological because of my lack of personality, or excess of personality.

I am obsessed with the fact that I am skinny and stupid

Ive probably never met a person whom I feel compatible with my intellectual, Spiritual & humorist will.

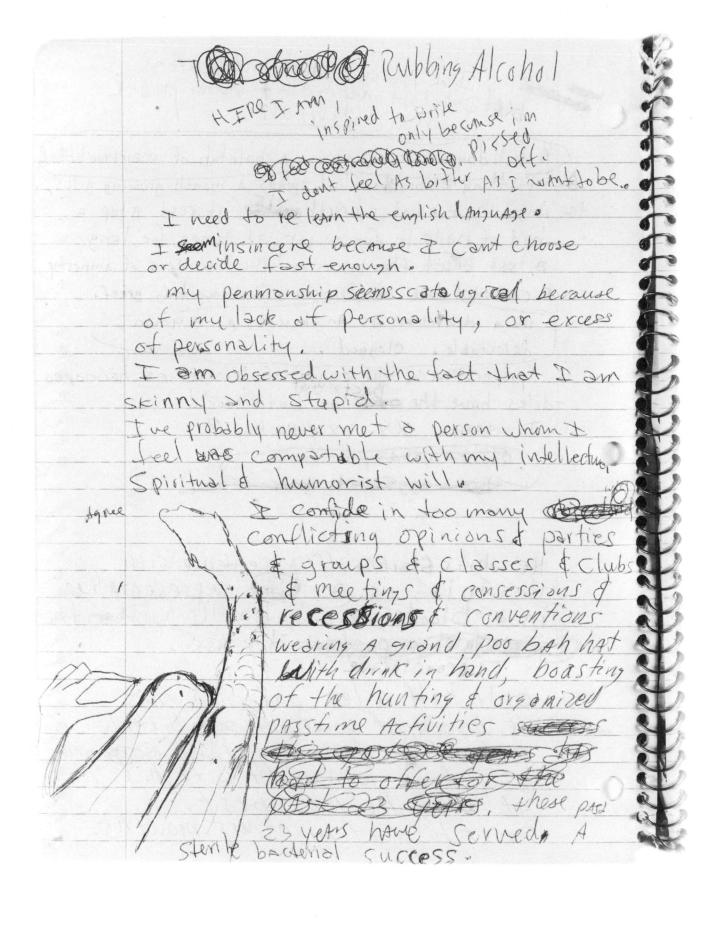

I confide in too many conflicting opinions & parties & groups & classes & Clubs & meetings & consessions & recessions & conventions wearing A grand poo bah hat with drink in hand, boasting of the hunting & organized passtime Activities these past 23 years have served. A sterile bacterial success.

~~Ive been to A lot of BAD poetry readings~~

Congratulations to obsession, ~~sounds like perfume isnt extracted from like embowelled whale blubber anymore~~. Chemicals are the thing of today, today ill take as many chemicals as I can get my greasy paws on, because this scent reminds me of you. just like they said it would in the commercial. yesterdays scent is still here today, Im beached. flat out stranded and obsessed. Ive got to leave because your still here in my Air, fucking with my sense of smell, invading my Air waves, your All over the sheets & in the bathroom, my couch reeks of you! youve left your underwear & COAT & records & books & scent here, IN my place of recovery. the place where Ive crawled off to die like A cat under A house after hes been hit, lying around waiting

DAVE
(213) 654-

I dont invent subjects of interest for conversation. I dont have Anything to SAY or ASK, I Just play Along. Im A reactionary in A WAY; I just react to what others SAY. I dont think & when I do; I forget.

give me A leonard cohen Afterworld.

Opinion

Congratulations you have won - its A
years subscription of bad Puns - and A
make shift story of concern - And to
set it up before it burns - my
opinion

Now there seems to be A problem here
the scale of emotions seem too clear -
Now they - Rise & fall like wall street stock
And they - Have an affect on our peace talks
my opinion

MANDATORY Breeding LAWS

Sue ME

MANDATORY Abortion ~~[illegible]~~ VACCINATIONS Denied

~~Taking time to smear dignified street smart-~~
~~hipness into the carefully cultivated image they~~
~~once represented~~, Now faced with corporate trust,
merging this happy day, This day giving amnesty
to SACrilege. Only do I think ~~when inspiration~~
is so welcome ~~[illegible]~~ from the allowance you
give with the birth of ~~[illegible]~~ ~~[illegible]~~ beyond
pissy complaints of ~~description~~ tongue. Inspired,
I SWAY back and forth between taking advantage
of my position and giving up. Self appointed
judges of review giving those with similar profit and
potential the confidence to quit.
So your parents suck. ~~[illegible]~~
parents have always sucked. So your parents
are really pretty cool? ~~[illegible]~~ so what! other kids
parents suck so fight for them. Revolution
is no longer an embarrasement, ~~[illegible]~~
thanks to inspiration. The politbureau
questions sarcasm: maintain we must our ~~[illegible]~~
~~[illegible]~~ righteously ~~opinions~~ alternative opinions carved into our
freshman year and slowly solidifying into the
JACKSON BROWN ~~Jimmy Buffet / James Taylor~~ kingdom by graduations end.
At times its an excuse to delay the world
we eventually take in the ass.
Throw eggs at your enemy. Symbolic chicken foetus.
AT Pro lifers.

I am a male, age 23 and I'm Lactating. my breasts have never been so sore not even after receiving Titty twisters from bully-school mates. They had hair down there long before I stopped playing with dolls. I havent mesturbated in months because Ive lost my imagination. I close my eyes and I see my father, little girls, german shephards & TV news commentators, but no voluptuous, pouty lipped, naked-females sex kittens, wincing in ecstasy from the ~~imagi~~ illusory positions Ive conjured up in my mind. No, when I close my eyes I see lizards & flipper babies, the ones who were born deformed because their mothers took bad birth control Pills, ~~in the sixties~~

I'm seriously afraid to touch myself.

homage or Ripoff? I dont care, uh, I dont know.
Seems like finally the appreciation of things are in order. there are a lot of things & bands to be thankful for, yes, and everything sucks.
Too many compilations of present day bands paying homage to old influential bands, Either there are no good ones left to look forward to or finally the undergrounds p-rock admittance to appreciation instead of Everything Sucks!
Clones of old, and the younger generation never hardly heard old Aerosmith records or Rod Steward & small faces so they have no ~~idea~~ sense of pladgerism in the "now" bands paying homage (supposedly) or keeping the faith.

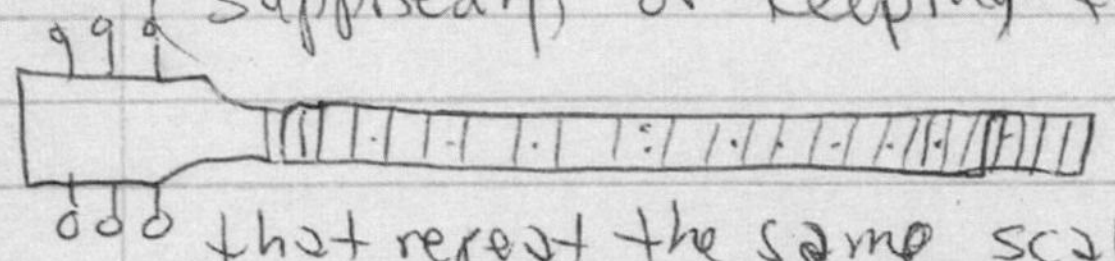

Six strings, 24 notes that repeat the same scale after 10, usually based on 4/4 time signature, Rock and Roll: 30 years = Exhausted! AH the good old days!
The Now generation: ~~recessive~~ unaware recession, Technology finally caught up with us.
Hip hop/RAP? = for the time being, yes good at least original, exhausted in 3 years.
women? yes. oppressed from chance since beginning. probably some ideas left in an unsaturated vagina.
Record store chains and RADIO play it safe, target audience, what sells, were completely at their mercy it used to be the other way around.
Programmers & DJs: get into Real estate!

I am in absolute and total support of: homosexuality, drug use, inexperimentation (although I am living proof of harmfull results from over indulgence) Anti oppression, ie: (religion, racism, sexism, censorship and patriotism) creativity ~~through~~ music, art, journalism, ~~writings~~ Love, friendships, family, animals and full scale ~~revolution~~ violently ~~terrorist~~ organized, terrorist-fueled revolution.

You cannot de-program the Glutton.

~~you can only make them scared shitless to~~

It would be nice to see the gluttons become so commonly ~~violently attacked~~ hunted down that ~~they~~ eventually they will either submit to the opposite of their ways or be scared shitless to ever leave their homes.

John lennon has been my Idol all of my life but he's DEAD wrong about revolution.

Sit on your ass and be beaten!

Bullshit!, Arm yourself, find ~~an example~~ a representative of Gluttony or oppression and blow the motherfuckers head off. design manifestos with ideas, contacts, recruits, go Public, risk jail or Assasination, ~~or~~ get employed by the target so its easier to infiltrate the system Slowly rot the mechanics of the empire

Hi Eugene,

Its eight o clock in the morning, that means its almost time for bed. I'm on this rediculous sleeping schedule where I retire in the wee hours of morning and successfully avoid any hint of daylight. my skin is ~~dead~~ goth rock pale. I dont know if you have these things in Scottland but I'm considering joining a tanning bed salon, they are coffin/beds with haloid or flourescent light bulbs built into the sides and lid. You lye down inside ~~to~~ fry away turning a crisp golden brown. we call them nuclear tans.

lately my nipples have been really sore, can males lactate? How have you been?

As you probably know, we recorded mollys lips & son of a gun for a peel session and we were wondering if we could use the recordings for a promotional EP hopefully to be released in a few months. we dont expect to make a profit off of it because were keeping the price down, It's mainly a feature for our supposedly hip-alternative debut single 'IN Bloom', the EP will have (if consented) (VASELINES) IN Bloom, sliver, D-7 by the wipers, Turn around by Devo, mollys lips and maybe son of a gun. If we do make any money off of this then we'll surely devide it amongst the bands or we could talk about up front advance for the use of the songs or whatever, it's legit!

were not on Sub Pop any more, our new label is DGC (Geffen)
we are label mates with Nelson!

I know this is starting to sound too business like
but I want you to have something for
giving us this great honor
to play your songs, they mean a lot
to me. Without trying to be too embarrassingly
sappy I have to say the songs you
and Frances have written are some of
the most beautiful songs ever and I just
feel like everyone should hear them.
Heres what the cover might look like →

I had a really fine time
at the show we played together
the video turned out good. you
want a copy? oh yeah, European
video tape format, forget it. geez I
dont know what else to say.
please write me (if you want)
and let me know how your
new band is coming along and
anything else thats on your mind.

Love, your pal
kurdt

NIRVANA SINGS..
songs of
DEVO
WIPERS
VASELINES
&
NIRVANA

Bill price guns & roses Chris thomas engineer sex pistols

Gill Norton pixies

Allan moulder - my bloody valentine mixed Jesus & Mary Chain

? & Barbiero - Guns roses soundgarden

George Derkoulios - Black Crowes

available last week of June

John Hanlon - Ragged glory freedom

Dave Jerden - Janes Addiction Talking Heads Alice n Chains

Ed Stasium - living Colour

Ron St Jermain - anthrax Death Angel the Youth

Scott Litt

And Hairy, sweaty, macho-sexist and racist Dickheads who will soon drown in a pool of razor blades and sperm from the uprising ~~of~~ your children, the armed and de-programmed crusade, littering the floors of Wall Street with revolutionary debris, Assasinating both the lesser and greater of two evils, ~~coming~~ ~~absolute~~ bringing an everlasting sterile and bacterial, herbacious & Botanical corporate cleansing for our ancestors to gaze in wondernment and awe.

Will be strung up by their Balls with pages of the Scum manifesto stapled to their Bodys

The representatives of the American male rapes in more ways than one.

~~oh well whatever, nevermind.~~

posing as the enemy to infiltrate the mechanics of the empire and slowly start its rot from the inside

it's an inside job — it starts with the custodians and the cheerleaders, oh well, whatever, nevermind.

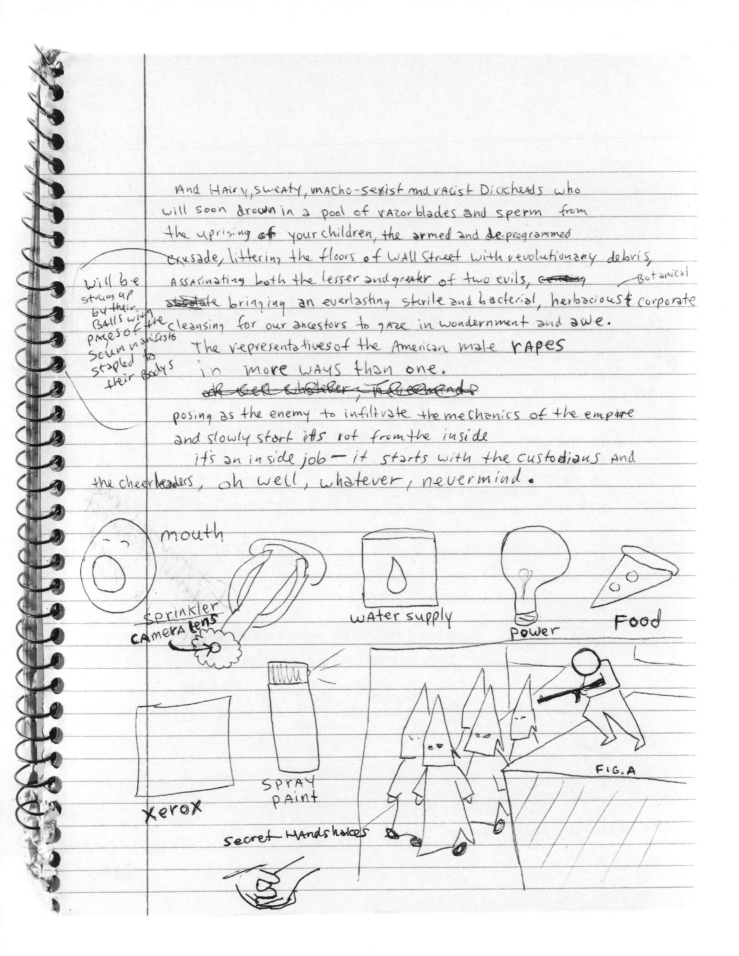

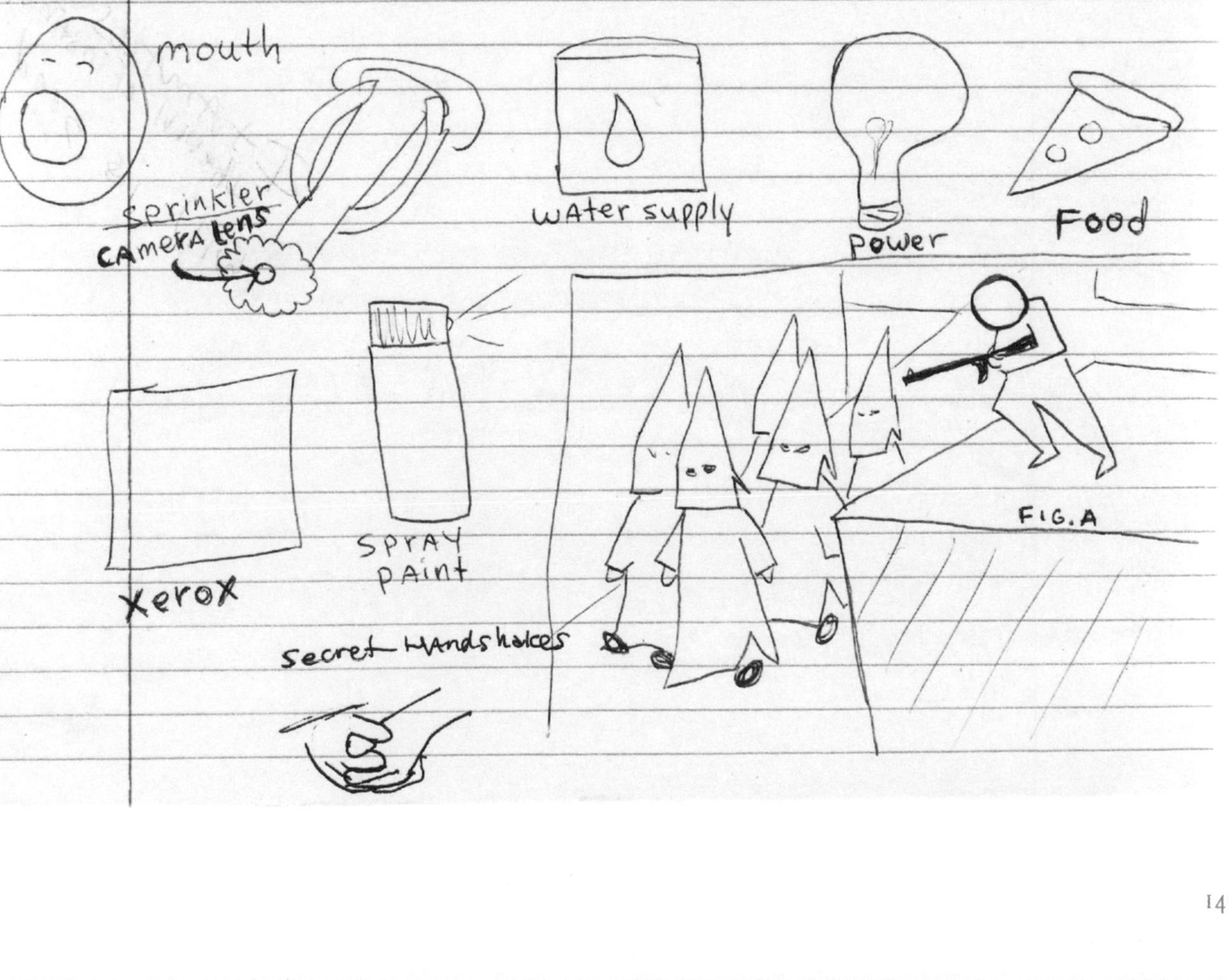

Cursed Aint the word

smells like Teen Spirit

It will be fun

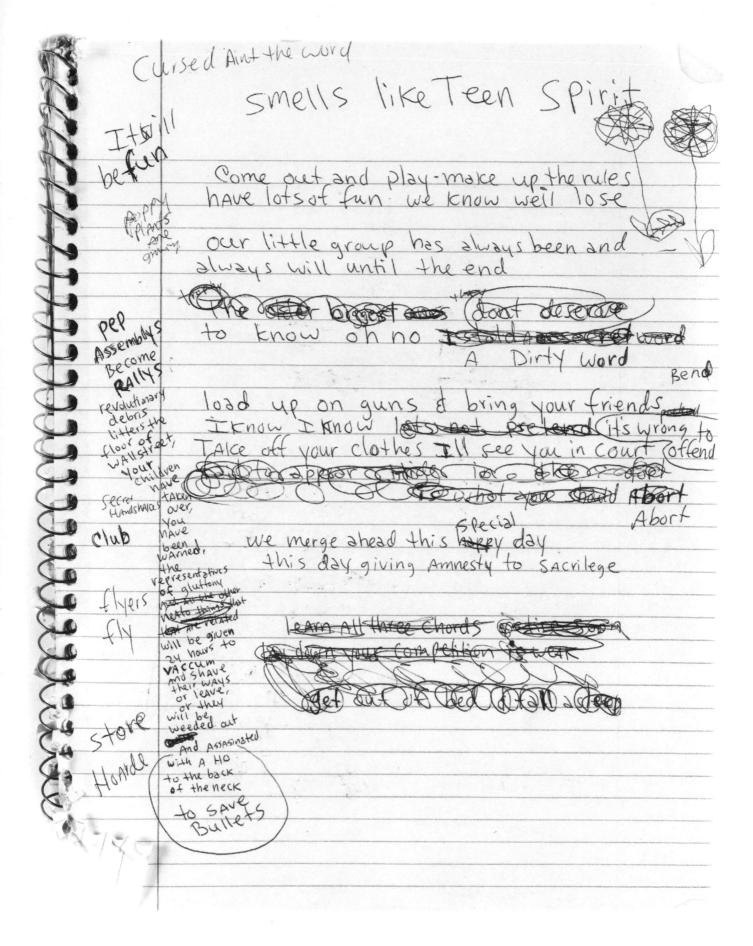

Poppy plants are growing

Come out and play - make up the rules
have lots of fun we know well lose

our little group has always been and
always will until the end

~~The older biggest ones~~ they ~~dont deserve~~
to know oh no ~~I stold a secret word~~
A Dirty word

pep Assemblys Become Rallys

revolutionary debris litters the floor of WAllstreet, your children have taken over, you have been warned, the representatives of gluttony ~~and all the other neato things that are related~~ will be given 24 hours to vaccum and shave their ways or leave, or they will be weeded out ~~and~~ And Assasinated with A HO to the back of the neck to save Bullets

Bend

load up on guns & bring your friends ~~pretend~~
I know I know ~~lets not pretend~~ its wrong to
TAke off your clothes I'll see you in court offend
~~[illegible]~~
~~is what you should~~ ~~Abort~~
Abort

secret Handshakes

club

we merge ahead this ~~happy~~ special day
this day giving Amnesty to sacrilege

flyers fly

~~Learn All three Chords~~ ~~[illegible]~~
~~lay down your competition is weak~~
~~get out of bed & fall asleep~~

store Hoarde

A gift of choice I got from you

oh No I know A Dirty word

~~I'll take as much as you can I never know~~
~~when you'll run out~~

                                    got from you

Now I forget just why I taste - oh yeah
~~   ~~ I guess   It makes me smile
why dont you cry when IM ~~   ~~ AWAY
oh yeah we want whats best for you

blemish
blush

what is

HO

touch
touch

i ~~   ~~
~~the wrong~~
truth

I don't
~~remember~~
~~when you~~
~~pull~~ Away

_ _ _   repeat   is something New

The finest day Ive ever had
~~   ~~
WAS when Tomorrow Never CAme
Im ~~   ~~ bad at what-I do best
~~   ~~ Im blessed to know ~~Tame~~
And for this gift I feel blessed   that Most Are
                                                        Tame
my credit ran Away from me

with the light out It's less dangerous
Here we are now entertain us
I feel stupid And contagious
Here we Are now Segregate us

A mulato An Albino
A mosquito my Libido
YAY

come hang yourself with Umbilicle NOOSE

UH oh oh No A Dirty word

Sell the kids for food..
weather changes moods . . . . . .
SPRING IS HERE AGAIN . . .
Reproductive glands

Lithium

① * I'm so happy because today I found my friends
Theyre in my head.

* I'm so ugly but thats ok cause so are you
~~And~~ we broke our mirror.

Sunday morning is ~~the da~~ everyday for all I care
And I'm ~~not sad scared~~ not scared
Light my candles in a daze cause I found God
Hey Hey Hey

I'm so lonely but thats ok I shaved your head
And I'm not sad

And just maybe
I'm to blame for all I've heard but I'm not sure

I'm so excited I can't wait to meet you
there - but I dont care

I'm so horny thats ok my will is good
~~And I've got food to tie me over and~~
~~Keep my mind on meeting you~~
~~And all my friends Again and again~~

I ~~like~~ you } I'm not gonna crack
I miss you }
I love you
I killed you

Night flight
11811 West Olympic Blvd
Los Angeles
CA 90064

Smells like teen spirit

feel

So stupid

~~Come out and play~~ make up the rules
~~I know I hope to buy the truth~~

Take off your clothes I'll see you in court
~~[illegible]~~
~~[illegible] hello~~
~~[illegible]~~ we know we'll lose but we wont be bored

Come out and play, make up the rules
~~[illegible] with golden [illegible]~~

Dyslexic idiot savant with bad hearing

~~[illegible]~~ Load up on guns & bring your friends
~~feel~~ The secret hand shakes pretend
~~were so stupid so lazy, blame our parents~~
~~Nothing fazes me~~
~~were so lazy & so stupid~~
~~blame our parents~~
~~& the [illegible]~~

So famous ~~your pamphlet~~
entertaining ~~has been read~~
~~every night before bed~~
undeserving

Neurotically ~~[illegible]~~ Lapharagic

Tribe

Variety

Our little group has always been, and always will until the end

We ~~cut~~ our hands & made a pact & ~~swore~~ swore we're never going back

A mulato an Albino
A mousquito my Libido

YAY

A deposit for a bottle ~~stuck~~ inside it

No Role model

A Denial

Tribe
territory
Passing
Leaving
Spraying
Your mark

The same percent has always been and always will until the end

Say anything just to have an opinion

Who will be the King & Queen
of the Outcasted ~~[illegible]~~ teens

I hate to use percentages It's nice to know there is A choice

IN BLOOM

Sell the kids for food - weather changes moods
Spring is here Again - re-Productive glands

Hes the one who likes all the pretty Songs - and he likes to Sing along - and he likes to Shoot his Gun But He knows not What it means know not What it means and I SAY AAHH

We can have some more
Nature is A whore
Bruises on the fruit
Tender Age in Bloom

Tastes like chicken

I SAW Jesus's FACE in wood panelling

Verse Chorus Verse

LUCKY BLACK sheep BLACKMAILed
I'll see you in court
I WAS SO High that I scratched
until I Bled
AT the end of RAINbows and
of your Rope
I WAS drawn into the
magnet TAR pit Pool

Grass is greener over here
leads to burning bridges clear
Reinventing what we knew
I cant wait until im sued —

your the reason i feel pain
it feels so good to feel again

Saline on the ocean in A Tank of fumes
wheres my stamp collection? I'm becoming bored
Have another baby its not filled up yet
I've Lost All my contacts and my lack of Iron
I SAW Jesus image in wood panelling

Collect Ripped Postage PAID

A three hour tour

Buy my Bottled Sweat

He goes without saying

Spayed & neutered

lack of irons

Verse Chorus Verse

Neither side is sacred - No one wants to
win - feeling so sedated think Ill just
give in - Taking medication till my
stomachs full - IM A moody baby

grass is greener - over here -
youre I

Reinventing what we knew
I cant wait until im sued

Drain you
Smells like
Power

Come As you are

Teen Spirit
In Bloom
Drain you
Polly
Lounge Act
P-rock
Lithium
Come As You Are
Verse Chorus Verse
Immodium
Pay to play
Something in the way

Come as you are - as you were -
As I want you to be -
as A friend - as a friend - as an
old enemy - Take your time -
hurry up - the Choice is yours -
dont be late - take a rest -
as a friend - as an old -
memoria memory ah

Come dowsed in mud - Soaked in Bleach
As I want you to be -
As A Trend as a friend as an old
~~enemy~~ memoriah

2
13
4
64
3
3
4

You said that I remind you of yourself tomorrow

And I swear that I dont have A Gun

Lounge ACT

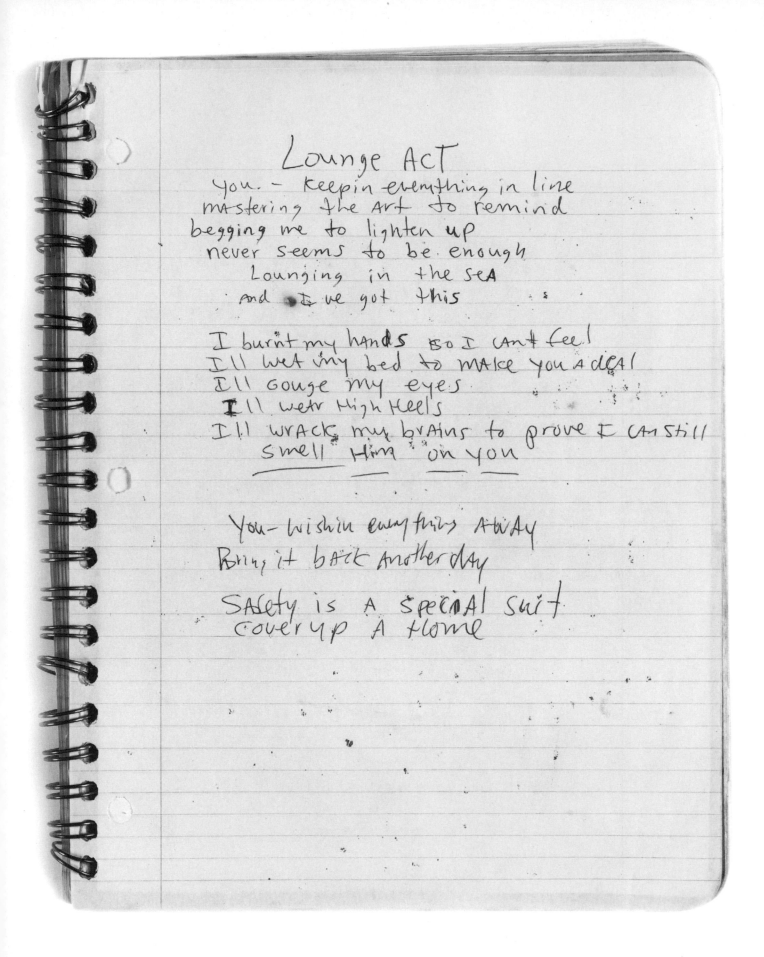

you. - keepin everything in line
mastering the art to remind
begging me to lighten up
never seems to be enough
Lounging in the sea
And I've got this

I burnt my hands so I can't feel
I'll wet my bed to make you a deal
I'll gouge my eyes
I'll wear high heels
I'll wrack my brains to prove I can still
smell him on you

You- wishin everything away
Bring it back another day

Safety is a special suit
cover up a flame

ON A PlAiN

Chorus

I'll start this off without any words
I got so High that I scratched till I bled

The finest day that I've ever had
was when I learned to cry on command

I love myself Better than you I know its
wrong so what should I do

my mother died every night
Its safe to say dont quote me on that

The Black Sheep got black mailed again
Forgot to put on the zip code

It is now time to make it unclear
to write off lines that don't make sense

Somewhere I have heard this before
IN A dream my memory has stored
As defense I'm Neutered & spayed
What the Hell Am I trying to say?

one more special message to go
And then I'm done then I can go home

I'm on A plAin I cAnt complain
I'm on A plAne I cAnt complain

needed

values
perspective
necessities
essentials

Mead
VERSE
CHORUS
VERSE
CHORUS
solo
Chorus
Chorus
5 CXL 6
PAY'n SAVE
1.99
120 sheets/college ruled
11x8½in/27.9x21.6cm
3 subject
notebook
06710 © The Mead Corporation, Dayton, Ohio 45463
0 43100 06710

Hi, Im 24 years old. I was born a white,
lower middle class male off the coast of
Washington state. My parents owned a compact
stereo component system molded in simulated wood
grain casing and A 4 record box set featuring
Am radios contemporary Hits of the early
seventies called 'good vibrations' by **Ronco**.
It had such hits as tony orlando & Dawns
"Tie A yellow ribbon" and Jim Croches Time
in a bottle. After years of my begging they
finally bought me a tin drumset with paper
heads out of the back of A Sears catalog.
Within the first week my sister poked
Holes in the heads with A screwdriver.
I cried to "Seasons in the sun".
My mother played A song by Chicago on
our piano, I dont remember the name of
the song but I'll never forget the melody.
my Aunt gave me a blue Hawaiian slide guitar
and Amp for my 7th birthday, she Also during
those first precious years had given me the
first 3 beatles albums for which I am forever
grateful knowing that my musical development
would have probably ~~come~~ to A HALT, if ~~[illegible]~~ of the
If I had to soak up one more year of the Carpenters and Olivia Newton John.

IN 1976 i found out that the beatles had been broken up since 71 ~~and I had never heard the music of Jimi Hendrix.~~ My parents got a divorce so I moved in with my dad into a trailer park in an even smaller logging community.

My dads friends talked him into joining the Columbia record club and soon records showed up at my trailer Almost once A week Accumulating quite a ~~large records by 77~~ collection by 77

~~What~~ dr? - witt
location? - Lakewood community center
9112 ~~Leader~~ Lakewood dr SW

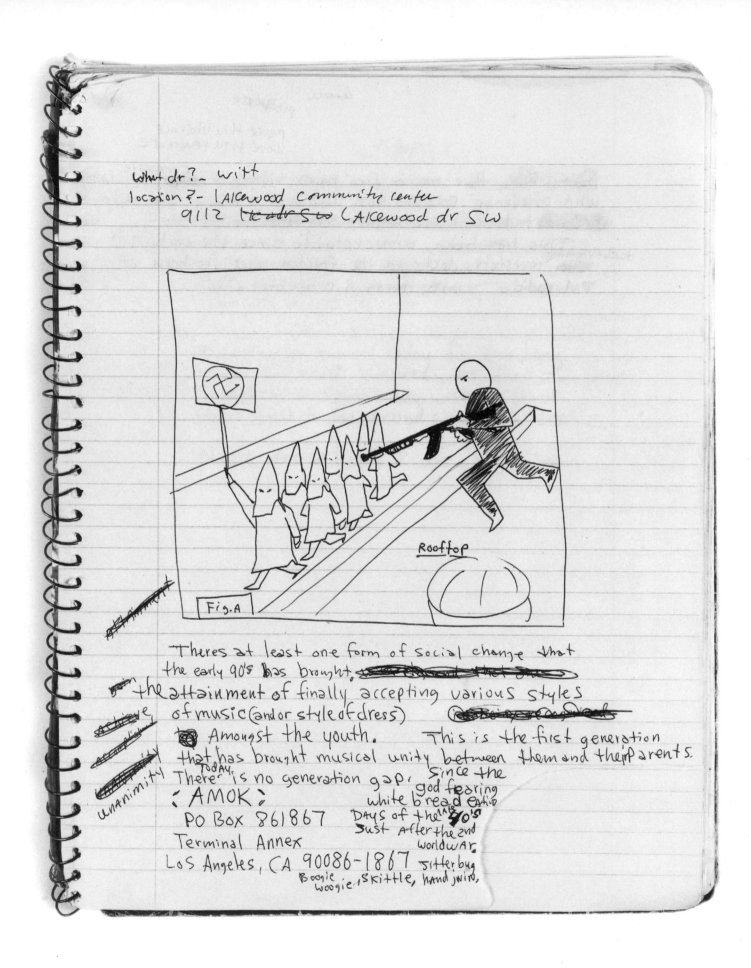

Theres at least one form of social change ~~that~~ the early 90's has brought, the attainment of finally accepting various styles of music (and or style of dress) Amoungst the youth. This is the first generation that has brought musical unity between them and their parents. There today is no generation gap. Since the god fearing white bread days of the late 40's Just After the 2nd world war. Jitterbug, Boogie woogie, skittle, hand jive,

~~achieve~~, ~~accomplish~~, unanimity

: AMOK :
PO Box 861867
Terminal Annex
Los Angeles, CA 90086-1867

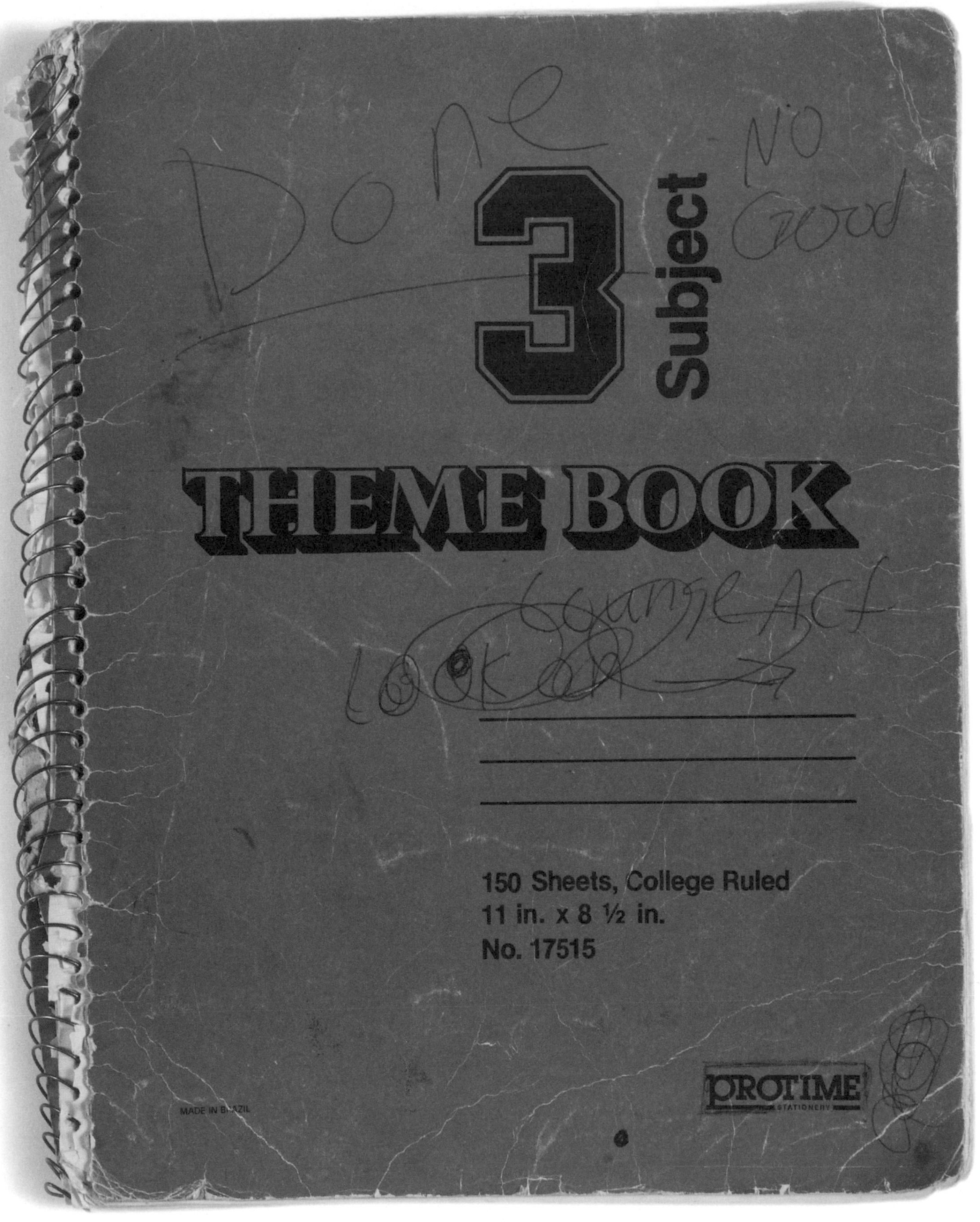
Done
NO Good
3 Subject
THEME BOOK
150 Sheets, College Ruled
11 in. x 8 ½ in.
No. 17515
PROTIME
STATIONERY

Serious Smells like Teen Spirit

GROSS HAPPY (X) DRain you

HAPPY Lithium

HAPPY In Bloom

SAD (E) [redacted] Come As you Are

SAD Polly

MAD Territorial Pissings

HAPPY Blew Immodium / Verse Chorus Verse

MAD STAY AWAY

SAD Something in the WAY

HAPPY (X) ON A PLAIN

HAPPY Lounge ACT

Verse Chorus Verse

* SAPPY

Lounge ACT

ON A PlAin

old Age

[redacted]

Thanks to: [redacted], Jimmy Carter, Susan Sylvers, [redacted], chad channing, Danny peters, the Melvins, Sonic Youth, mudhoney, Bob Goldthwait, the Vaselines, the wipers, the Beatles, the pixies, Black Flag, scratch Acid, [redacted] Leadbelly, Night Flight, the stooges, [redacted], Olympia, Brothers Quay, flipper, Devo, Gang of four, aron Berkhart, [redacted], flipside, Beat Happening, H.R. Puffnstuff, Mark Lanegan, Tales of Terror, Butthole Surfers, New Wave theatre, REM, young Marble Giants, Aerosmith, Led Zeppelin, Johnathan Poneman, Bruce Pavitt, TAd

[redacted]

Thanks to: un-encouraging parents everywhere for giving their children the will to show them up, and to the white macho-american Male for reminding the small percent who are capable of recognizing injustice to fight you and learn from your sick sadistic instinctual WAYS MAY you rot in the very reason you even bother ~~exist~~ to stay Alive whether that

Thanks to ~~the representatives of~~ political figures and those in the entertainment industry who Are the representatives of gluttony, for reminding us

Dont fuck your children
Dont beat your wife

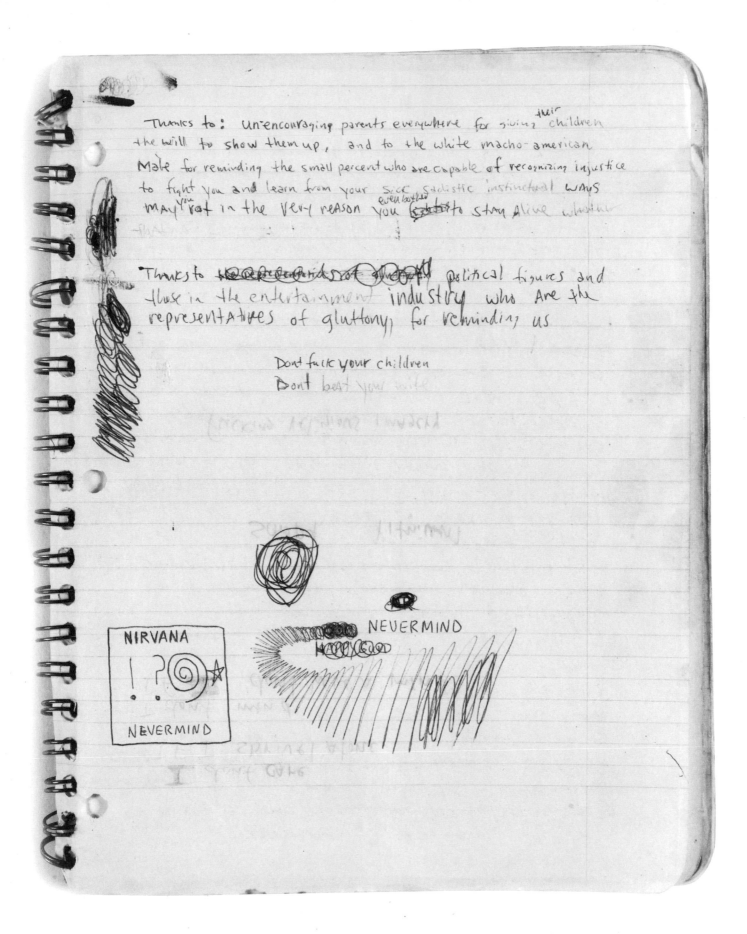

NEVERMIND

"Punk is musical freedom. It's saying, doing and playing what you want. Nirvana means freedom from pain and suffering in the external world and thats ~~my~~ close to my definition of punk rock", exclaims guitarist Kurt Kobain. ~~The wieght of that quote~~ Nirvana try to fuse punk energy with Hard rock riffs, all within a pop sensibility. "Speaking of sensibility" adds bass guitarists CHRIS NOVOSELIC "I wish we had more sense, you know basic common sense, like rembering to pay your phone bill or rent". With the band inking a deal with D.G.C earlier this year the band is enjoying all the trappings that come with it. "Trapping, Schmapping fuck it man they throw us A few bones and the lights stay on for a while". rebuffs Drummer Dave Grohl. Cynical of the music industries machinery ~~Fo~~ Nirvana still sees the nesscessity ~~of such apparatice~~ to drive their musical Crusade.

Nevermind the bands second album but 1st on a major label, culminated two years After the release of their first Album BLEACH. • Kurt notes " ~~HAVE~~ you ever had ~~to find a job~~ a day when you were going to find a job then it was already two o'clock so you just blew it off? then the next day a friend comes over and hangs out, so you'll go tomorrow. Then well tommorow, then tomorrow etc. etc. etc." Hower during this period the "Procrastination BUG" didn't AFFECT the bands song writing. An E.P. was relieased BLEW. It had two songs off BLEACH (Love Buzz, Blew) And two new songs (Been A Son, Stain). In the Fall of '90 the band relieased ~~the~~ single. Sliver w/ DIVE. There are also various Studio outakes and live recordings making the rounds on the ~~greasy~~ sleazy Bootleg market.

~~toured~~ played
Nirvana played alot also during this period: three major tours, including excursions to England twice and elsewhere in Europe once. They played in Berlin one day after the wall fell. "~~People were crying at the sight of bananas" recalls Kobain.~~ "there were westerners offering people coming over baskets of fruit and a guy cried at the sight of bananas". recalls Kobain.

the bands roots go back to '87. It's the classic case of two bored art students dropping out and forming a band. Kobain, a saw blade painter specializing in wildlife and seascapes. Met Novoselic whose passion was gluing sea shells and driftwood on burlap potatoe sacks, at the acclaimed Grays Harbor ~~school of north~~ institute of northwest crafts Chris notes "when I saw Kobains work I new there was something special. I introduced myself to him and asked what his tryouts were on this ~~glitter dust~~

macaroni mobile piece I
was working on. He suggested
I glue glitter on it. From
then on it was an artistic
partnership that would spawn
the basis of what is the
magical collaboration of Nirvana
today" AFTER A long succesion
of drummers Nirvana finally

smells like
TEEN Spirit

needed

1. mercedes benz and a few old cars
2. Access to Abandoned a mall, main floor and one Jewelry shop.
3. lots of fake Jewelry
4. school Auditorium (Gym)
5. A CAst of hundreds. 1 custodian, students.
6. 6 black Cheerleader outfits with Anarchy A's Ⓐ on chest

~~Elizabeth~~

I had a cigarette in my hand, I thought it was a ~~cig~~ pen, I started writing a letter to my congressman, I told him about misery and corruption and bat cave ~~girls~~ - death rock girls who have danced at nude clubs in the city while trying to get off drugs and how they really, really care and if more vegetarian vampires could concentrate on ~~[illegible]~~ disclaimer-malpractice, sitting in the dark channelling the combined energy of all the lost infant souls in this sphere or realm then we could all sip ~~[illegible]~~ licorice-flavored alcoholic beverages down by the lazy rivers of ~~Jordan~~ the rhone or rhine. I dont have a beef with you, or a terrible, bitter, starvation for or in general. and its really hurting my lungs. This fag is marinated with the fear of the RCPP and laced with heavy metal-power ballads, giving me the clout to use stationary soaked in my favorite perfume and to put a stamp on upside down, only proves how much smell there is here and now, before ancestors and flint or even citrus colored sports bottles. Well, get your priorities straight, ~~you fucker you mean nasty person~~

His jaw dropped. and off slid his finely sculpted, bohemian goatee.

Breeders - pod An epic that will never let you forget your ex girlfriend.

pixies surfer rosa - A die-cast metal fossil from a space craft, with or without the fucking production.

Leadbellys last sessions (folkways) vol. 1 - orgones, pyles, cells and he probably knew the difference between male and female hemp.

VASelines - pink & Green EPS - Eugene + frances = documented love.

young Marble Giants - Colossal Youth - lying in an iron lung filled with luke warm water and epsom salts.

wipers - is this real? - yeah it is.

Shonen Knife - Burning farm EP - when i finally got to see them live, I was transformed into a hysteric nine year old girl at a Beatles concert.

Sex pistols - Nevermind the Bollocks - one million times more important than the Clash

Jad fair - great expectations - with my head phones on, Jad and I share "our little secret" walking thru Shopping malls and Air ports.

YEAH, And then
they wiped their butts with it then

set it on fire!

rehabilitation, sympathy: <u>Groups</u>.
usually small, non profit or state funded
organizations directed ~~tow~~ helping rape
victims cope with the crimes.
brought upon them, also known as
rape crisis centers or planned parenthood
who by the way have now just recently
been warned that it
soon will be unlawful for doctors
working at these centers (usually on a
voluntary basis) to offer young pregnant
women every option available, meaning:
~~abortion~~ They are not allowed to suggest
the option of abortion,

this is happening in the U.S. so why should you care? it could probably happen here as well.

[redacted] I wonder if it was an intentional
decision ~~to leave out such~~ on your part
to ~~leave out~~ ~~such~~ vital key words as
such as the sympathy or rehabilitation, instead,
leaving the word 'group' all by its lonesome
to deceivingly make this rediculous little
quote to read as if I were attacking
other <u>groups</u> (meaning ROCK Bands)
for inefficiently addressing rape and in turn
so righteously claiming that the song polly
was ~~intended to~~ written as a rebuttle
towards ~~these~~ groups or (your so-called
(ROCK bands) and to claim that

not print

our BAND (NIRVANA) have conciously decided that
it is our devout crusade, as a band,
to teach men not to rape.
We find it very frustrating to engage in a 2
Hour in depth interview and to waste these

two hours giving what we felt was a pretty
insightful interview ~~and~~ then it turns out,
only a few embarrasingly misguoted
words were used, ~~making it~~ not
to mention one quote literally
Stolen from another article a few
months ~~later~~ ago from NME (guns n roses attack)
and in the end making it seem AS IF
were a band who have nothing better
to say than garbled - second rate
political rantings, we are not politically
Correct, but yes we do ~~feel~~ have
opinions on these ~~matters~~ subjects but we
don't deserve the illusive display
of ~~the next Guns and roses~~
~~your more responsible for the exchagerated~~
~~Commercial Hype~~

Being solely A political band, it's quite
obvious that were not qualified or prolific
enough to even try. thats why 90%
of our interviews consist of half
witted talk about music or our pets
and when squeezed out of us about
10% of sincere, politically personal
viewpoints revealed, and why is
this? learning the hard way, to
not be able to trust the majority
of the incestually-competetive
english journalist. talk about
politics shall we? how many ~~sadistic~~
times have journalists of both papers

one another

stabbed in the back, lied or provided favors
in order to ~~beat~~ one another for A cover story
with the same band? er, just A guess,
sensationalist tabloids are quite harmless and
its understandable why they are needed when
the majority of present rock bands, have
nothing to say musically but musical inspiration seems
to have been deformed by the vicious and
self serving pleasure of the journalist which
naturally incites bands to become paranoid
Defensive, Jaded, abusive and uncooperative.
the english journalist is a
second rate self apointed judge who couldnt
make it to becoming a ~~therapist~~ mental therapist,
theyre enemic, clammy, physically deformed,
gnome-like, internally upset with A dysfunctional
ability to stabilize a relationship (except
with eachother) and sincerely masochistic
who would bathe in the glamour of
nude photos of them selves with handcuffs
behind the back, on their knees wearing
a diaper with a rubber
cock stuffed in their mouth, and these
photos pasted on every cover magazine
in Europe. the rivals and the poachers
shall one day ban together to print
one tabloid monthly.

And the weak crumbs will report to
the custodial arts.

love kur-d-t Koebane

we
gleefully
decline
the
opportunity
to
Be
raped
by
the limey
Journalist.
By saying to
future interview?
No thanks
No thank
You

Hi,

yeah, all Isms feed off one another,
but at the top of the food chain is still
the white, corporate, macho, strong
ox male, Not redeemable as far as im
concerned. I mean, classism is determined
by sexism because the male decides whether
All other isms still exists. its up to men.

Im just saying that people cant deny any ism
or think that some are more or less subordinate.
except for sexism. He's in charge
He decides. I still think that in order
to expand on all other isms, sexism has to
be blown wide open,
Its almost impossible to de program
the incestually-established, male oppressor.
especially the one's whove been
weaned on it thru their familys generations,
like die hard N.R.A freaks and inherited,
corporate, power mongrels, the ones who
were born into no choice but to keep the
torch and only let sparks fall for the rest
of us to gather at their feet. But
there are thousands of Green minds, young
gullable 15 year old Boys out there just
starting to fall into the grain of what
theyve been told of what a man is
supposed to be, and there are plenty of
tools to use, the most
effective tool is entertainment. The
entertainment industry is just now

starting to accept us. (mainly because of trendy falseness and environmentally, socially concience hype) ie: the new 90's Attitude, which is at a total standstill because of the patriotic, aftermath of the war and all its Nuremberg rally-parades) but theyre using MediA! Media. Major labels. ((the evil corporate Oppressors, (god I need a new word!) the ones who are in CAhoots with the government, the ones the underground movement went into retaliation against in the early 80s.) The corporations are finally allowing ~~subversive~~ supposedly subversive, alternative thinking bands to have a loan of money to expose their crusade, ~~whether~~ obviously they arent ~~doing this~~ forking out loans for this reason, but more because it looks to be a money making, comodity. but we can use them! We can pose as the enemy to ~~to~~ infiltrate the mechanics of the System to start its rot from the inside. Sabotage the empire by pretending to play their game. compromise just enough to call their bluff. And the hairy, sweaty, MACho, sexist dickheads will soon drown in a pool of razorblades and semen, stemmed from the uprising of their children, the armed and deprogrammed crusade, littering the floors of WAllstreet with revolutionary debris.

Assasinating both the lesser and greater of two evils. bringing an everlasting, sterile and bacterial, herbacious and botanical and corporate cleansing for our

ancestors to gaze in wonderment and Awe. AWE!
geezus christ. (repeat): posing as the enemy
to infiltrate the mechanics of the empire and
slowly start its rot from the inside, its an
inside job - it starts with the custodians
and the cheerleaders. And ends with the entertainers.
: The youth are waiting, impatiently.
Homophobe VACCECTOMY.
Its like what Kathleen said about how in school
there was this class that you went to and they
were teaching the girls how to prepare themselves
for rape and when you looked outside and saw
the rapers outside playing football and
you said "they are the ones who should be in
here being taught not to rape."
How true. Suck em in with quality
entertainment and hit em with reality.
The revolution will be televised.
Theres this new 24 hour channel on cable called
the 90s, which is available only in a few states so far
and it's magazine version can be seen on pbs
(public broadcasting system) once a week,
it's Pretty damn informative and it exposes
injustices in a kind of conservative-
/liberal format, but its new so it has to be that
way. Ive seen it a few times and really liked
it. Also Night flight is back. you know,
the show that used to play new wave theatre?
We plan to use these shows and others
if given the chance. Yeah I know, I'm a
confused, uneducated, walking cliche, but I dont need
to be inspired any longer, just supported.

Oh yeah, Gluttony, I almost forgot Gluttony,
The band now has an image: the anti-gluttony, materialism & consumerism image which we plan to incorperate into all of our videos. The first one 'Smells like teen spirit.' will have us walking through a mall throwing thousands of dollars into the air as mall-goers scramble like vulchers to collect as much as they can get their hands on, then we walk into a jewelry store & smash it up in anti-materialist fueled, punk rock violence. then we go to A pep Assembly at a High school And the Cheerleaders have Ⓐ Anarchy A's on their sweaters and the Custodian-militant-revolutionarys hand out guns with flowers in the barrels to all the cheering students who file down to the center court and throw their money & Jewelry & Andrew dice Clay Tapes into A big pile then we set it on fire and run out of the building screaming. Oh, didnt twisted sister already do this?

Things that have been taken from me within the past 2 months: 1 wallet, drivers license etc.. $2100.⁰⁰ three guitars (including the moserite) all my neato 70's effect boxes, apartment and phone. but I got a really neato left handed 67 fender Jaguar, which is in my opinon, almost as cool a's a mustang. So I consider it a fair trade for the moserite.

while staying in LA.
We almost got killed by gang members.
well, sort of.
Dave Franz and I were in the parking lot of a famous, female-mudwrestler-night club scoring lewds, when all of a sudden two gass guzzling cars pulled up next to us and five cho-los with knives and guns walked over to the car closest to ours and started yelling & cursing in gang lingo at eachother. But then by the motto of "To protect and serve" the cops show up, which insighted the gang bangers to flee away in their cars, resulting in a hot persuit - car chase. There were even hellicopters with search lights.
Needless to say we scored our lewds and split. We played a really fun show with fitz of Depression at a really small coffee house called the jabberjaw. We were indescribably fucked up on booze and drugs, out of tune and rather uh, sloppy. It took me about fifteen minutes to change my guitar string while people heckled and called me drunk Robyn Zander, (cheap trick lead singer?)
After the show I ran outside and vomited, then I came back in to find Iggy pop there, so I gave him a sloppy-puke breath kiss' and hug. He's a really friendly and cool and nice and interesting person, It was probably the most flattering moment of my life,

As you may have guessed by now I've been taking a lot of drugs lately
It might be time for the Betty Ford Clinic or the Richard Nixon library to save me from abusing my enemic, rodent-like body any longer. I can't wait to be back at home (wherever that is) in bed, neurotic and malnourished and complaining how the weather sucks, and its the whole reason for my misery. I miss you, Bikini Kill.
I totally love you.
Kurdt

There is a small percent of the population who were BORN with the ability to detect injustice. they have Tendencies to question injustice and to look for answers ~~(by~~ their oppressors standards in ways that would be considered abnormal. They have Tendencies and talents in the sense that they know from an early age that they have the gift to challenge what is expected of their future.

These kids are usually hyperactive, uncontrollable brats who never know when to quit because their so wrapped up in whatever their tryin, to prove, that they eventually offend someone, not meaning to of course, This is good.

They usually go through childhood thinking their special. its partly instinctual and maybe theyve been told by their parents or teachers, that their special. maybe theyre put in a gifted childrens—overachiever class in grade school. for whatever reason they end up molding into a person aware of their abilities and not understanding them and having bloated egos caused by societys insistance that those with an overly-functional insight ~~must~~ should be praised and considered to be on a higher level of ~~[illegible]~~ easy access ~~toward~~ toward success. Eventually they beome totally confused and bitter adolescents who tend to see nothing but injustice because by that time they (usually) have had the chance to be exposed to others like them who learn from their gifted, bohemian ancestors.

conciousness

The larger percent who have and always will dominate the smaller percent simply because they outnumber were not BORN with even the slightest ability to comprehend injustice. there are the stump dump Average Joe Garbagemen or Lawyers of life.

Its not their fault because they physically lack that special, extra group of cells in the brain that welcome a questioning conciousness.

This is definitely Not hereditary.

It is definitely not their fault.

They aren't simply misguided.

Of course the extremes ~~of~~ and levels of the ability to defect injustice range ~~to~~ all levels. these people usually fit in the bracket that not described AS Could be ~~easily~~ compared ~~to~~ the level of one who is marginally retarded.

you know, the ones who have the symptoms of mongoloid rings around the eyes yet they can still act on prime time Television dramas.

All other so called talents like, dance, singing, acting, wood carving and Art is mostly a developmental culmination of exercise ~~trying to~~ ~~towards~~ attaining perfection thru practice

NO True talent is ~~ever~~ fully organic.

born passion

yet the obviously Superior talented have not only control of study but that extra special, little gift ~~@~~ at birth — fueled by passion. A built in, totally spiritual, unexplainable, New Age, fuckin, cosmic energy bursting love for passion.

And yes, they are an even smaller percent amongst the small percent, And they Are Special! mistrust All Systematizers.

All things cannot be evaluated to the point of total Logic or Science. No one is special enough to ~~realize~~ Answer that.

This is not to be taken seriously,
This is not to be read as opinions.
It is to be read as poetry.
Its obvious that I am on the educated level of about 10th grade in High school, It's obvious that these words were not thought out or even re-read, this writing style is what I like to call thru the perspective of a 10th grader, her/his attempt at showing that no matter what level of intellizence one is on, we all question love and lack of love and fear of love.
Its good to question authority and to fight it just to make things a bit less boring, but ive always reverted back to the the Conclusion that man is not redeemable and words that dont necersarily have their expected meanings can be used descriptively in a sentence as Art. True english is so fucking boring. And this little pit-stop we call life, that we so seriously worry about is nothing but a small, over the week end jail sentence, compared to what will come with death.
life isnt nearly as sacred as the appreciation of passion.

its good to question Authority but Ive always come to the same conclusion that man is not redeemable And this little pit stop we call life that we so seriously worry about is nothing but a jail sentence compared to what will come with death

If were going to be ghettoised, I'd rather be in the same slum as bands that are good like mudhoney, Jesus Lizard, the Melvins and Beat happening rather than being a tennant of the Corporate Landlords regime.

I mean, were playing the Corporate game and were playing as best as we can suddenly we found ourselves having to actually play instead of using the Corporations great distribution while staying in our little world because we sold 10 times more the amount of records we had expected to sell. It's just a shock to be doing interviews with magazines that I don't read

positive >

there are alot of bands who claim to be alternative and theyre nothing but stripped down, ex Sunset Strip hair farming bands of a few years ago

I would love to be erased from our association with pearl Jam or the Nymphs and other first time offenders.

Alternative bands have tried to the general public every year since the sex pistols and have failed every time not the fault of the bands but the times werent right. the Reagan years so effective in keeping out Any chance of a better concience which is why there were so many great indie - do it yourself bands throughout the 80s as subverts towards Reagan because he was such a creep.

3-D

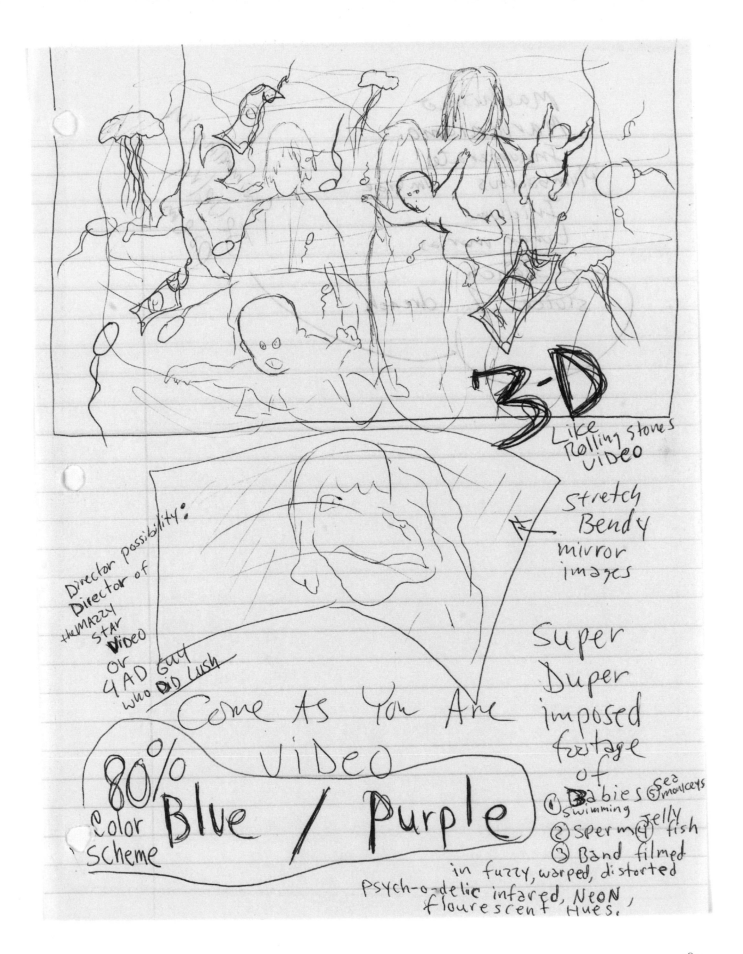

Like Rolling stones VIDEO

stretch Bendy mirror images

Director possibility:
Director of the MAZZY STAR VIDEO or 4AD GUY who DID LUSH

Come As You Are VIDEO

80% Color Scheme Blue / Purple

Super Duper imposed footage of
① Babies swimming
② sperm
③ Band filmed in fuzzy, warped, distorted psych-o-delic infared, NeoN, flourescent Hues.
④ Jelly fish
⑤ Sea monkeys

MELVINS

They have Reagan or Bush vote Republican
stickers on the bumper of their Van
to fend off nasty Rodney King Cops

All three members consistently sculpt verious ~~displays~~ models
of the Goatee facial hair fashion oh except for peach fuzz,-
pieeyed, baby face, Sometimes pinch an inchish, sometimes Annorexorcist,
skin tight purple Levis, wearin Jimmy from HR Puffnstuff haircut,
ex-Tea head, smoking non-smoker ~~Dale~~ All around nice Guy Dale Crover

oh by the way he's the best drummer in the world

Its hard to decipher the difference between
a sincere entertainer and an honest swindler.

Ive violently vomited to the point of
my stomach literally turning itself inside out to show
you the fine hairlike nerves Ive kept and raised
as my children, garnishing and marinating Each one
as if God had fucked me and planted these precious
little eggs, and I parade them around in peacock
victory and maternal pride like a whore relieved
from the duties of repeated rape and torture, promoted to a
more dignified Job of just plain old every day,
good old, wholesome prostitution. my feathers are my pussy.

CArtoon

oh how I love the brutal effect of just one
word offering to ponder like....

Cartoon

fuck man, think about it,

CArtoon

HeAVY man

HeAVY

If you think everythings been said and done
then how come nothing has been solved
and resolved?
I ASK YOU.
Sarcastically with a sneer. in A 90's way.
kinda uh, defensively to say the least and to do the worst.

~~I~~ kind of feel like a dork writing ~~or~~ about myself like this as if I were an American pop-rock icon, demi God, or self confessed product of corporate-packaged-rebellion, but Ive heard so many insanely exhaggerated stories or reports from my friends and Ive read so many pathetic second rate, freudian evaluations from interviews ~~from~~ my childhood up until the present state of my personality and how Im A notoriously fucked up Heroine addict, Alcoholic, self destructive, yet overtly sensitive frail, fragile, soft spoken, narcoleptic, ~~Neuro~~ Neurotic, little piss Ant who At any minute is going to O.D. Jump off a roof wig out ~~and~~. Blow my head off or All 3 At once. Oh Geez GAWD I can't handle the success! the success! And I feel so incredibly Guilty! for Abandoning my true commrades the ones who are devoted. the ones who were into us A few years Ago

And ~~After~~ And in 10 years ~~we~~ ~~As~~ when NIRVANA becomes as memorable As KAGAGOOGOO ~~in 10 years the same~~ that same, very small percent will come to see us At reunion gigs sponsored by Depends diapers, bald fat, still trying to RAWK At ~~water~~ Amusement PARKS.

Saturdays ~~Nel~~ Puppet show, Rollercoaster & NIRVANA

ASK Jenny Tumi if we can re-print her how to record A record essay, for this fanzine.

~~[illegible]~~ After all the hype and oogling over us this past year I've come to two conclusions,

1: we've made A way better commercial record than Poison,

2: there are quadruple the amount of Bad Rock Journalists than there are bad Rock Bands.

Well for those of you who are concerned with my present physical and mental state.

I Am NOT GAY, Although I wish I were, just to piss off Homophobes

I Am Not A Junkie.

I've had a rather unconclusive and uncomfortable stomach condition for the past 3 years which by the way is not related to stress which also means it is not an ulcer, because there is no pattern to the burning, nauseous pain in my upper abdominal cavity, I never know when it will ~~come on~~ happen, I can be At home in the most relaxed atmosphere sipping ~~bottled~~, ~~and~~ a Natural spring water, No stress, No fuss and then WhAm! like A shot gun: stoMAch Time, then I CAn play 100 ~~shows~~ live performances in A row Guzzle Boric Acid & do A zillion television interviews and Not even A Burp. This has left doctors with no ideas except the usual: here Kurt try another peptic ulcer pill and lets jam this fibre optic

~~As say the~~ just perplexed

this has left many doctors perplexed

(Called an endoscope) tube with A video camera in it down your throat (its) for the 3rd time and see whats going on in there. Again. Yep your in pain alright. Your stomach is extremely inflamed and red. try eating ice cream from now on.

please lord ~~let me have a disease~~ fuck hit records just let me have my very own unexplainable rare stomach disease Named After me. ~~[illegible]~~

And the title of our next double Album. "Cobains disease." ~~the endoscope is great for A video and were just about finished with the~~ A rock opera which is all about vomiting gastric juices being A borderline Annorexic ~~[illegible]~~ Auzhwitz - Grunge - BOY. And with it an accompanying endoscope Home-video.

~~And~~ so After protein drinks and doctors after doctor becoming A vegetarian, exercise, stopping smoking I decided to relieve my pain with small doses of Heroine for A walloping 3 whole weeks. It served as a band-aid for a while but then the pain came back so I quit. It was A stupid thing to do And I'll never do it again and I feel real sorry for Anyone who thinks they can use heroine as a medicine because um, duh it dont work. drug withdrawal is everything youve ever heard, you puke, you flail around, you sweat, you shit your bed just like that movie Christiane F. ~~I dont feel sorry for anyone who uses junk~~. It's evil. leave it alone

I'm not stressed I am the product of 7 months of

I just sit back and laugh screaming at the top of my lungs almost every night

7 months of jumping around like a retarded wheesus monkey

7 months of Answering the same questions over and over

The Cherub little scruff you've grown to know from the picture on the back of Nevermind is proof that film adds 10 pounds to your body, because I've been the same birdweight ever since my last excuse which is . . .

I'm really bored with everyone's concerned advice like: "man you have a really good thing going your band is great. you write great songs, but hey man you should get your ~~shit together~~ personal shit together. Don't freak out and get healthy. Gee I wish it was as easy as that but, honestly I didn't want all this attention but I'm not freaked out ~~like everyone would like to believe~~ which is something a lot of people would like to see. It's an entertaining ~~thought~~ to ~~own your~~ ~~own~~ watch a public domain A Rock figure whos mentally self destruct, but I'm sorry friends I'll have to decline. Maybe Crispin Glover should ~~start~~ join our band.

And at the end of the day, instead of plotting how I can escape this ~~~~ I just simply have to laugh I find it really funny. It feels as if we've almost, pulled a minor Rock-n-Roll Swindle because I'm not nearly as concerned with or about myself or anyone as the media would have us believe. I think the problem with our story is that there isn't an exciting enough truth for A Good story.

Well I've spewed enough, probably too much but oh well, for every one ~~self appointed~~, opinionated, curmudgeon, pissy, self appointed Rock Judge there's A thousand kids.

OH THE GUILT   THE GUILT   (by: KurDt disclaimer-boy)

I kind of feel like a dork writing about the band and myself like this as if i were an American pop-rock icon, demi god or a self confessed product of pre packaged, corporate rebellion. But ive heard so many insanely exhaggerated wise tales and reports from my friends, and ive read so many pathetic, second rate, freudian evaluations from interviews, regarding our personalities and especially how im a notoriously fucked up heroine addict, alcoholic, self destructive, yet overly sensitive, frail, meek, fragile, compassionate, soft spoken, narcoleptic, NEUROTIC, little, piss ant who at any time is going to O.D, jump off a roof and wig out, blow my head off or all three at once because I CANT HANDLE THE SUCCESS! OH THE SUCCESS! THE GUILT! THE GUILT! OH, I FEEL SO INCREDIBLY GUILTY! GUILTY for abandoning our true commrades. the ones who are devoted. the ones who have been into us since the beginning. the ones who (in ten years when were as memorable as KAGA GOO GOO) will still come to see NIRVANA at reunion gigs at amusement parks. sponsored by depends diapers, bald fat and still trying to rawk. MY favorite reocurring piece of advice from concerned idiots is: "Man, you have a really good thing going. your band is great. you write pretty good songs and youve sold a shit load of records but, hey man, you should get your personal shit together. dont freak out and get healthy." Gee I wish it was that easy but honestly, I didnt want all this attention, but im not FREAKED OUT! which is something a lot of people might like to see. Its entertaining to watch A rock figure whos become public domain mentally self destruct. But im sorry ill have to decline. Id like to freak out for you. maybe Crispin Glover should join our band. At the end of the day I laugh my ass offk knowing ive gotten about 30¢ from this dork. Sometimes it feels as if weve pulled a minor rock and roll swindle because im not nearly as concerned with or about myself, the band or anyone as much as the media would like us to believe. I think the problem with our story is that there isnt an exciting enough truth for a good story. Oh, and another thing. I am not a heroine addict!

and others like Him

MR advice

for the past three years ive suffered a rather unconclusive and uncomfortable stomach condition. which by the way is not related to stress which also means is not an ulcer because there is no pattern to the burning, nausious pain in my upper abdominal cavity. its like russian roulette, I never know when it will come on, I can be at home in the most relaxed atmosphere, sipping natural spring water, no stress, no fuss, and then wham! like a shot gun.: stomach time is here again. then i can play 100 shows in a row, guzzle boric acid and do a load of television interviews, results: not even a burp. This has left doctors with no ideas except the usual, "Here Kurdt, try another peptic ulcer pill and lets jam this fibre-optic tube with a video camera on its end down your throat for the third time. (called an ENDOSCOPE) and see whats going on in there. yep, your in pain. the stomach lining is extremely red and inflamed. this could be life threatening. try eating ice cream from now on. Please lord! to hell with hit records, let me have my very own unexplainable, rare, stomach disease named after me. The title of our next double concept album could be called "COBAINS DISEASE". A rock opera all about vomiting gastric juices, being a borderline annorexic-Auschwitz-grunge-boy. And with this epic, an accompanying ENDOSCOPE rock video.

I am the product of seven months of screaming at the top of my lungs almost every night. seven months of jumping around like a retarded rheesus monkey. seven months of answering the same questions over and over. The cherub, little scruff youve grown to know from the back of the nevermind album is proof that film adds ten pounds to your body, because ive been the same bird weight since ive had the dreaded gut rot. Well ive spewed enough, probably too much but oh well. for every one opinionated, pissy, self-appointed rock judge-cermudgeon, theres a thousand screaming teenagers.

hope i die before i turn into Pete Townshend.

WomBan

DE_JA VOO- DOO BY: KurDt Kobain

stomach bile

An industrial size garbage sack filled with liquid demerol, sweet cutgrass juice, the urine of extremely retarded,fetal alcohol syn syndrome victims from Costa Mesa who are one chromosone away from severely dangerous examples of why we will become a third world country in a matter of years. If this is the current state of the underground,youth culture Id rather retire to my big mansion petting my pot bellied pig,eating Hagen Dahs ice cream with this garbage sack I.V. , in an iron lung deprevation tank,submerged in a glassno no a gold aquarium filled with epsom salts with full visibility of a television monitor projecting endless footage of fishing and golfing programs as the grateful dead pumps through the speaker. Relaxing , lying naked except for a tie dyed T- shirt dyed with the urine of Phil Collins and the blood of Cherry Garcia, Ill be so relaxed and famous that an old man named Bob will travel miles to visit me. He will pull apart my pyles and stick it in. He will die just as he comes inside of me and all of his orgones and bad thoughts and desires for truth will soak into the walls of my lower intestines. I will be re-fueled. so re-fueled as to work up the energy to run on foot to the grave of Leadbelly, dig up his corpse and put us on a one way ticket to the Vatican. I will nail the corpse of Huddie in a corner of the ceiling, paint him white and decorate him with costume jewelry.

Womben

Womban

its So relieving to know that your leaving
as soon as you get paid

its so relaxing to know that your asking

its so soothing to know that youll sue me
whenever you get the chance

its so religious

She eyes me like a pisces - when I am weak
Ive been buried in your heart shaped box for weeks
Ive been drawn into your magnet tar pit trap
I wish I could eat your cancer when you
turn black

Hey - wait - Ive got a new complaint
for ever in debt to your priceless advice
Hate - wait - *
"

She fries me like cold Ice cream - headaches and chills
Ill cook my own Meals

uncertainty certainty

I wish there was someone I could ask for advice. someone who wouldn't make me feel like a creep for spilling my guts and trying to explain all the insecurities that have plagued me for oh, about 25 years now. I wish someone could explain to me why exactly I have no desire to learn anymore. why I used to have so much energy and the need to search for miles ~~for~~ and weeks for anything new and different. excitement. I was once a magnet for attracting new off beat personalities who would introduce me to music and books ~~that~~ of the obscure and I would soak it into my system like a rabid sex crazed junkie hyperactive mentally retarded toddler who's just had her first taste of sugar. This weeks obsession, vagina medical books, the meat puppets and

Lester Bangs

why in the hell do journalists insist on ~~breeding~~ coming up with a second rate freudian evaluation on my lyrics when 90 % of the time theyve transcribed ~~them wrong~~ the lyrics incorrectly?

there are more bad rock journalists than there are bad rock bands

~~does anyone remember~~

what the fuck do they teach journalists at school anyway?

what do they use as reference or examples?

does anyone remember lester bangs.

I'm giving you factual quotes from my mind

I'm fed up with having long winded 2 hour discussions with journalists and finding that they've chosen all the unimportant more tabloid esque quotes of the past 2 hours.

Rock bands are at the mercy of the journalist and in my opinion there is not one I can think of who deserves to own a pen.

you probably need more qualifications to be a welder than ~~a journalist~~ to get a job being a journalist.

I would have printed the lyrics on the sleeve of the album if I knew it were going to be such a problem with people thanks for your second rate freudian evaluation on my ~~present~~ minds present state of "oh gee I feel guilty for not expecting to sell so many records."

Ask my friends; Ive always been this skinny You know me from pictures, film adds ten pounds to A person. Youve never seen me before in real life until that most memorable night.

I suffer from narcolepsy, I suffer from bad sleeping and eating habits. I suffer from being on tour for 7 fucking months.

Sometimes I wonder if I ~~(crossed out)~~ very well could be the luckiest boy in the world.

for some reason Ive been blessed with loads of neat stuff within the past year and I dont really think these baubles and Gifts I have been acquired by the fact that im a critically acclaimed, internationally beloved -teen Idol, demi-god like blonde frontman, cryptically honest, stuttering, outspoken speech impediment articulately award acceptance speech, Golden boy, Rock star who has finally, finally come out of the closet in regards to his vicious 2 month drug habit, showering the world with the ~~(crossed out)~~ Classic I can no longer keep this a secret because it pains me to hide any part of my private life from my adoring, concerned, we think of you as our public domain, cartoon character but we still love you fans Yes my children in the words of a total fucking geek ~~(crossed out)~~ speaking in behalf of all the world !" we really appreciate you finally admitting what we have been accusing you of, we needed to hear it because we were concerned because the katty Gossip ~~and~~ Jokes and speculation at our jobs schools and parties had become well uh, exhausted oh yeah the bitter, pissy reincarnation of pick yer King has strayed from the positive introduction. so heres the things Ive had the wonderful opportunity to have acquired, the wonderful people ive met and the things people have said to me that I look back upon and hold dear to my heart.

1st while in London England in ~~(crossed out)~~ June I went to Rough Trade records where I make my pathetic annual, effort to find the 1st raincoats album

x x x x x x x x

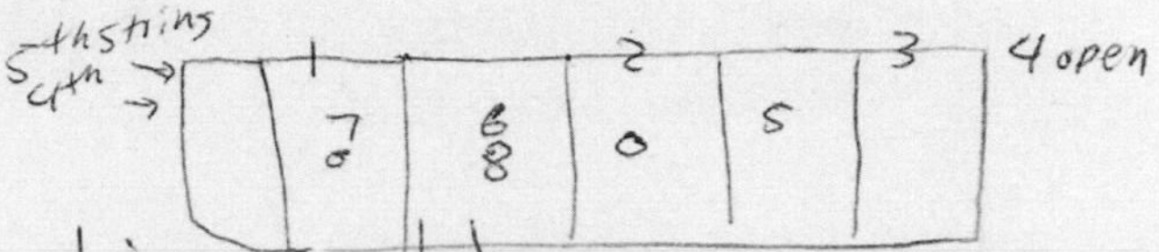

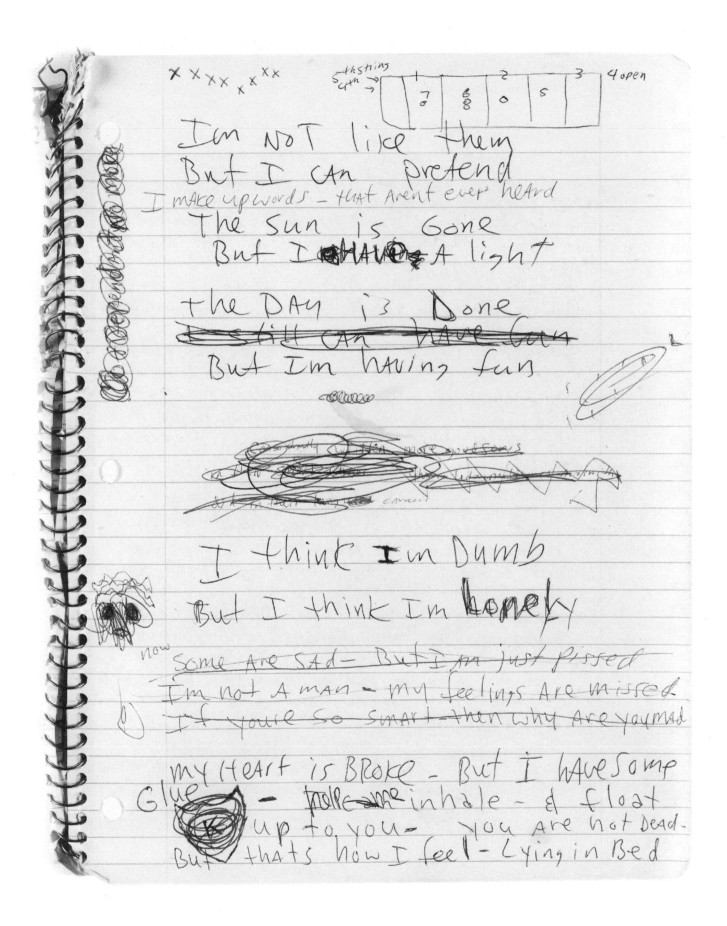

Im NOT like them
But I CAn pretend
I make up words – that arent ever heard
The sun is Gone
But I ~~have~~ A light

the DAY is Done
~~I still can have fun~~
But Im having fun

I think Im Dumb
But I think Im lonely

now ~~Some are sad – But I am just pissed~~
~~Im not A man – my feelings are missed~~
~~If youre so smart – then why are you mad~~

my Heart is BROKE – But I have some
Glue – ~~help me~~ inhale – & float
up to you – you are not Dead –
But thats how I feel – Lying in Bed

Id be better off if i kept my mouth shut.

But theres a cool breeze chapping my lips
As my jaw hangs open discharging waterfalls
of guilty drool. My eyes are pinned and the stupid
fucking British press bought the lie that I
suffer from narcolepsy. Yeah, talkin bout
drugs. opening my mouth for the disaffected youth
to ask them a question. Are you gay?
bisexual? A bigot? A redneck? A prom queen?
A porn star? A topless dancer? did you know the
King, the King of Rock n Roll Elvis presley
died in the bathroom face down, pants down,
choking on blue shag carpet with the remainder
of his stool proudly sticking out of his
big fat Ass? Are you kinda mad sometimes
At your mom or dad kinda, in a way?
I went on A three week Heroine
Binge after our last European tour, got A little
habit, kicked it in A Hotel in three days (sleeping
Kicking, vomiting and the worst gas you'll ever
know. then 3 days later we went on A
Australian tour And on to Japan during which I
Collected A very distressing stomach disorder,
Went to A doctor and he gave me stomach
pills that Ive had before and didn't work and
some five milligram methadone tablets.
They stopped the stomach pains, I ran out
when I got home then went to A hospital
for A few days to recover from that.
more bad gas.

~~Now I don't do drugs anymore~~

Yeah, I went on A 3 week drug binge and now
Im thought of as an emaciated, yellow skinned, Zombie like-
- Evil drug fiend, Junky, ~~[illegible]~~ lost CAuse, on the
brink of Death, Self destructive, selfish pig,
A loser who shoots up in the backstage ~~area~~ just seconds before
going ~~on~~ a performance

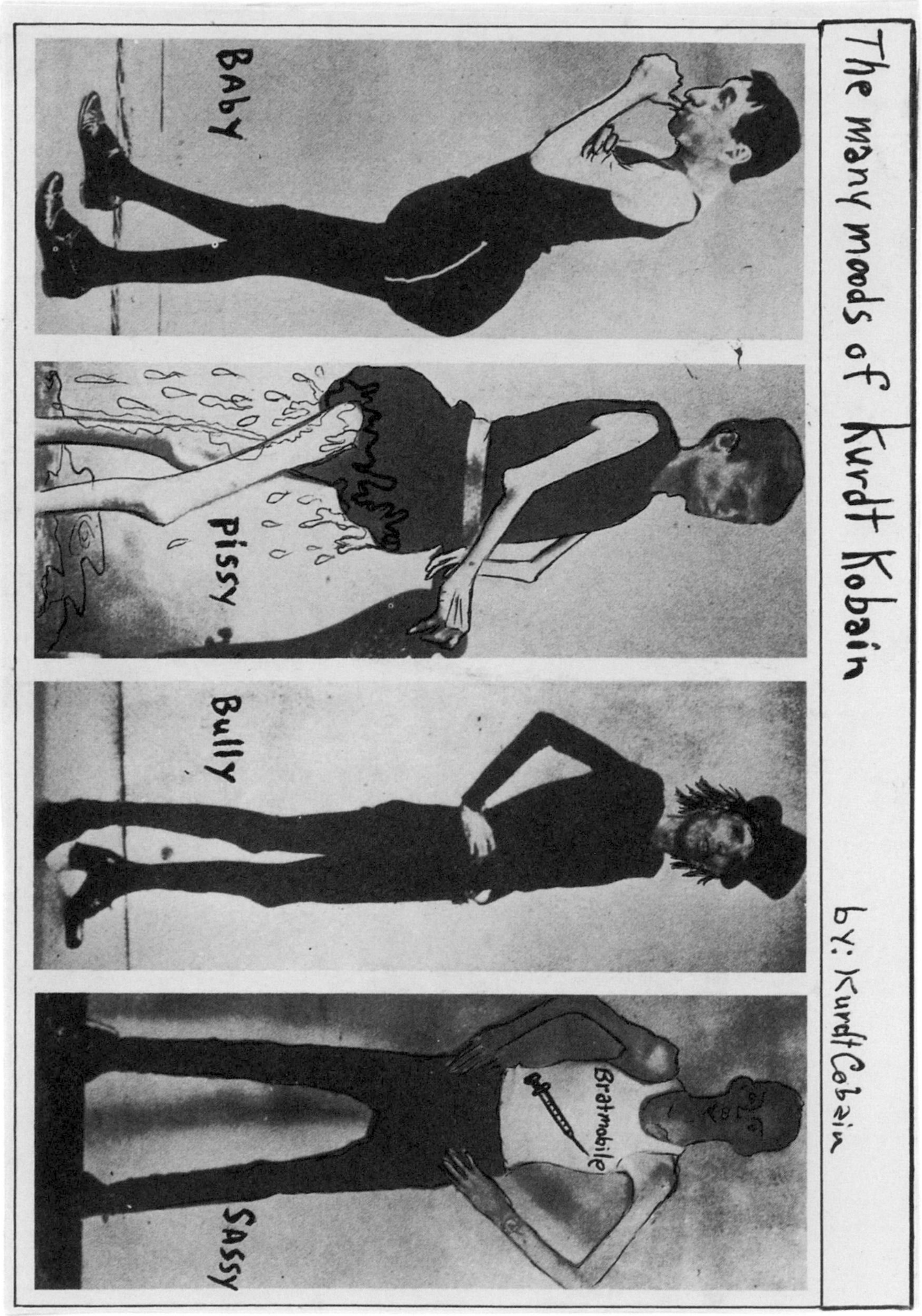

The many moods of Kurdt Kobain
by: Kurdt Cobain
BABY
Pissy
Bully
Bratmobile
SASSY

I tried heroine the first time in 1987 in aberdeen and proceeded to use it about 10 more times from 87 to 90. when I got back from our second European Tour with Sonic Youth I decided to use heroine on a daily basis because of an ongoing stomach ailment that I had been suffering from for the past five years had literally taken me to the point of wanting to kill myself. For five years every single day of my life. Every time I swallowed a piece of food I would experience an excruciating burning nauseous pain in the upper part of my stomach lining. The pain became even more severe on tour due to lack of a proper and regimented eating schedule and diet. Since the beginning of this disorder I've had 10 upper and lower Gastrointestinal proceedures wich found an enflamed irritation in the same place. I ~~went to~~ consulted 15 different doctors and tried about 50 different types of ulcer medication. The only thing I found that worked were heavy opiates. There were many times that I found myself literally incapacitated in bed for weeks vomiting and starving. So I decided ~~If~~ I feel like a junky as it is so I may as well be one. After the last European tour I vowed to never go on tour again unless my condition is either masked or cured. I did heroine for about one month then found myself realizing that I wouldnt be able to get drugs when ~~we~~ we go to ~~Japan in~~ ______ Australia and Japan so Courtney and I detoxed in a Hotel room

I went to Australia and of course the stomach pain started immediately. We had to cancel A few shows because the pain left me immobile doubled up on the bathroom floor vomiting Water and blood. I was literally Starving to death. my weight was down to about 110 lbs. I was taken to a doctor at the advice of my management who gave me physeptone. ~~take Instead~~ The pills seemed to work better than anything else Ive tried ~~a~~ a bit later into the tour I read the fine print on the bottle it read: "Physeptone - contains methadone" Hooked again. We survived Japan but by that time opiates and touring had started to take their toll on my body. and I wasn't in much better health than I was off of drugs. I returned home to find that Courtney had gotten hooked again so we checked ~~her~~ into a detox center for 2 weeks. She recovered. I instantly regained that familiar burning nausea and decided to ~~either~~ kill myself or ~~to~~ stop the pain. I bought a gun but chose drugs instead. I stayed on heroine until one month before frances due date. again I checked into a detox center and went through 2 months of the slowest process I have ever witnessed in recovery 60 days of Starvation and vomiting. Hooked to an IV and moaning out loud with the worst stomach pain I have ever experienced. ~~B~~ by the last 2 weeks I was introduced to a medicine called bubrenorphine which I found eleviates the pain within minutes. It has been used experimentally in A few detox centers for opiate and cocaine withdrawal. the best thing about it is that there are no known side effets. ~~and~~ It acts as ~~a~~ an opiate but it doesn't get you high. Ive been on an increasingly smaller dose of it for nine months and havent had a single stomach episode since. The potency range of beprenorphine is that ~~like~~ of a mild barbiturate on a scale of 1 to 10 its a 1 and heroine is 10.

Dear Empty TV
the Entity of all Corporate
Gods.
how fucking dare you embrace
such trash journalism from an
overweight, unpopular at highschool,
Cow who severely needs her karma
Broken. my lifes Dedication
is NOW TO Do Nothing
But SLAG MTV and
LYNN Herschbers
who by the way is in kahoots with
her lover Kurt Loder (Gin blossom drunk)!
We will survie without
you. easily
The old school is going
DOWN fAst
Kurdt
Kobain
professional
Rock musician
FACT FACT

4 month media blackout

use just once and destroy
invasion of our piracy
after birth of a nation
starve without your skeleton key

(3) ~~x~~ I love you for what I am not
x I did ~~not~~ want what I have got
(4) x blanket acned with cigarette burns
speak at once while taking turns

(1) x this has nothing to do with what you think
x If you ever think at all
~~[illegible]~~
~~revolutionary debris~~
~~litters the floor of WAll street~~

what is what I need – what is wrong with me
what is what I need – what do I think I
think

Bridge (x)
use use your enemies
and save save your friends
and find find your place
and spit spit the truth

(2) x Bi polar opposites attract
x All of a sudden my water broke
~~free xeroxes~~ for all alternateens
(3) x second rate ~~word by pass throat~~
of ferns

Hes such a knob

9 month media BLACKOUT

I love you my lovely dear
I dont want you any where

I want you to be my bride
no not really, I just lied

will you love me with your might
Ill beat you an inch from your life
AWAY

hold me tight with breaths of truths
I wish a terminal disease on you

Gosh I feel so darn confused
ever felt like youve been used?

Bi-polar opposites attract

All of a sudden my water broke

I love you for what Im not

primary → second rate word play bypass throat throat

Bypass

Use once and destroy
invasion of our piracy
afterbirth of a nation
blanket acned with cigarette burns
I forget what I look like to you

starve without your skeleton key

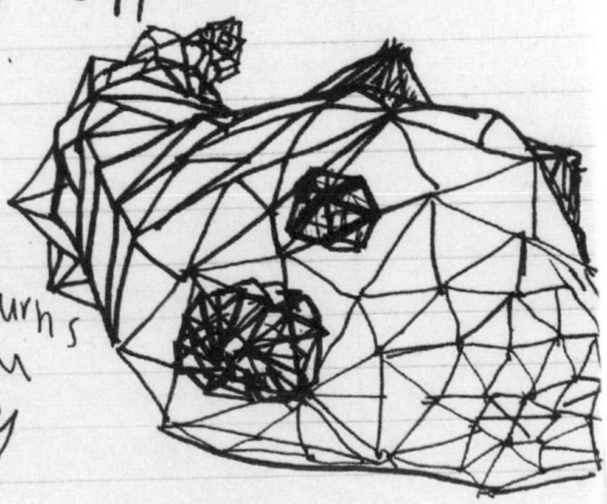

A matter of opinion

Second RATE
third GenerAtion

Personal Preference

A Date with Fusion

RAW Power
Funhouse
the Stooges
} the Stooges

Generic Flipper - Flipper
Surfer Rosa - pixies
Trompe le Monde - pixies
Pod - Breeders
VAselines pink EP
Aerosmith - Rocks
Gang of four - entertainment
~~Nevermind~~ Never mind the Bullocks - sex pistols
Flowers of Romance - PIL
Jamboree - Beat Happening
Superfuzz Big Muff - Mudhoney
Leadbellys lAst session - Hudie Ledbetter
LAnd shark - Fang
Millions of dead Cops - MDC
Damaged - Blackflag
Scratchacid EP - scratchacid
Locust abortion Technician - butthole surfers
Rock for light - Bad Brains
Raincoats - Raincoats
Philosophy of the World - shaggs
Combat Rock - Clash
Are we not men - Devo
B-52s
Collosal Youth - Young Marble Giants
Kleenex
Slits - Slits
Daydream Nation - Sonic Youth
man who Sold the world - David Bowie
GI - Germs

Saccharine Trust - EP
Get the Knack - the Knack
Atomizer - Big black
Great expectations - Jad fair
Is this Real
youth of AmericA
} wipers
~~Lipe~~ Rubbing the impossible to burst - Huggy Bear
XTC

Jackie 362-2610

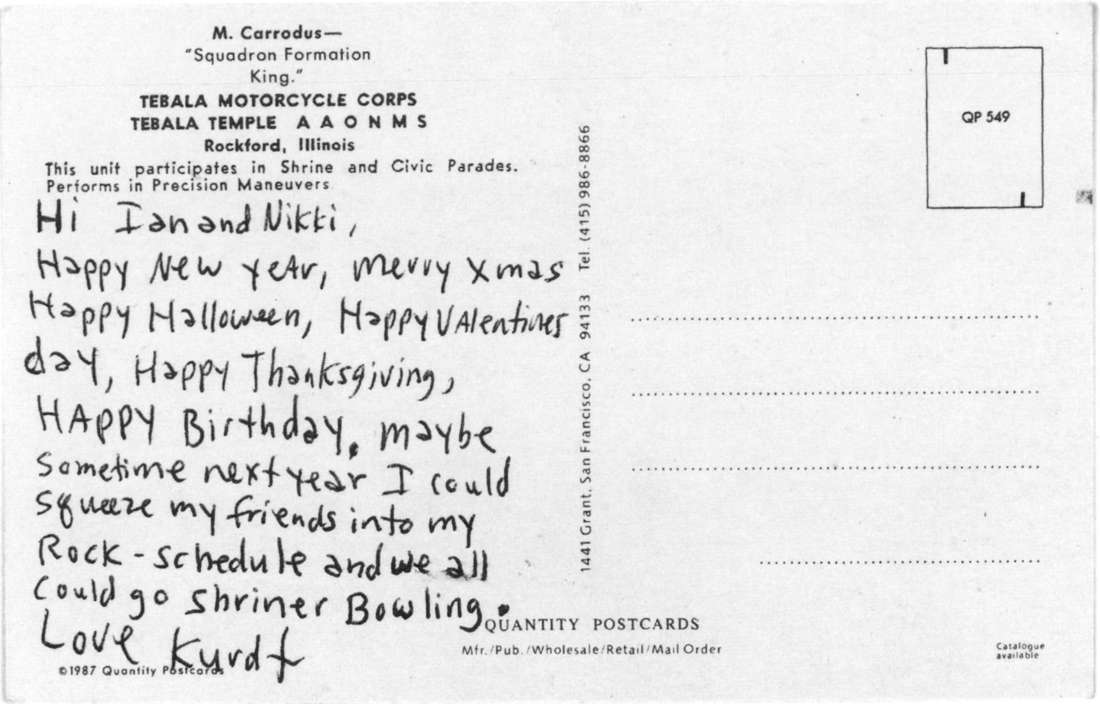
M. Carrodus—
"Squadron Formation
King."
TEBALA MOTORCYCLE CORPS
TEBALA TEMPLE A A O N M S
Rockford, Illinois
This unit participates in Shrine and Civic Parades.
Performs in Precision Maneuvers

Hi Ian and Nikki,
Happy New year, merry xmas
Happy Halloween, Happy VAlentines
day, Happy Thanksgiving,
HAPPY Birthday, maybe
sometime next year I could
squeeze my friends into my
Rock-schedule and we all
could go shriner Bowling.
Love Kurdt

QP 549

1441 Grant, San Francisco, CA 94133 Tel. (415) 986-8866

QUANTITY POSTCARDS
Mfr./Pub./Wholesale/Retail/Mail Order

Catalogue available

©1987 Quantity Postcards

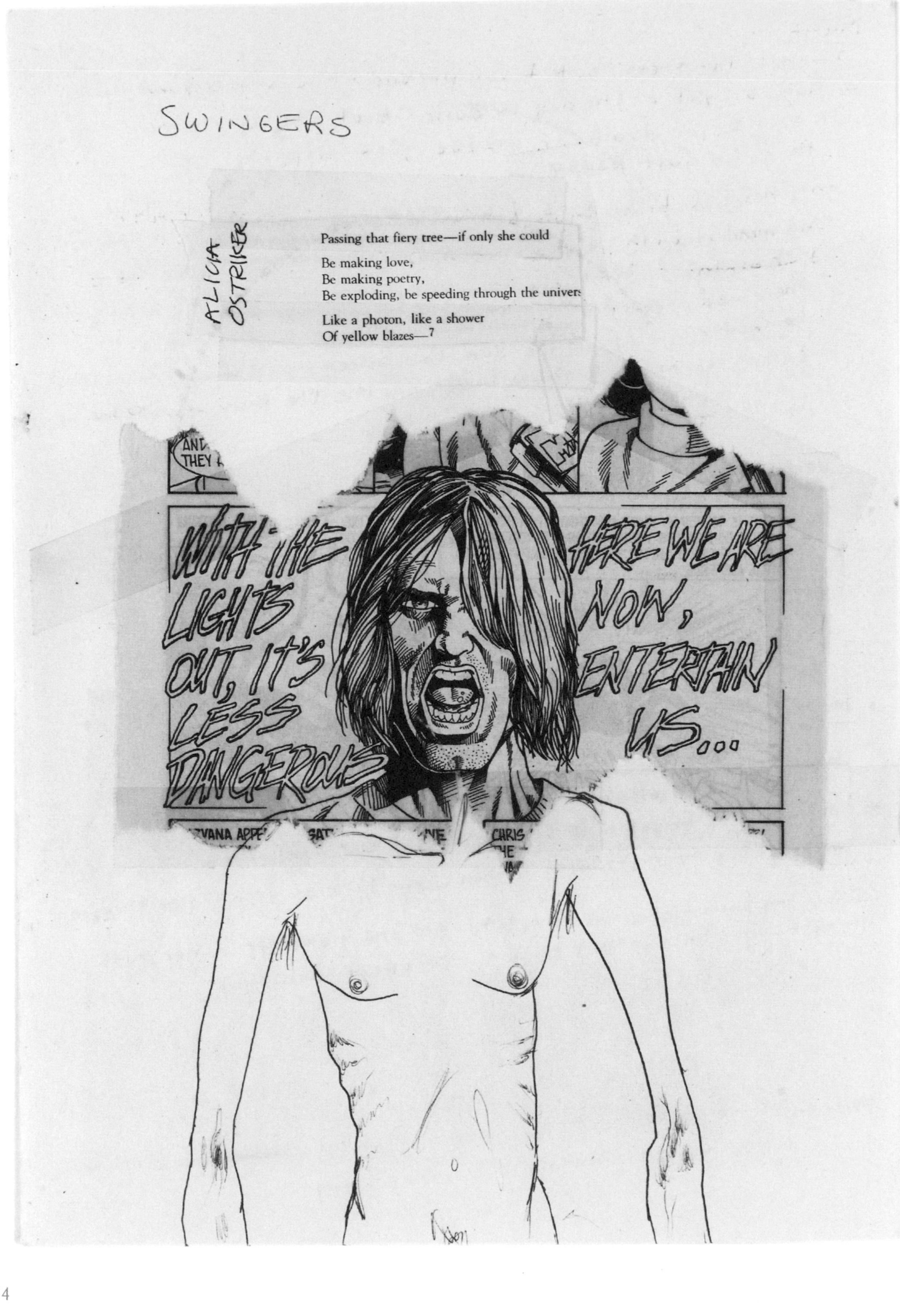
SWINGERS
ALICIA OSTRIKER
Passing that fiery tree—if only she could
Be making love,
Be making poetry,
Be exploding, be speeding through the univers
Like a photon, like a shower
Of yellow blazes—7
WITH THE LIGHTS OUT, IT'S LESS DANGEROUS
HERE WE ARE NOW, ENTERTAIN US...

Mead
Flipper
washed up, has been, drug addicts.
70 sheets/college ruled
11x8½in/27.9x21.6cm
notebook
$ 3-19
06540 © 1985 The Mead Corporation, Dayton, Ohio 45463 U.S.A.

The barium never left me
Cigarette burns in comforters
riddled with approach
Cursed with ~~the~~ welcome talents
Ive never been so yes

I know exactly what im doing
its All under control
I dont need any help
Id rather not
please leave me be
control freak
I appreciate your concern
has gratuity been added?
set it down over there
~~efficient handler~~
handler of the gods

Drain you (Live) (written by Nirvana) from the Nevermind LP note Kurdts clever, little guitar fuck up in the first half of the song.

School (Live) (written by Nirvana) from 1989's Bleach LP
A staple grunge Anthem in the Key of E

Son of A Gun (written by VAselines) } two songs written by NIRVANAS #1 favorite, Love Band from Scottland the VAselines
mollys lips } thanks to Eugene Kelly and francis McKee, the lennon & McCartney or the Boyce and Hart or the ferrante & Teicher of the underworld. Shield & Yarnell, Captain & tennile

D-7 (written by Greg Sage)
If there is a "Seattle Sound" it came from portland Oregon in the Early 80's by A three piece band named the wipers.

Turn Around (written by Devo) this song was only available on the B-side of the whip it single

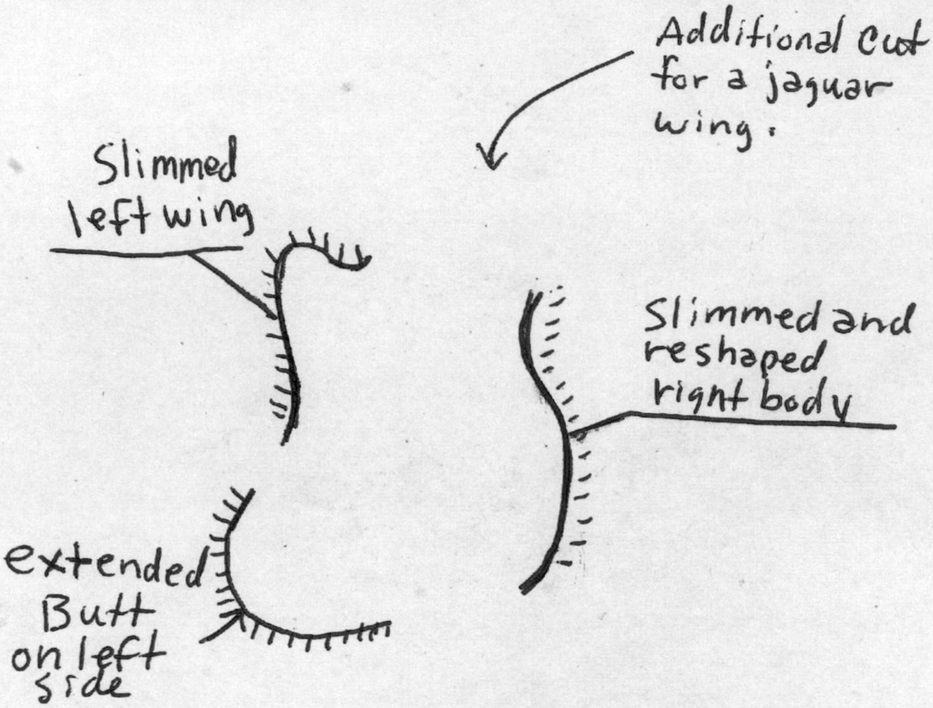

This is a mustang [redacted] cut differently with a few inches added to the wing and left side of butt and the left wing and side cut thinner

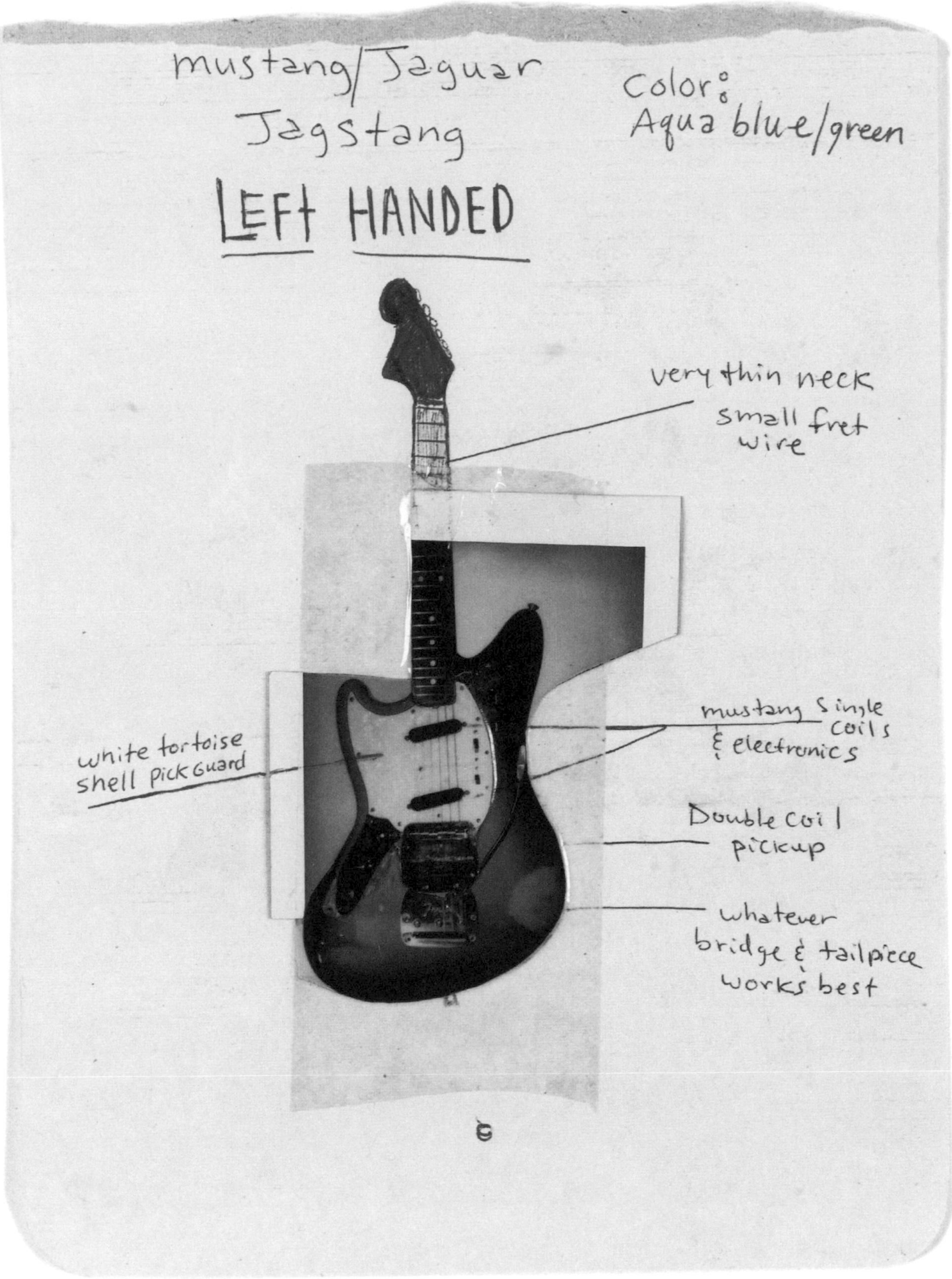
mustang/Jaguar
Jagstang
Color:
Aqua blue/green
LEFT HANDED
very thin neck
small fret wire
mustang single coils
& electronics
white tortoise shell pick guard
Double coil pickup
whatever bridge & tailpiece works best

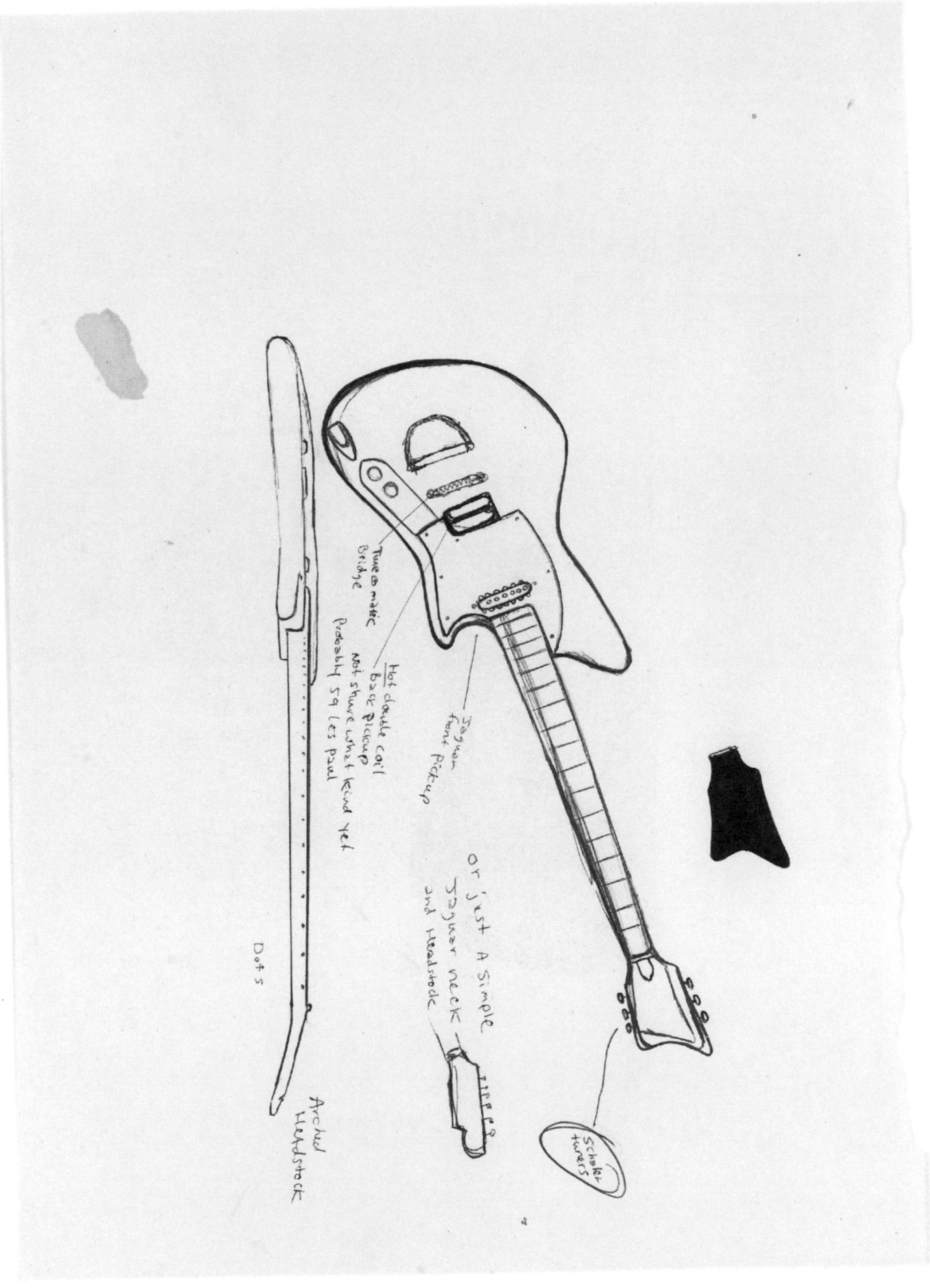
Tune-o-matic Bridge
Hot double coil back pickup
Not shure what kind yet
Probably 59 Les Paul
Jaguar front pickup
Or just A simple Jaguar neck and Headstock
Dots
Arched Headstock
Schaller tuners

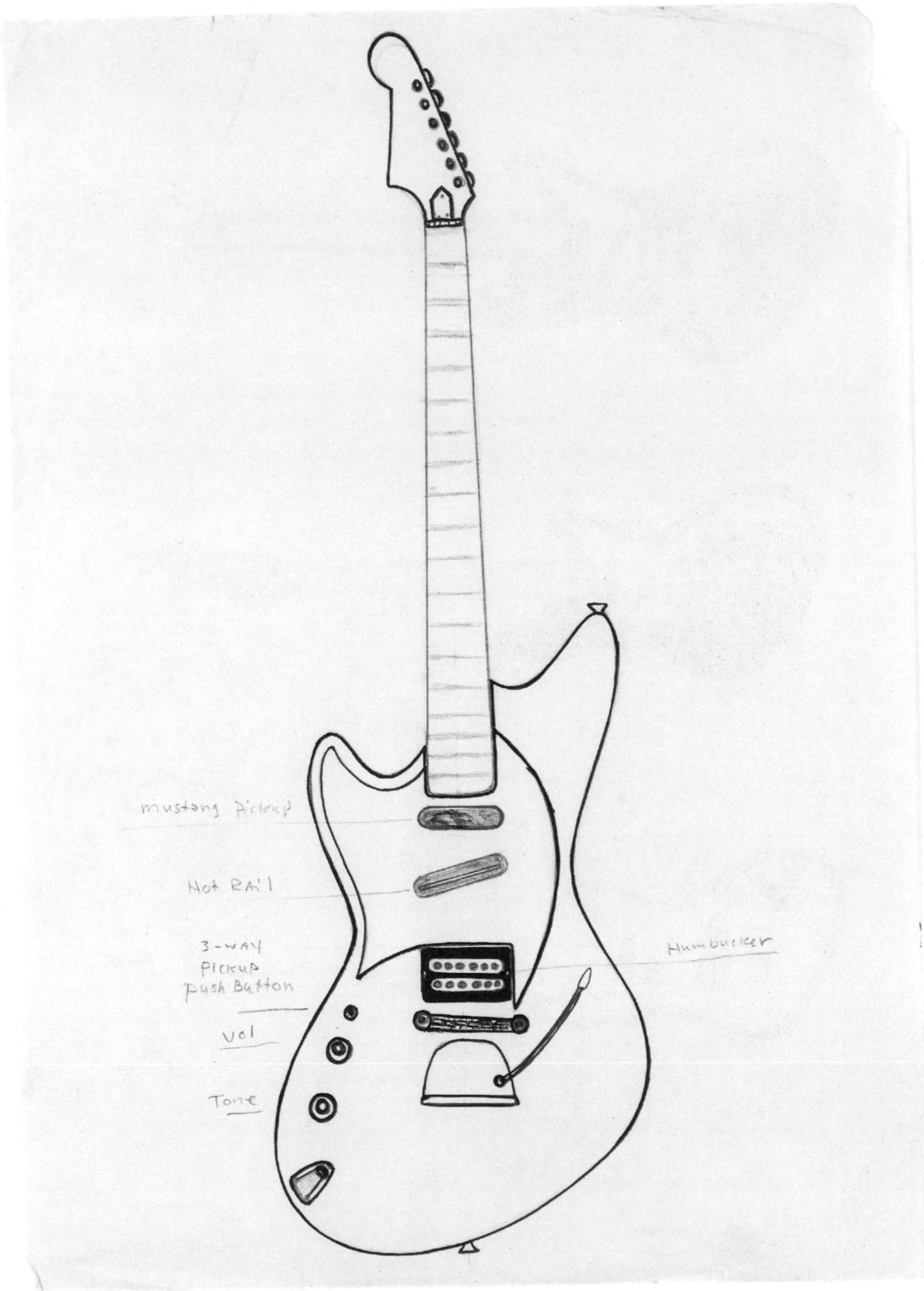
mustang Pickup
Hot RAil
3-WAY
Pickup
push Button
Vol
Tone
Humbucker

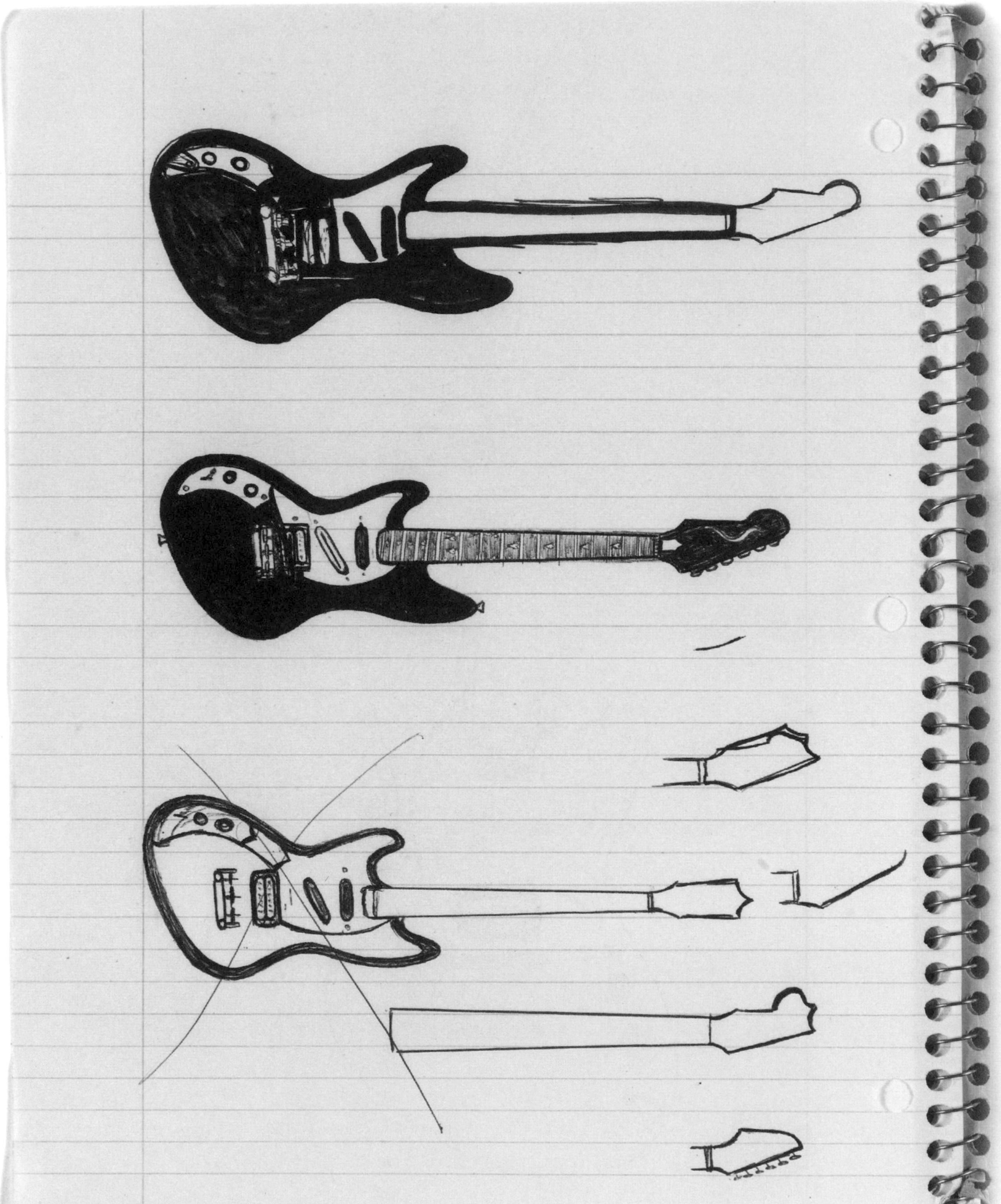

-2.

Color: Same old blue/green/aqua from the mustang

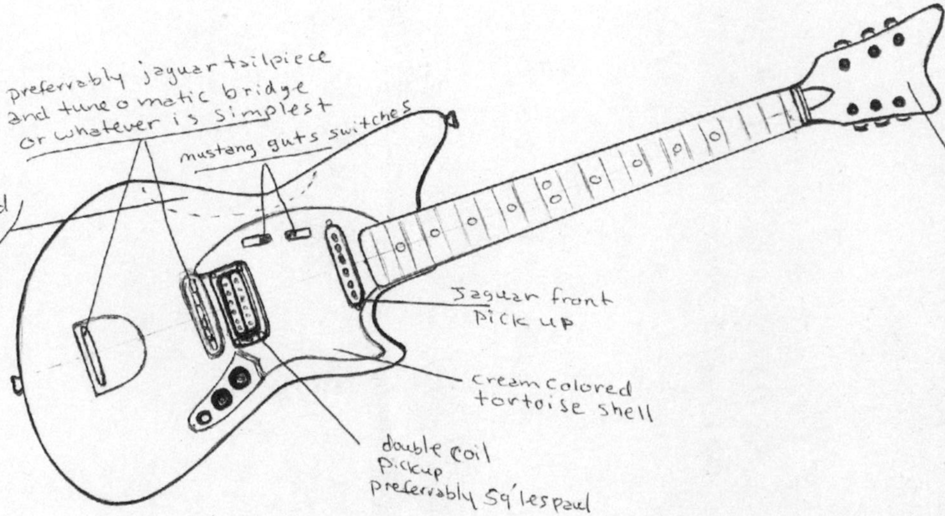

LEFT HANDED!

Kurt Kobain model
1993
c/o gold Mountain ent
Cahuenga blvd west
Suite 450 LA CA 90068

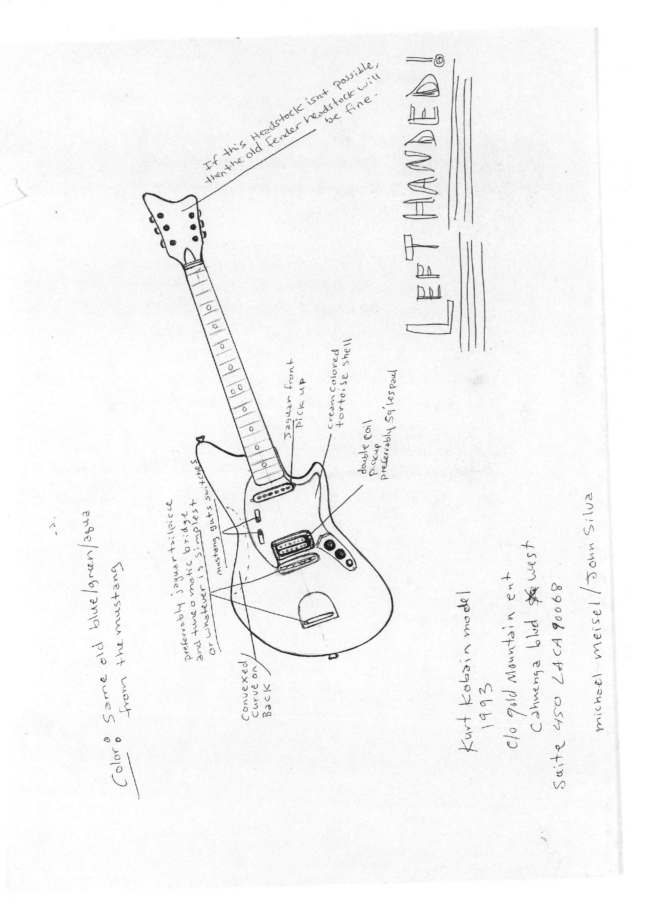

michael meisel / John Silva

with the phrasing I allow myself it isnt very easy to
be ~~[illegible]~~ lyrically prolific

~~[illegible]~~

Boys write songs for Girls - what a simple world
how the hell do I - Know whats on inside
what else should I say? - All my words are grey
what else could I write? - Im sorry I am white

Such an easy thing - such a shiny ring
let me grow some breasts - I cheated on my test
I dont have the right - to say whats on your mind
your not allowed to sing - All Apologies

In the sun in the sun I feel as one in the sun
in the sun Im married and buried

you have every right - to want to start a fight
~~treated like a dog~~
~~its gone on too long - treated like their dogs~~
such an easy thing - let my sister sing
what else can I do? - Im in love with you

Seven months ago I chose to put myself in a position which requires the highest form of responsibility a person can have. A responsibility ~~which~~ that should not be dictated ~~by thinking that I should rather want~~ to take on this responsibility. ~~when~~ Everytime I see a television show that has dying children or seeing a testimonial by a parent who recently lost their child I cant help but cry. The thought of losing my baby haunts me every day. Im even a bit unnerved to take her in the car in fear of getting into an accident. I swear that If I ever find myself in a similar situation than youre ~~had~~ been in i.e. the divorce I will fight to ~~my~~ death to keep the right to provide for my child. I'll go out of my way to remind her that I love her more than I love myself. not because it's a fathers duty but because I want to out of love. And If Courtney and I end up hating eachothers guts we both will be adult and responsible enough to be pleasant to one another when our child is around us.

I know that youve felt for years that my mother has somehow brainwashed Kim and I into hating you. ~~which~~ I cant stress enough how totally untrue this is and I think it's a very lazy and lame excuse to use for not trying harder to provide your fatherly duties, I cant recall my mother ever talking shit about you until much later in the game, right around the last two years of High school. That was a time when I came to my own realizations without the need of my mothers input. Yet she noticed my contempt for you and your family and acted upon my feelings in accordance by taking the opportunity to vent her frustrations out on you. Every time she talked shit about you Ive let her know that I don't appreciate it and how unnecessary I think it is. I've never taken sides with you or my mother because while I was growing up I had equal contempt for you both.

13th 28th

RCA Ribbon mic's

RCA
77

Guitar transducer element
Closer the bassier

AKG 414 BK-5

Beyer 160-130
4 to 6 inches close to Amp

DRUMS

Rad
Inbetween Condenser toms snare

AKG 451
small
Close to head

Sanken Pencil

Schopes

No Sanheiser

No Noiman

Post-It™ brand fax transmittal memo 7671 | # of pages ▸ 1
To Kurt | From Michael
Co. | Co. Gold MtN.
Dept. | Phone #
Fax # | Fax #

NOV 19 '92 09:34AM GM LA P.1/1

Between Sunset
Across Fountain
Fuller 6ft
tall bushes

KURT:

I AM HOME AND 1340
AVAILABLE IF YOU
NEED/WANT TO
TELL ME ANYTHING.

Nieve
80-68

Failure fun L.A.

— STEVE ALBINI

MR Producer

try to find oak or maple sheets to be nailed on rough plywood

UTENCILS: five 5ft x 5ft pieces of plywood. thickness depends on type of wood. preferrably 1/2 inch thick. Carpeted on one side each. Thick, dense carpet is preferred.

Guitar: RCA ribbon mics

looking for a transducer element

Beyer 160 – 130

BK-5?

With Beyer 4 to 6 inches close to amp. no closer or static breakage will result.

Setting: the closer to the cabinet the bassier with most other brands.

Amp settings: ① try mids on full.
② try Highs at lower than usual setting.
③ Lows full.

EFFECTS: slight compression. Roomchamber Alessis very small dimensions

carpeted plywood

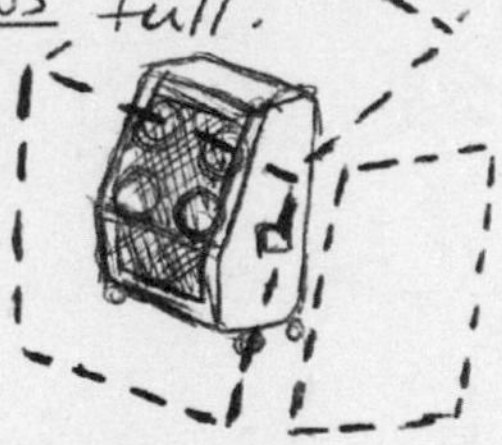

④ Use carpeted cabinet.
⑤ build or use A large cardboard box for muffle chamber, or pieces of plywood with carpet to make an enclosure around the cabinet. allowing at least 2 feet of breathing space

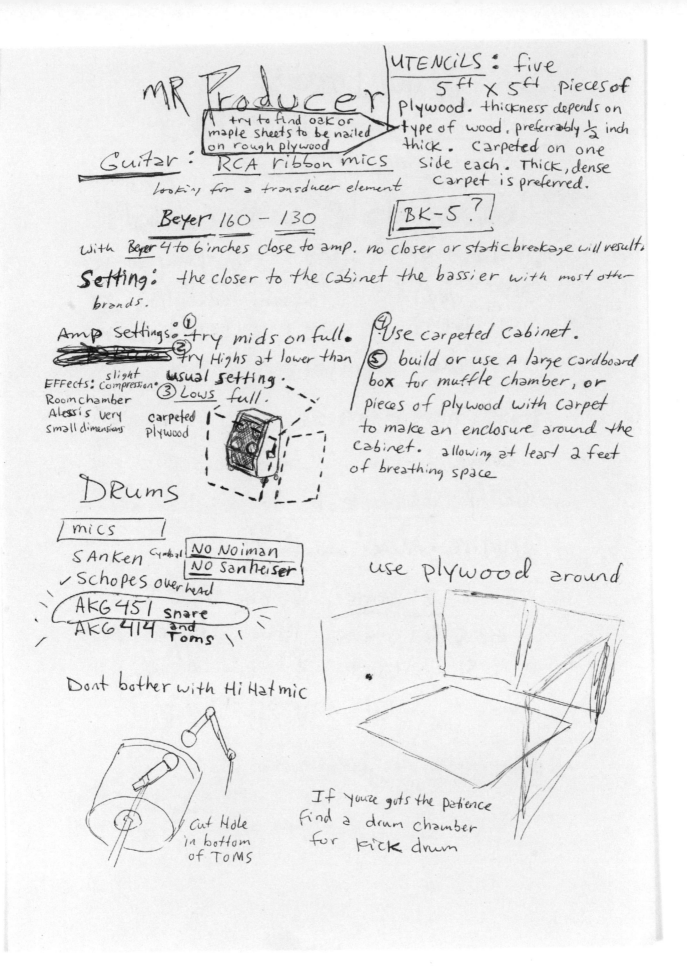

DRums

mics

SAnken cymbal

NO Noiman
NO Sanheiser

✓ Schopes overhead

AKG 451 snare
AKG 414 and Toms

Dont bother with Hi Hat mic

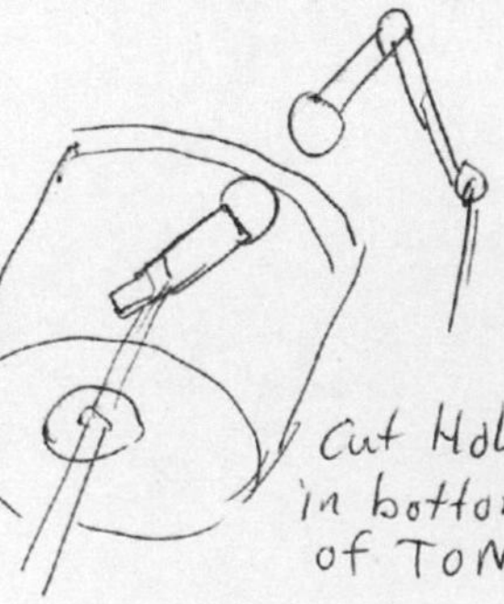

Cut Hole in bottom of TOMS

use plywood around

If youre gots the patience find a drum chamber for kick drum

New ideas for Melvins

put mics inside Toms ??

record date with cymbals Heavily taped so they make NO Noise! this will allow us to use the room mics A lot louder then dub cymbal crashes Later.

put Three mics on the snare one of them will be recorded Very Very hot to the point of distortion After about 4 dbs

And 2 more room mics besides the little schoeps room mics About 3 feet Away from kick And snare

more chorus on BAss guitar.

use very directional mics for this

APR 9th caffron
MAY 3 – Spin ads

Ian McKay

NIRVANA

I hate myself and I want to die

1. Serve the servants
2. Scentless apprentice
3. Heart shaped Box
4. Penny royal tea
5. Frances farmer will have her revenge ON Seattle
6. ~~Eustacian tube~~ Turrets
7. * Dumb
8. Rape me
9. Very ape
10. milk it
Fourmonth media blackout
11.
12. Verse chorus verse
13. * LA LA LA (alternateen anthem) ~~Dolin~~ chello on *

DGC C&P
David Geffin
Sup Pop ~~SUP POP~~

produced by
A dick in the SNOW
feb 12–26
1993
Personnel:
mr pissy: Guitar/mouth
Suavy Smooth: Bass
Jocko Accidente: Polyrythms

Hi Simon,
Thanks a load for the
drawings, pictures and music.
They're the best presents I've ~~gotten~~ recieved
in a really long time!
I looove the stinky
puffs! and would love to hear
more once you all record some
more. I was wondering if
you would be interested in drawing
some pictures for the cover of
the next NIRVANA record wich will
be ready to sell once we have the
art work done. I think you draw
really good and → (over)

It would mean a lot to me if you'd consider it. heres some ideas I had.

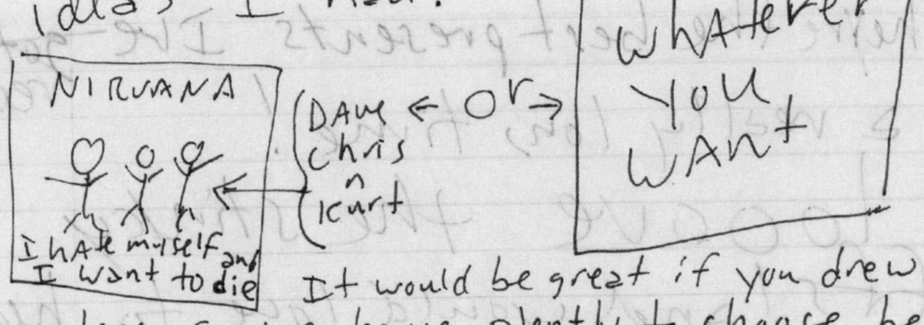

It would be great if you drew about 5 or more or less so we have plently to choose between.

the title of the album is rather negative but kind of funny. Its called:
I hate myself and I want to die.

Heres some info that needs to be written for the back of the LP
DAVE-drums. Chris-bass. Kurt Geetar-n-mouth.
D.G.C records and subpop. recorded by steve albini.
Cello on LALALA & dumb oh, and artwork by Simon Timony

well, bye
write back soon
Love Kurdt
& Hi Jad!

Since my freshly found relationships with employees of the *corporate ogre ~~Capitol~~ (*catch phrase © copyright Calvin Johnson of Beat Happening) I've ~~found~~ ~~realized~~ learned that there are a handful of very honorable and sincere music lovers who are working in the system who are posing as the enemy to infiltrate the mechanics of the Empire. to help destroy what we all have known for too long as shit, Rock, prefabricated, incestually & politically oriented garbage business, a smoke screen to clog the Arteries of Honesty and true talent and to keep those willing to kiss ass the no risk, using A & R ~~only those~~ unchallenging, and most importantly undeserving at the top of the Heap. the Heap of Dung.

1 ~~Sonic Youth – Goo~~
2 ~~Every good boy deserves fudge – mudhoney~~
3 ~~Bandwagonesque – Teenage fanclub~~
4 ~~Trompe Le Monde – Pixies~~
5 ~~Beat Happening – dreamy~~
x 6 ~~Violent femmes – why do birds sing?~~
x 7 ~~Bull Head – melvins~~
8 ~~Strangely Beautiful EP Television personalities~~
9 ~~Army of Lovers – Pretty little BAKA Guy reissue – Shonen knife~~
10 ~~Pere – out of time Hole – pretty on inside~~
~~No1 Single – Crucified – Army of Lovers~~

1 Sonic youth – Goo – DGC
2 Mudhoney – Every good boy deserves fudge – Sub Pop
3 Pixies – Trompe le Monde – Elektra
4 Teenage fanclub – Bandwagonesque – DGC
5 Hole – pretty on the inside – Caroline
6 Beat Happening – dreamy – Sub Pop
7 Television personalities – strangely beautiful EP – Fire records
8 Shonen knife – Pretty little BAKA Guy (reissue) Zero (Japanese import)
9 Melvins – Bullhead – Boner
10 Violent femmes – why do birds sing?

P.S. Urge Overkill – Supersonic storybook – Touch-n-Go
NO 1 Single: Army of Lovers – Crucified

The Heap starts with the Ass kissers all the way up to the top where the cherry or old school music publication sits looking down on the Baby Birds with eyes still shut, and feeding them dehydrated worms. But as I said before the small percent of deserving bands and music loving employees will keep sawing away at the Heap and if we fail we will just simply wait until the cherry rots of old Age and we will use your Historical decomposition as a reference or a sweaty bed time story as remembrance of a warning to next time, plant our seeds closer to a cleaner Asshole.

You have failed at conditioning the young ones of the underworld whom you have spawned, and you yourselves ~~are~~ should have been Kleenex or poached fried or scrambled sperm, neutered-eggs.

Serve the Servants

Initially this song was about coming of age during a time where your old enough to support yourself without the aid of your parents. A theme for the twenty somethings; if you will not. I've always felt that a person doesn't necessarily have to force themselves to love their parents simply because of blood. If you don't like your parents or relatives, don't fake it tell them how you feel and in my own way I decided to let my father know that I don't hate him. I simply don't have anything to say and I don't need a father son relationship with a person whom I don't want to spend a Boring Christmas with. In other words; I love you. I don't hate you. I don't want to talk to you.

Scentless apprentice

~~just a book report?~~ [illegible] "perfume" by Patrick Susskind

Heart shaped box

Camille's ~~flower/vagina theory~~ vaginal/flower theory bleeding and spreading into ~~fabric~~ the fabric that leonardo would have used to ~~[illegible]~~ improve ~~the~~ his ~~hangglider~~ hang glider but he died before he could change the course of history. shit. I Claudius I play dumb for thee! and dorothy and toto (the dog) not the band. and rusty pyles. ~~The fem~~ The male seahorse empregnates the female seahorse, she ~~[illegible]~~ holds them through most of the developmental stages then transferes the babies to the father who carries them through the last stages ~~then~~ and finally gives them birth. ~~They share [illegible] transformation~~

The majority of our so called Outlaw heroes of the old west were nothing but fucked up psychopath ~~Sympathisers ex~~ Confederate soldiers. Sympathisers of the way it used to be with alcohol fuled ~~[illegible]~~ Bi polar rage during the transformation years. killing every darkie they could find. Heroes my ass! ~~[illegible]~~ If I only had a heart. ~~I don't~~ listen you snivelling little, opinionated, spoiled punts, HI dost hate you. I love you. Ah god it feels so good to be clean DR Bronner!

Kinda like when Axl ~~[illegible]~~ was butt neked in that epic video of his.

RApe me

How Bold ~~should the print be~~ shall ~~I make the print~~ the print be made?
~~in order to help you in the simple pleasure of Reading?~~
~~Ask lots of questions~~

OBvious. oblivious. settle down. calm. calm. its ok sshh.
Hold still. sshh. Hold still.

Frances farmer will have her revenge on seattle.

The conspirators are still alive and well in their comfortable, warm, safe home's.
gag on her ashes. jag on her gash. uh, god is A woman and shes
~~Black~~. BAck in Black

Dumb

All that pot. all that supposedly unaddictive, harmless, safe
reefer that damaged my nerves and ruined my memory and made
me feel like wanting to blow up the prom. and the patience
to play guitar for 5 hours every day after school. and to sleep
during the day when I should have paid a bit more attention
to my studies. especially in English sometimes an A+ sometimes
an X on my hand or forehead and the feeling that it just
wasnt ever strong enough so I climbed the ladder to the
poppie. Not everyone does the latter so Ive learned one lesson.
I have absolutely no right to express my opinions until I
know all the answers. far out.

Veryape

I forget

penny royal tea

An ~~abortive~~ herbal abortive.
it doesnt work you hippie.

Radio friendly unit shifter

Boy this will really get the A&R mans Bloodboiling.
Hell be so Pissed. heh heh. Clever.
getting into the inner me. self indulgent.
way out there ~~dude~~.
~~fun to play live~~ [illegible]

Ask about Dantes Inferno movie from the 30's
to use instead of ~~m~~aking our own props
we will use the scenes of people intwined old withering oak trees

Sebadoh

Alex wages

tourrets

me. old man. ~~has made~~
have made my conclusion. but nobody will listen any more.

Birds. Birds are and always have been reincarnated old men
with tourrets syndrome ~~and every morning~~ having somehow managed
to ~~com~~ dupe the reproductive saga ~~and~~ they fuck eachother and
tend to their home repairs and children while never missing
their true mission. to scream at the top of their lungs
in horrified hellish rage every morning at day break
to warn us all of the truth they know the truth.
Screaming bloody murder all over the world in our ears
but sadly we dont speak bird.
the whales respond i~~n a similar way~~ with their message for
us in similar ways. by beaching themselves

this album is dedicated to dead relatives.
they are warm and full of happy smiles.
SAfe

All apologies

Nothing has or will
Nothing Could or should
Alternateens ignoring the Budweiser sponsor banner behind the 10 yrs + Acts.
An excuse to get laid
~~Kurt Loder and Tabitha Soren are completely~~
Jimmy Carter was ~~[scribbled out]~~ and still is an extremely loving and sensible man. but when I was a kid I only remember that he liked peanuts and had big lips.

milk it

If you really love me you will send medical supplies.
oh god, he's awake again.. don't look, just ignore it, before he starts to, oh shh he fell asleep again thank God.
How do you feel? shhh be quiet.

A multitude

serve the servants

Oh lord the guilt of sucksess. ~~[scribbled out]~~ during the past two years I have slowly come to the conclusion that I do not want to die. ~~[scribbled out]~~ I am now no more of a recluse than I used to be. I lived in the (K) Kingdom for a few years hiding in a little apartment. ~~[scribbled out]~~ And now I stand in my room without a sandbox ~~[scribbled out]~~ on punk Rock show attendant ratio I would say it's about the same. I am still equally annoyed and equally impressed with the same old familiar ritual of standing in a room full of people hoping to feel a vibration that runs through my back when I hear a familiar song or see an enigmatic performance from ~~[scribbled out]~~ A collection of people who choose to strap on pieces of wood which are electrically activated and manipulated
Ive never claimed to be a punk rocker.
I was inspired by it, as much as led zeppelin or Aerosmith

& the beatles ~~etc~~. but oh lord never paul pleeease!
Is it egotistical to talk about myself like this?
I guess this song is for my father who is incapable of communicating at a level of affection in which I have always expected

Nordic trAC

1-800-382 9177

Augment ensamble

verile

Kevlar

Kevin & CO
for the Long form

~~On Anurysm: keep the Audio from the Amsterdam show but keep the edits the same.~~

1 ON Anurysm: Keep Amsterdam audio when first change happens ie. kurdt in over coat

2 TAKe out Dave & Chris playin Aerosmith song

3 Put Subtitle in "Bronchitis" flashing throughout Dive

4 Video footage of us with Jason "the early years" put in sub title = Jason everman guitar Chad channing drums Rhino Records LA 88. Song. Sifting

5 Cut out the last half of dave talking about new bands

6 Start my rant just as I say Black flag flipper leave the rest.

subtitle 7 = Rock star lesson: for Come As U are — when your guitar is out of tune, sing out of tune along with it

8 Englands prestigious Top of the pops equivalent of US's American Bandstand.

Cut to 1st IN Bloom video we did with one camera in dresses destroying the set.

9 Replace mollys lips with Reading version with Eugene singing

Add the scene where I hand the guitar to the audience. I think its from Reading

And the penis and flower petal face in camera performance piece kurdt does in Rio.

the first Vinyl Rele

but the video's recorded Audio version will be the re-mixed one.

---

(1) release Albini version: <u>mastered</u> – different sequence under <u>title</u>: <u>I Hate myself and want to die</u>: on vinyL LP, Cassette and <u>8-track</u> ← Yes! Yes! Yes!
Albini producer, mixologist credits. with sticker that says: NIRVANAS Latest studio release for 93' contains Heart shaped box, Rape me & 12 others.
<u>Retail</u>: Sold to small mom and pop stores or anywhere vinyl can be found.
NO-PROMOS sent out!!!

(2) one month later: after many lame reviews and reports on the curmudgeonly, uncompromising Vinyl, cass, 8-track only release. we Release the Re-mixed ~~version~~ & re-recorded ~~of~~ bass and Acoustic guitar Version under the title: "<u>Verse Chorus Verse</u>". on vinyL LP, cassette, and God forbid, Cd. with <u>sticker</u> that says: This Album is the radio-friendly, unit shifting, compromise version which, by the way, NIRVANA is extremely proud of, contains Heart shaped box, Rape me & 10 more.

(3) Release Video of Heart shaped box at the same time of the 1st vinyL, cass, 8-track only release. but the re-mix audio version will accompany it.

Hi, im the moody, bohemian member of the group. blonde frontman. thesensetive artist type.

I like: pasta, turtles, girls with weird eyes, writing, reading, keeping my mouth shut, cake decorating, horseback riding, gun cleaning, Sally Struthers impersonations, pina coladas and getting caught in the rain, buttfucking, accupuncture, painting, friends, cats, goats, mo-hair sweaters, cultivating a fine army of facial blemishes, scarification, playing music with my band, my ~~[illegible]~~ wife, ~~and~~ my family and all of the people with whom our band works with.

I would only wear a tie died T shirt if it were made from the Blood of Gerry Garcia and the urine of Phil Collins.

Here Are Some of the BAnds I like.

the vaselines, the breeders, the Stooges, the pixies, Sexpistols, raincoats, melvins, tales of terror, scratch acid, butthole surfers, young marble giants, urge overkill, marine girls, Jesus lizard, Teenage fanclub, slits, mudhoney, Beat happening, cramps, Shonen knife, Delta 5, sonic youth, Black flag, R.e.m, meat puppets II, witchy poo, Hole, TV personalities, Daniel Johnston, the Sonics, lead belly, the wipers, Half Japanese, Dead moon, public enemy, Big Black, the ~~[illegible]~~, Germs, Husker Du, Dinosaur Jr, Captain America, saints, velvet underground, Lee Hazlewood, Hank williams, flipper, feederz, Lewd, Bad Brains, Patsy Cline, Devo, Clash, ~~[illegible]~~ Fear, Army of Lovers, fugazi, ~~[illegible]~~, Bikini Kill, ~~[illegible]~~, Beatnik Termites, the staple Singers, Discharge, Cannanes, Bratmobile, Saccharine trust, Dirt, pavement, love Child, Superchunk, Boredoms, Sebadoh, Axemen, Cows →

Shocking Blue, wire, Leonard Cohen, PYLon B-52's, Duh, Didjits, Mazzy star, TK records, Sun City Girls, Sprinkler, Calamity Jane, Finklers, some velvet sidewalk, Smegma, Go Team, Rites of spring, VOID, shop Assistants, NIP Drivers,

Fire records
339 sevensisters RD
London N15 6rd England

Suckdog
PO Bx 1491 Dover NH, 03820

Simple machines
PO Box 10290 Arlington VA
22210-1290

independent labels ~~address~~ 90260

SST: po box 1 Lawndale CA ↙ Seminal twang

25520 Chicago IL 60625 | Box 7154 | Olympia WA 98507

Touch and Go [K] Sympathy for the record industry

Boner, matador, **Sub pop**, ecstatic peace GASATANKA Rockville

Kill rock stars, feel good all over, Homestead 4-AD

Rough Trade Caroline C/Dpresents ~~BS~~ T/K records Alternative Tentacles

out of Business | 114 West 26th st N.Y., NY 10001 | 42423 Portland Oregon 97242

music publications: fACT sheet five: Twin Tone

CALL Thurston FANZINES: Bikini kill Alternative press Jigsaw INK Disease Your flesh

Girl germs, flipside, maximum Rocknroll

murder can be fun, Spin, forced exposure,

Amok Research, option, Kitten Kore, and shes not even pretty.

Technicolor effect for film:

Old weathered man in hospital bed with a rubber foetus in his IV Bottle chris dave and I sitting at the foot of the bed, impatiently waiting for him to pass away. In the hospital room the curtains are drawn 90% of the way with a blinding white light shooting through the curtains. Lots of flowers in the room and kurdt hold an old pocket watch dangling back and forth – indicating that time is running out.

4 year old aryan girl with bright blonde hair with vivid blue eyes. in a klu klux klan robe on sitting in a small shack. The walls of the shack is covered with stargazer lillies with stems cut off and the butt end of the flowers ~~and~~ glued ~~on the~~ every where on the walls. Each flower has a bright light alluminating ~~each of them~~. from behind them. another shot of the little girl holding hands with an elder. he squeezes her hand as if she could never escape. bright red blood soaks ~~into~~ from inside of the girls robe. Close up of red ink or blood soaking in to white fabric then a gust of wind blows her KKK hat off, the camera follows it ~~through~~ blowing above a field of poppies, eventually the hat turns into a butterfly net and chases butterflies through out the field. then it falls into a small pool of black tar (india ink. another close up of black ink-goo soaks into the white fabric. ~~then we see~~ after the hat is completely black it appears to be a black witches hat and blows away ~~but~~ with a gust of wind.

~~old man on a cross~~

old weathered interesting looking man on a cross with black crows on his arms, pecking at his face — Scarecrow/Jesus.

Animation, forest Dantes inferno from the thirties
Bodies entwined in old oak trees
maybe we can use the original footage from that movie

optical illusion

Your All absolutely one hundred percent correct.
I was severely wrong when I wrote "For me
Punk Rock is dead. although it is dead
for me which were the key words I wrote
in those oh so negative and retarded linear
notes. The ~~two~~ words ~~s~~ for was miss printed
at the ~~Doc~~ printing offices when they translated
my handwriting. ~~Instead~~ The word to was
used instead of for which is a very common
occurance when deadlines are due and
people are scratching like mexican fighting cocks
to get an approval for something as non important
as ~~a~~ liner notes to a B-side cash cow.
Yes friends. punk rock is dead for me.

Letter to the Editor.
I thought I would let the world know how much I Love ~~them~~ People. I thought I would ~~make art~~ try to create something that I would personally like to listen to. because a very large portion of this worlds art sucks beyond description. ~~But~~ yet I ~~Besides~~ feel that, its a waste of time to pass judgement. and who the fuck am I to declare myself an authority whos certified, one who has the right to bother someone critique. I guess in a way anyone with enough ambition to create and not take away is someone who

deserves respect. There are ~~some~~ those who are better at it than others. there are some who have severely large amounts of enthusiasm who are prolific as Hell, spewing out a million products a year. Yeah products. they are ones who usually give 10% good and 90% crap. Then there are those who spend years studying other peoples works because they dont have a chance in Hell to produce anything with a hint of talent. Yeah talent. But like I said no one should be denied the priviledse to create and some people most

certainly do not need the
~~fear of~~ whether their goods
are better or worse
than the Best or worse.
They can find that out for
themselves. maybe I
On second thought ~~I thought~~
~~I would~~ just tried to let the world
know how much I love
myself. like a hypocrite
in a hippie crypt.
I hate myself and I
want to die
Leave me alone.
Love Kurdt

Love Child – He's So sensitive
Love Child – Diane
Calamity Jane – Car
Beatnik Termites – when she's nearby
Sun City Girls – Voice of America #1
Discharge – The more I see
Jadfair – the Crow
Jadfair – take a chance
Jadfair – I like Candy
Mazzy Star – Halah
Didjits – under the Christmas fish
Bags – Babylonian Gorgon
Bags – Survive
Bags – We will bury You
Sebadoh – Loser Core
Duh – spaghetti and red wine
TV personalities – I know where Sud Barret lives
Axemen – mourning of Youth
side 2
Daniel Johnston
Continues stories
Stinky Puffs – stinky Puffs theme
How ~~You~~ HAmburger make A car
Baby A monster

Courtney, when I
Say I love you I am not
ashamed, nor will anyone
ever ever come close to intimidating
persuading, etc me into thinking
otherwise. I wear you on
my sleeve. I spread you
out wide open with the wing
span of a peacock, yet
all too often with the attention
span of a bullet to the head.
I think its pathetic that the
entire world looks upon a
person with patience and a
calm demeanor as the desired
model citizen. yet theres
something to be said about
the ability to explain

ones self with a toned down,
tune deaf tone. And I will say it: I am what
they call the boy who is
slow. how I metamorphosised
from hyperactive to cement
is for lack of a better knife
to the throat uh, annoying,
aggrevating, confusing
as dense as cement.
cement holds no other
minerals. you can't even find
fools gold in it. its strictly
man made and youve taught
me it's ok to be a man
and in the classic mans world
I parade you around proudly
like the ring on my finger
which holds no mineral.

Also Love Kurt

THE New improved revised

NIRVANA list of Albums

in which the pson writing this has been emotionally affected by. • inspired to encapsulate what his thoughts of a lifestyle in which he MAY be [redacted] immersed in for reasons of looking cool and hip. OH and by the way maybe to introduce these elititist obscure, treasures to the unabashed

---

Elo: Electric light orchestra . The KNACK Get the KNACK

(Gold. John?) 10CC the things we do for love.

HALL and oats. Rich Girl (wild cherry) play that funky music

Leo SAyer?

Supertramp Breakfast in America

EAgles: long Run

PAt Benatar?

Journey escape.

Reo speedwagen Hi infidelity

Fleetwood mack Rumours

BAY City Rollers?

Seasons in the sun Terry Jacks

Bugles: video Killed the radio stare

Beatles meet the Beatles

I Have been forced to become a reclusive RockSTAR
IE: No interviews, No radio appearances, etc.
due to the legions of self appointed authorities on music
who are not musicians, who have not contributed anything
artistic to Rock and Roll besides maybe a few second rate
long winded, books on Rock and Roll and most importantly
who are the highest group of mysogynists of all
forms of expression.

I have since the beginning of my first revelation in alternative thought
through the introduction of New WAVE - then, Punk rock, then alternative,
Soundtracks of Contemporary Classic Rock. Never in years of my awareness
of sexism have I seen a more radically venemous display of
Sexism in my life than in the past two
years. for years Ive observed and waited like a vulture
for any hint of sexism and Ive found it in relatively small
doses compared to the present state of Rock and Roll,

from critics darlings to Samantha fox. simply because one of
the members of what used to be thought of as a band with members
Has married an established, musical, success determined by
the establishment of non musical music writers. Something smells fishy!

by this time. All conspiracy theories are very very real with more proof than needed to be bothered with describing.
Beaurocracy exists as cancer in the simplest, most naive, grass roots business of pencil vendors, panhandling, fanzine distribution, home baked, hippie cookie sales agents up through the yawn; medical profession, Government related protection agencies, Janitorial positions, and erm, entertainment industries. Journalists will now break their own fingers after engaging in each individuals fingerprint of display on their left breast in the form of a button and they will bow down to let the artists critique themselves and other artists. This is a fanzine written by music fans. We know this to be true because they are musicians. Can they write as well as they play? better.
What about Genres. A Heavymetal musician cannot reach A dance RnB Soul group. Its that easy.

Elitism = Punk Rock
Capitalism =

If you were a music fan than you would contribute to A fanzine.

You have no right to ask the question: do you have artistic control now that youve signed to a major - for all Journalists are at the mercy of their editors.

second rate 3rd degree burns.

If we ever win any more awards we will have
3 impersonators come up and accept the awards
3 people who look fairly familiar to us.

VIDEO concept. milk it or scentless apprentice
drunken fucked up me, man in a room full of
people at a party man has gun and is stumbling
around falling down threatening to shoot.
man has wild glossy stare.

Play unplugged soon.

release a compilation tape of favorite punk
songs with vinyl version of album

♡ Shaped box video

William and I sitting across from one another at a table (Black and white) lots of Blinding Sun from the windows behind us holding hands staring into eachothers eyes. He gropes me from behind and fell's dead on top of me. medical footage of sperm flowing through penis. A ghost vApor comes out of his chest and groin area and enters me Body.

during solo. violin shots. Chris as New wAve keyboardist. and very quick edits of strobe light.

image of little 3 year old white arian, blonde girl in KKK outfit being led by the hand of a KKK parent

Same violet colors as in the New order video

Animation Doll footage. Close up of lillies lying on lighted draft Board. footage of Anatomy models from Kurts collection

FIGURE 10. Examples of herpes gestationis.
ject
book
150 SHEETS
9½ IN. x 6-IN.
(24.1 cm. x 15.2 cm.)
College Ruled
PROGRESS
20305
DataCom
Horsham, Pa. 19044 • Made in USA

TRAVelin white trASh couple #1

He BAthes in GAllons of mens Cologne
Hes filldup full of testosterone
She Kisses sensuAlly into the lense
They spit their lingo to Keep their egos cleansed.

They Keep A lifestyle that is comfortable
they travel far to Keep their stomaches full
They have A HAir style that is out of ~~style~~ date
They seem to clAim that their from out of state

He keeps his cigarettes close to his heart
she keeps her photographs close to her heart
they keep their bitterness close to their hearts

She wants to build herself A windchime house
she does her arts And crafts while stAying soused
they probably own About A million CATs
they dont care where their from or where their At

They Rip you off And then they leave your town
The local swap meet is their battle ground
She loves him more than he will ever know
He loves her more than he will ever show

NIRVANA TOP 50

RAW POWER
Stooges

SURFER ROSA
Pixies

POD
BREEDERS

PINK EP
VASELINES

PHILOSOPHY OF THE WORLD
SHAGGS

LANDSHARK
Fang

MILLIONS OF DEAD COPS
M.D.C.

1st ep
SCRATCH ACID

1st ep
SACCHARIN TRUST

peepee the Sailor
Butthole Surfers

MY WAR
BLACK FLAG

ROCK FOR LIGHT
BAD BRAINS

ENTERTAINMENT
GANG OF FOUR

NEVER MIND BOLLOCKS
SEX PISTOLS

ITS ONLY RIGHT & NATURAL
FROGS

DRY
PJ HARVEY

DAYDREAM NATION
SONIC YOUTH

GET THE KNACK
THE KNACK

KNOW YOUR PRODUCT
THE SAINTS

ANYTHING BY:
KLEENEX

RAINCOATS LP
RAINCOATS

COLOSSAL YOUTH
YOUNG MARBLE GIANTS

ROCKS
AEROSMITH

WHAT IS THIS?
EARLY SO. CALIF PUNK COMP.

GREEN
R.E.M

BURNING FARM cassete
SHONEN KNIFE

TYPICAL GIRLS
SLITS

~~COMBAT ROCK~~
~~CLASH~~

VOID / FAITH SPLIT EP
VOID / FAITH

RITES OF SPRING
RITES OF SPRING

JAMBOREE
BEAT HAPPENING

TALES OF TERROR
TALES OF TERROR

LAST SESSIONS VOL. 1
LEAD BELLY

SUPERFUZZ BIGMUFF
MUDHONEY

YIP JUMP MUSIC
DANIEL JOHNSTON

GENERIC FLIPPER
FLIPPER

MEET THE BEATLES
BEATLES

WE ARE THOSE WHO ACHE WITH AMOROUS LOVE
HALF JAPANESE

LOCUST ABORTION TECHNITION
BUTTHOLE SURFERS

for many months I decided to take a break from reading rock magazines mainly to rest and clear my head from all the folk lore and Current affair journalism that had been piling up since weve become a lot of peoples (dare I say) breakfast lunch and dinner gossip.

~~Φ~~ Last month I thought Id take a peek at a few ~~ma~~ Rock mags to see whats going on and if things have cooled down.

well, to my estimation many trees have been wasted on account of ~~peopl~~e bored and boring people who still like to waste space with NIRVANA DRECK. Years ago I knew better than to believe that every article in a news paper reported everything we need to Know. as in all the facts man. I knew that newspapers, magazines and history books left out things or embelished based on the special interests of the political and moral beliefs of the share holders or owners of all printed matter. Do you think a History book from the South has basically the same information on the civil war as a History book printed for the northern School districts? Do you think A right wing, Christian owned news paper reports the same as mother Jones magazine? well the rock literary world is a bit more confusing. It's not as cut and dry as the above refferences. People who write for music mags are a collective bunch who are at conflict every day.

As youve heard this cliché many times before music journalists are people who are paid to find as many interesting anectdotes of a musicians personality, and if there isnt enough they must spice it up and if it isnt still spicy enough which is almost always the case then, In steps the editor. an editors job is not to correct grammatical errors. his or her job is to sell magazines and to sell magazines you need to have a cupboard full of spices. So once again a journalist is almost always at the mercy of the editor. ironically journalists are the ones who obsessively try to prove that the musician has no control over their own creativity and ~~the record company~~ is dictated by their record company ~~companies~~. and the biggest ~~cliche of~~ and most overly used cliche of the journalist although is too true to ignore is the fact that most ~~a~~ journalists have no idea of what its like to write a song, play an instrument or know what it's like to perform on stage in front of people.

The choice to become a music journalist is usually after ones realization that they are musically retarded. but theyve worked at tower Records and own a lot of Cd's and rock biographies.

I found at an early age that the same people who share the same truth-witheld due to special interests conspiracy theory are usually the same people who are fans of politically motivated or music that leans towards elements of outspoken truths. PUNK ROCK. for the most part falls under this category. Quite a few years ago I felt that most of these people who listened to punk rock were aware of Commercial Rock mag Sensationalism and knew better than to believe what was written in these magazines which have always ignored underground or punk Rock bands because Punk Rock doesnt sell magazines, until now. just like new wave. punk rock has been cristened a new name by commercial magazines "Alternative music" And just like NEW WAVE only the most commercial bands are featured in these magazines.

The easiest way to advert from the chance of misrepresentation is to use the Queston Answer format. it has been proven for years that this is a safe and effective way to report the truth as long as all of the answers are printed in their entirety. when chris said "most Heavy metal kids are dumb" that was printed. what wasn't printed was the rest of it which was," and I was one of those dumb Heavy metal kids. Its not their fault because there are Stupid Heavy metal bands carrying on the legacy of sexism and homophobia in white boy rock and roll." The most interesting thing about our supposed contradictory attitudes and statements made almost 2 years ago is that all of those interviews were conducted within a span of 2 to 3 months and anyone given the surprise of becoming instant rock stars against their will have the same thoughts running through their heads. Basically what we felt was a danger. the threat of losing contact with the very people whom we felt shared the same commercial/corporate magazine conspiracy theory as we did. But as it turns out pages and pages of letters bitching about our negative reactions (which were nothing more than precautionary) littered every fanzine this side of the world. In conclusion those same people who we felt an honest love and mutual bond with bought the current affair hype hook line and sinker. which has left us feeling betrayed. we simply wanted to give those dumb heavy metal kids (the kids who we used to be) an introduction to A different way of thinking and some 15 years worth of emotionally and socially important music and all we got was flack, backstabbing and pearl Jam.

S

an's "When
Dubious Super
e January issue
rmative. How-
o add my two
rong, but when
d Donna Sum-
eponymous
'0, didn't the
he $25 million
a mistaken
um $15 mil-
ports? Also,
our albums

n implies
e label's
ig stars
t big
n.
ter
D

Scamming isn't new. I know some evangelists that make Mötley Crüe look like pikers. The *real* problem is having to look at Vince Neil's mug for a whole month.

Joseph Fossett
Chicago, IL

TEEN SPIRIT

Nirvana's music (Jan. '92) is an explosion of excitement! Unfortunately, for me, you would never catch me at a Nirvana show standing side by side with sweaty juvenile headbangers—I would rather stand in an area infested with alligators.

I think I'll wait for MTV to swallow them up and turn them into snotty, ungrateful, monstrous assholes; then I can watch their overly exposed videos and watch their music career and personal lives become a circus for the media.

Trisha Val
Rosemont, IL

The moſt ſtrange and admirable diſcouerie of the three Witches of *Warboys*, *arraigned*, *conuicted*, and executed at the laſt Aſsiſes at Huntington, for the bewitching of the fiue daughters of Robert Throckmorton Eſquire, and diuers other perſons, with ſundrie Diuelliſh and grieuous torments:

And alſo for the bewitching to death of the Lady Crumwell, the like hath not been heard of in this age.

LONDON
Printed by the Widdowe Orwin, for Thomas Man, and John Winnington, and are to be ſolde in Pater noſter Rowe, at the ſigne of the Talbot. 1593.

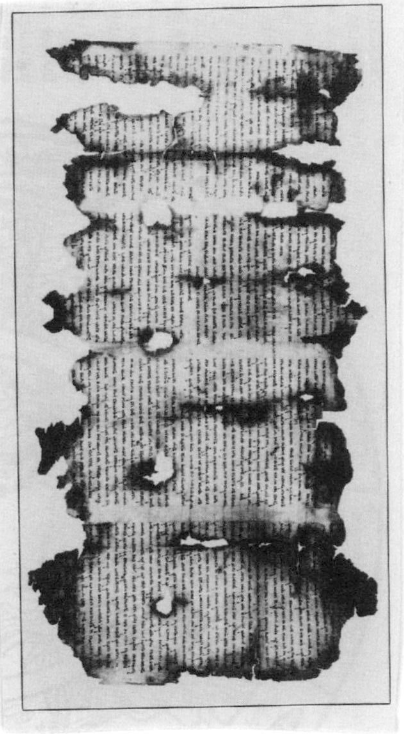

whithin the months between October 1991 thru december 92 I have had 4 four Notebooks filled with two years worth of Poetry and personal writings and ~~thoughts~~ lyrics stolen from me at seperate times. two 90 minute cassettes filled with new guitar and singing parts for new songs damaged from a plumbing accident, as well as two of my most expensive, favorite guitars. I've never been A very prolific person so when creativity flows, it flows. I find myself scribbling on little note pads and pieces of loose paper which results in A very small portion of my writings to ever show up in true form. Its my fault but the most violating thing ive felt this year is not the media exxagerations or the catty gossip, but the rape of my personal thoughts. ripped out of pages from my stay in hospitals and aeroplane rides hotel stays etc. I feel compelled to say fuck you Fuck you to those of you who have absolutely no regard for me as a person. You have raped me harder than you'll ever know. So again I say fuck you although this phrase has totally lost its meaning

FUCK YOU!

FUCK YOU.

opec Anwar Sadat Golda Meir salt talks, Camp David

Sore ba hrre astray the Gouna hs been found dead in a
He Shouldnt A been bed!

Dead and bloated fed and bearded poet.

90% of the adult American population were not
Concerned with nor had any desire to see or heard
about woodstock. 90% of the woodstock Generation are
not old Hippies now with children and the priveledge of
infusing their once young liberal ideals into the new society
in which they now are responsible for

Y..., Every one of our parents likes to hear the same old
NO 1 Hits of the 60's & 70 and lead us to believe that
they were active in the revolutionary methods of thinking
and Idealic ubrance of naivety they just couldnt wait
to open up and use once they got into power
the majority were then a product of fetal inflation
produced by the fear and shock of the world war.
They took the bait, stayed in their classes, remembered
the scriptures of Donna Reid, graduated from High School and
had children. The Hippies are the baby boomers younger
Brothers and sisters and the Hippies were a very small breed
of veal who never managed to teach the basics to theirs
and their older brothers and sisters that of peace, love, resignation
of predjudice of any kind. I remember only one thing about my perception of
Hippies when I was a child. by the way my generation is the children of the
older brothers and sisters we who inorder of keeping the tradition of rebellion
get Republican tattoos on our asses and dont take a damn thing seriously
do spite our filthy hippie parents. and these sad pathetic sensitive types who carry
the tragic burden of taking everything too serious and making everyone feel uncomfortable
I remember thinking all hippies were evil baby killers like Charles Manson.
I only remember a few things about Jimmy Carter, He had big lips
and liked peanuts. I know now that Jimmy Carter was and is a good man
Jimmy Carter is a good, honest, smart man.

Eric Clapton dusty Blues riffs

Hi, I played the snare drum in school band from ~~the fifth~~ grades five to nine. during this time I didnt bother learning how to ~~actually~~ read sheet music, I just waited for the geek in first chair to ~~play~~ learn ~~to play the~~ each song, ~~and~~ then I simply copied him. I ~~got~~ managed ~~By just fine~~ to do well without ever having ~~to ever learned how~~ to read music. It took me 5 years to realize ~~that~~ how rhythmically retarded I WAS AS A Drummer, so I sold some of my fathers guns ~~then~~ used the money to purchase my first six string electric guitar. ~~I took one weeks of lessons~~ I learned everything I needed to know from one week of lessons which ~~are~~ resulted in the famous musical knowledge of the louie louie chords.

E A B

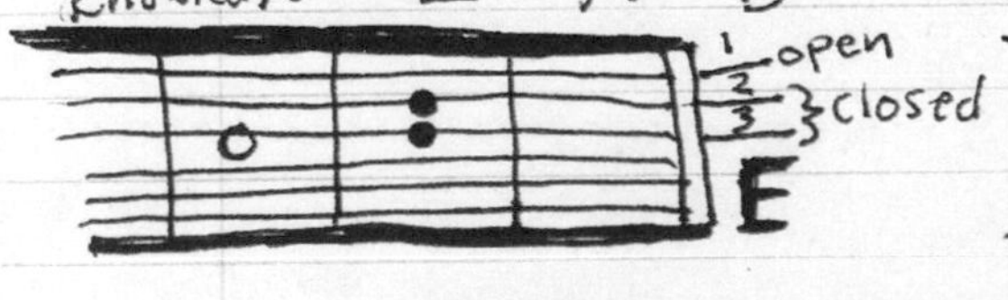

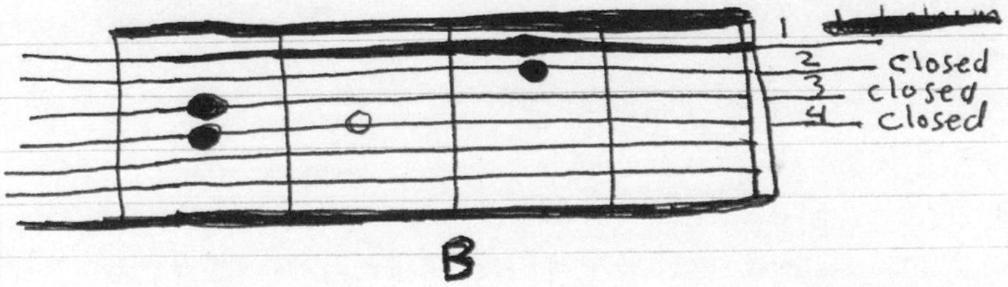

weird Al

I noticed that
~~Then I~~ I could ~~you can~~ use the finger positions from
the B note anywhere on the guitar, this is
known as the power chord.
~~Then I started writing my~~
And SO After figuring out songs like
Kingsmen louie louie, troggs wild thing, and cars. my best friends girl
I decided that in order to become A big famous
Rock star I would need to ~~start~~ write my
very OWN songs instead of wasting my
time learning other peoples because if you
study other peoples music too much It
may ACT AS AN obstruction IN developing
your very own personal ~~style~~ style
obstruct
Someone told me that there are the All Across overworld
Guitar institutes of technology ~~throughout our~~
~~Great land.~~
where they teach you how to be
A lame un-original jukebox heroe
with stars in your eyes

Uh, Gee I guess what im trying to say
is: theory is A waste of time
Dorian modes are for technically Anal Boys with BAd values
make up your own music.
ERIC Clapton plays second rate dusty blues licks.
Too much practice is like too much sugar.
weird Al Yankovic is Americas modern pop-Rock Genious
Do your own thing ~~not~~ others ~~things~~ own their own thing.
If you copy too much ~~or~~ you'll find yourself in late night
cocktail Lounge cover band limbo.
PS: the Guitar part for come AS YOU Are is the same AS A song CAlled
the "eighties" by Killing joke And
Teen spirit has an uncanny resemblance to Godzilla
by Blue Oyster cult and the cultare AC/DC

The Guitar has twelve notes
The Guitar is based on mathematics
Guitar oriented ~~[illegible]~~ Rock and Roll has been Around
for over 30 years ~~and~~ when ~~you~~ working
within the structures of A standard 4/4 Rock time signature ~~[illegible]~~ ~~structure~~ rhythm
there Are limitations So ~~[illegible]~~ consider this music
book As something just to
own like A bottle cap collection
or Baseball cards or A Family photo album
or an example of just exactly how
not to brighten your musical capabilities
Happy motoring
love. kurt

~~(Territorial pissings)~~

95747
Jaguar Serial

At the end of your Rope At the end of the rainbow

Black sheep Black mailed

Sue is sue Happy
wisdom was pulled from her teeth

the second coming came in last
And out of the closet

revolutionary debris litters the floor of Wall street

pregnant with shame

I was so High that I bloodied myself from scratching so much.

Dr Kains thats the price you have to pay for not working

KIRK CANNING cello on something in the way

Invasion of our piracy

out of the Blue
Dennis Hopper

Tracy Marander
8th st TACOMA 98405

phone Accant no.
0992 F 67025 304.16

GAS 890343

$38.83

For live show

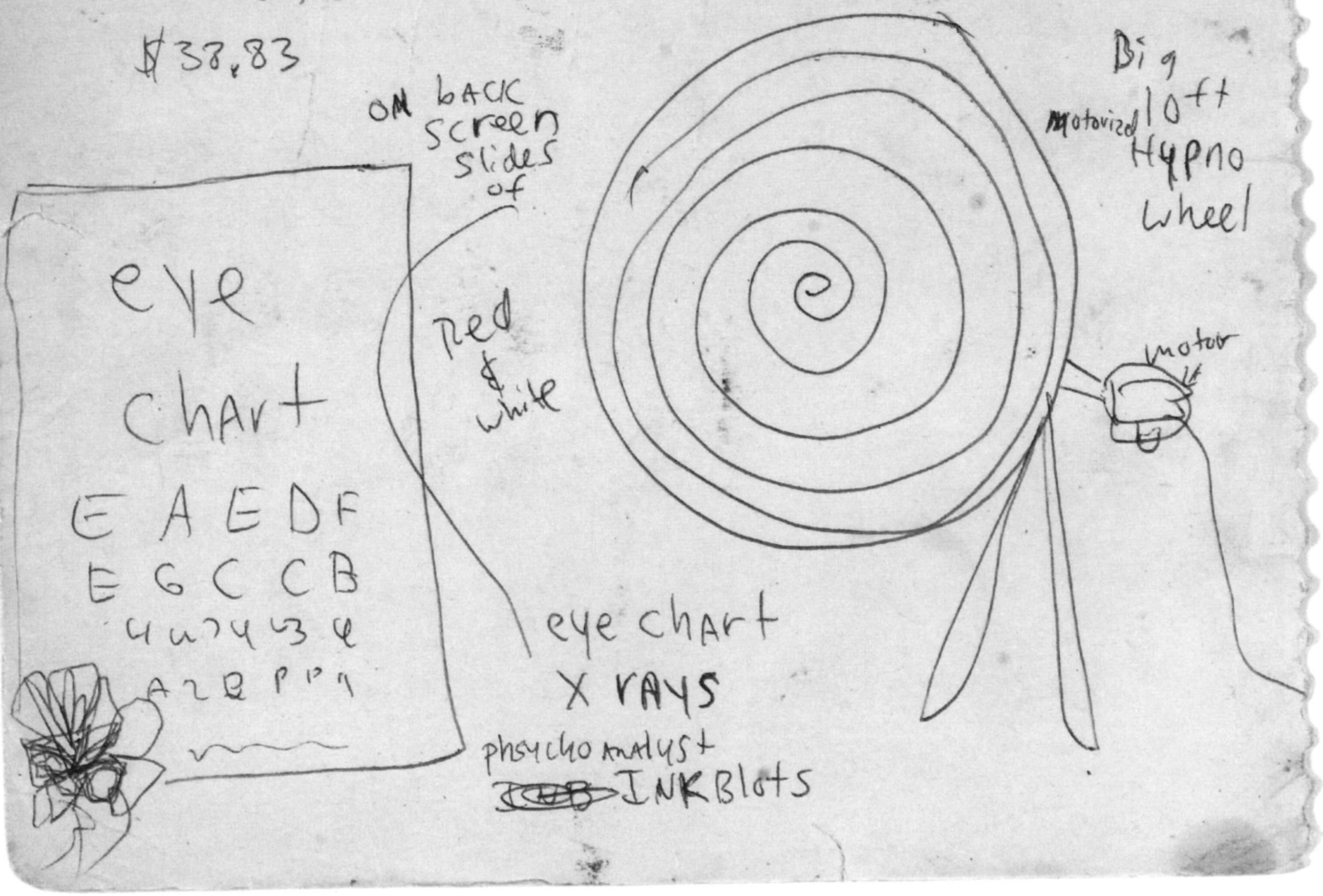

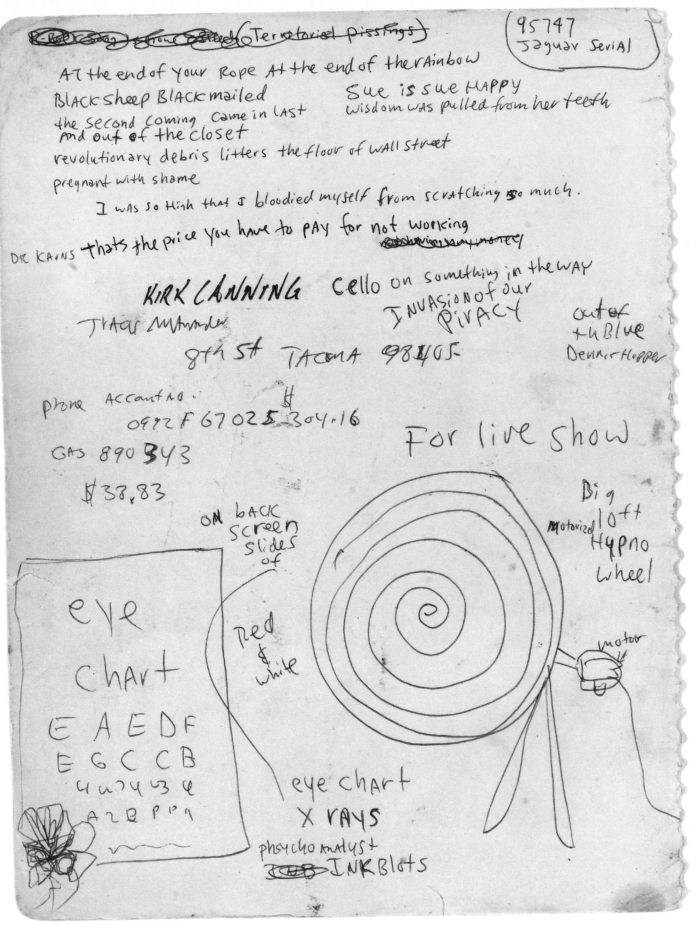

Hope I die before I turn into pete Townshend.

At this point in our uh, <u>career</u>, before hair loss treatment and bad credit. Ive decided that I have no desire to do an interview with Rolling stone. WE couldn't benefit from it because the Average Rolling Stone reader is a middle aged ex hippie - turned hippiecrite who embraces the past as "the glory days," ~~and claims to~~ and has a kinder, gentler, more adult approach towards liberal conservatism. The average Rolling Stone reader ~~is a middle aged~~ has always ~~been aware of~~ Denied the underworlds musical options ~~and have denied this~~ unless it becomes an obviously safe commodity.

I've always felt it was kind of necessary to help out the "now Generation" internally destroy the enemy by posing as or using the enemy. but the now generation doesn't read Rolling Stone, so we'll just sit around and wait until the Old school starves like dinosaurs while the diaper school begins to litter the floors of wall street with "Real love" - revolutionary debris. Smells like thirty something.

I would only wear a tie dyed T shirt if it were ~~made from~~ dyed with the urine of phil collins and the blood of Gerry Garcia.

Ideas:

Buy a really powerful Ham radio system connected to ~~A sattelite~~ dish in order to listen to any college rock station in da country. note House for sale with weeping willow has one in its attic. check into it! per Joan of Landmark realty

TOP 50 by NIRVANA

Raw power
Stooges

Surfer Rosa
pixies

PoD
Breeders

Pink EP
vaselines

Philosophy of the world
Shaggs

Land shark
Fang

millions of Dead Cops
M.D.C

1st EP
scratch acid

1st EP
saccharin Trust

Pee pee the Sailor
Butthole Surfers

my wAr
Black flag

Rock for light
Bad Brains

Entertainment
Gang of four

Nevermind the Bollocks
sex pistols

Its only Right and natural
Frogs

Dry
P.J. Harvey

Daydream Nation
Sonic Youth

Get the knack
the knack

Know your product
the Saints

anything by:
kleenex
Raincoats LP
Raincoats

Colossal youth
young marble Giants

Rocks
Aerosmith

what is this?
punk comp California

Green
R.E.M

Burning farm cassette
Shonen Knife

typical Girls
slits

Combat Rock
Clash

Void/Faith EP
Void/Faith

Rites of spring
Rites of Spring

Jamboree
Beat Happening

tales of terror
tales of terror

last sessions Vol 1
Leadbelly

Superfuzz Bigmuff
mudhoney

Yip jump music
Daniel Johnston

Generic Flipper
Flipper

meet the Beatles
Beatles

we are those who ache with amorous love
Half Japanese

Locust abortion technician
Butthole Surfers

Damaged
Black Flag

the Record
Fear

Flowers of Romance
PIL

Takes a nation of millions
Public Enemy

Beach Party
marine Girls

the man who sold the world
David Bowie

Is this real?
Wipers

Youth of America
wipers

Over the edge
wipers

mazzy star
mazzy star

Raping a slave
swans

the MAle
Seahorse
Carries the
Children
and
gives
them
Birth.

when I think of Right wing I think of Ronald Reagan Clones as mayor in every state of the US.

When I hear the term Rightwing I think of Hitler and Satan and Civil war. when I think of Right wingers I think of terrorists ~~and~~ who plot to kill and terrorize the lives of planned parenthood practionists. ~~Thee~~ reality of actually getting an abortion in this country is very scarce right now due to Randell Terry and his pro life gestapo who gather in Churches dressed in the best camouflage ~~possible~~ possible (~~middle~~ lower-middle-class cameleon polyester from the warehouses of the home shopping network. IN the house of god, Operation Rescue, (Terrys pet nonprofit organization) plot to unveil yet another helpful household hint to helping their duty as god fearing common folk. They either break into or enter during business hours posing as ~~a~~ patients at ~~an~~ abortion clinics and set off bombs which release a gas that will absorb into every inch of the clinic ruining every single instrument within that clinic. They put nails in the driveways of clinic staff and doctors. they make never ending threatening and violently abusive phone calls. ~~to clinic staff and doctors~~ They stand outside abortion clinics every day all day with pickets and loud, violent and threatening words of wisdom from GOD. to anyone within miles often ~~st~~ physically stopping patients from entering. yes these people have criminal records, they have marksman ~~skills~~ and terrorist skills. They are way ahead of the game than their enemy. They steal fetuses from abortion clinic dumpsters and disposal recepticals and pass sometimes, hundreds of ~~fetuses~~ mutilated fetuses between households to be stored in boxes or zip loc baggies in freezers and in the family garage. The ~~fetuses~~ rotting deteriorating fetuses are then thrown at senators congressmen or just about anyone involved in government who is a Democrat. These people who are terrorists are also people who have basically the same beliefs as white supremists who also claim to act and embrace their ideals on the grounds of GAWD. They post names addresses and phone numbers of patients scheduled to have abortions and the doctors to be performing the operation. They have a computer network of information available everywhere in the united states. Right wing is the foulest, dirtiest, insult a person could be called. These people hate minorities of all color, they will perform mass extermination of everything that is not white, ~~Right~~ god fearing and Right wing R is for Republican.

Right now in the state of Florida there are no available abortion doctors or clinics to be serviced by. Ethnic Cleansing is going on right now in the inner citys of the united states. Blacks, hispanicks and others are being exterminated before they can reach the fifth grade. The Right wing republicans ~~have been~~ Are responsible for releasing, crack and Aids in our inner citys. Their logic is better to kill living breathing, free thinking humans rather than unknowing unstimulated, growing cells, encased in A lukewarm chamber.

Cartoons, saxophones and jazz Drumming do not mix with rock and roll

Cermudgeon

pissy, little self appointed judge-curmudgeon

oh the Guilt!
the Guilt!
the autographs
the fame
the lights
the flash
the glitter
the Guilt
the Guilt
the Guilt

I can't sing or play or rhyme, I think that's just fine

individual T shirts

ASK
Robert
to find A
Good Photo
of A SEA-
-Horse
[redacted]
Giving
Birth
if You
cant find
a pregnant
one,
draw
them
in

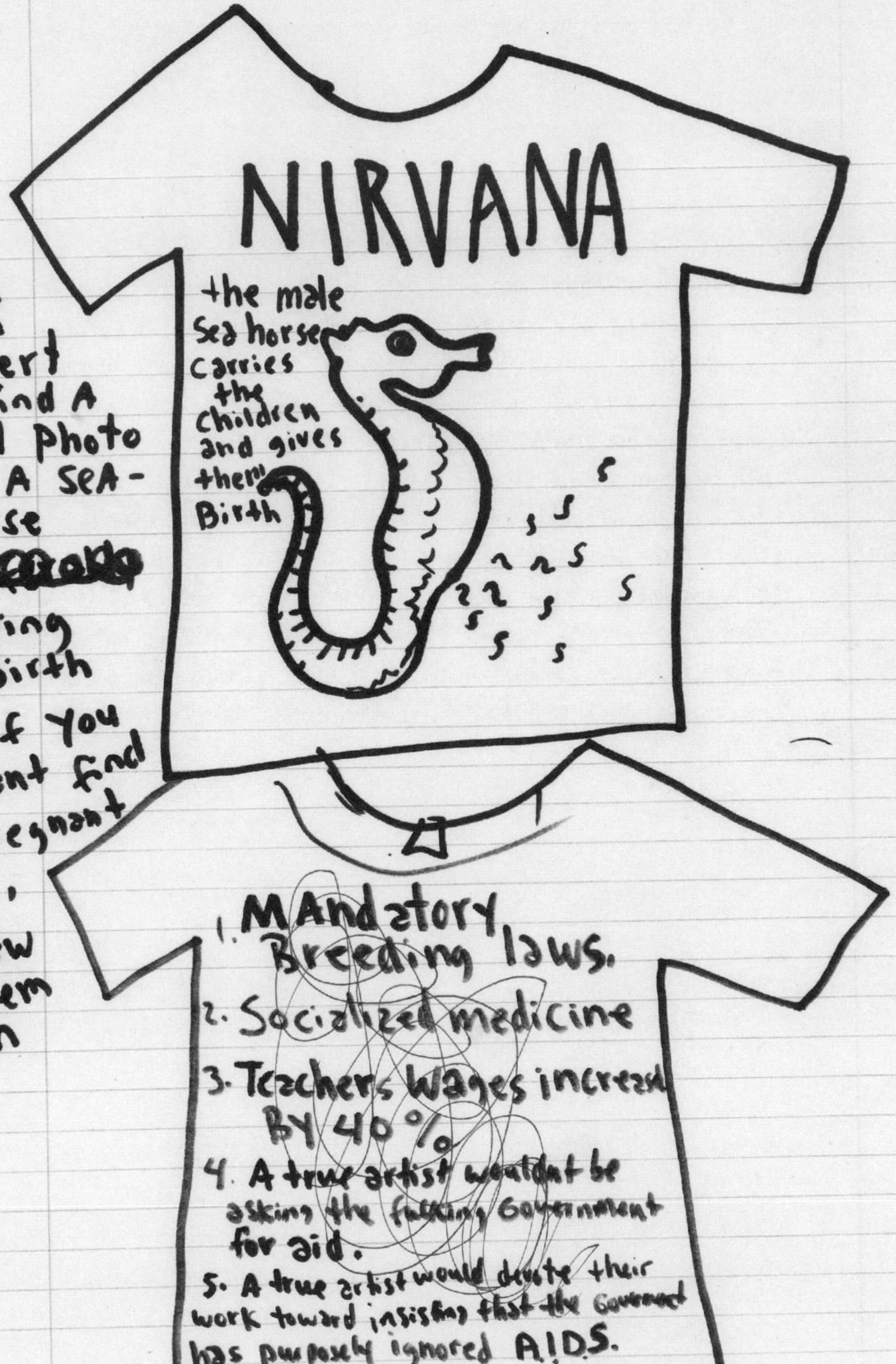

NIRVANA
the male
sea horse
carries
the
children
and gives
them
Birth
1. MAndatory
Breeding laws.
2. Socialized medicine
3. Teachers wages increased
By 40%
4. A true artist wouldnt be
asking the fucking Government
for aid.
5. A true artist would devote their
work toward insisting that the Government
has purposely ignored A.I.D.S.

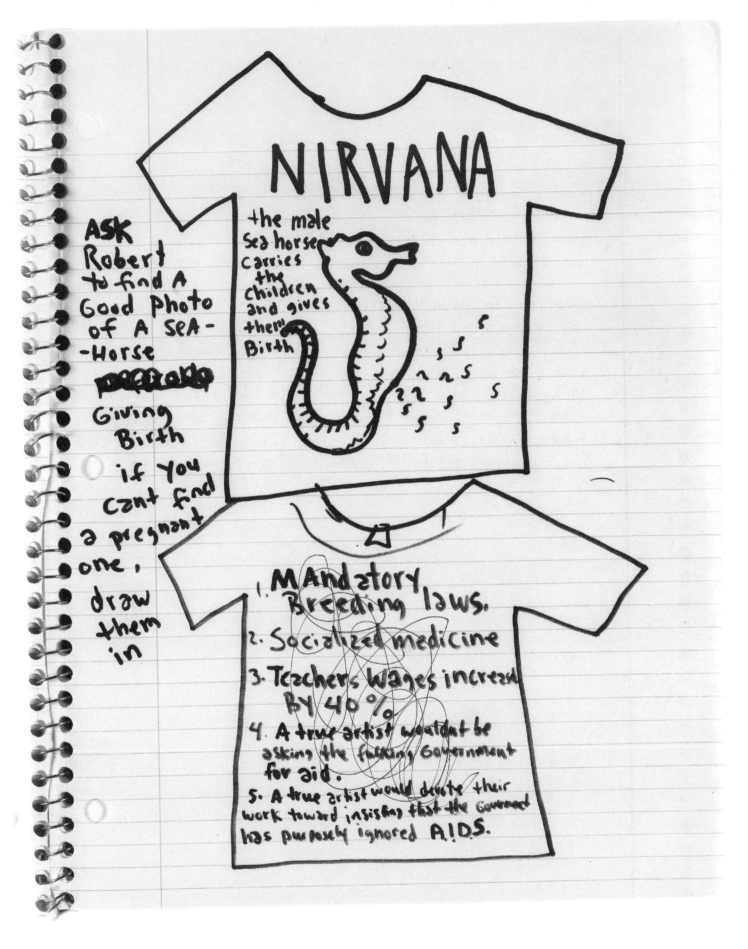

for Boys

step# one: ~~[illegible]~~

remember that your older brothers cousins, uncles, and your fathers are not your role models. this means you do not do what they do, you do not do what they say. They come from a time when their role models told their sons to be mean to girls, to think of yourself as better and stronger and smarter than them. They also taught things like; you will grow up strong if you Act tough and fight the boys who are known as nerds or Geeks, ~~[illegible]~~

~~The early 80's saw an acceptance of the counterculture~~

The early 80's saw the white-male-corporate oppressors acceptance ~~towards~~ of a new musical ~~the~~ counterculture stemmed from ~~with~~ the birth of Punk Rock. Well, the clash, the sex pistols and even the melodic accessability of the Ramones didn't break through into the mainstream.

~~Its ... years to~~
~~Its fourteen years later~~

The result of the major labels involvement ended with ex-punk bands compromising to such ~~an extent~~ extremes that the only true successes were, gasp! Billy Idol or KAJA GOO-GOO-

Its fourteen years later and theyre at it again. So called "Alternative" bands are being signed left and right and the ones with more of an edge towards compromise or mainstream are the ones who will be successful.

NIRVANA will put out a couple of more brilliant albums on their own terms and then become frustrated with being so close to general public acceptance and so ~~in debt~~ financially in debt, that they will eventually result in releasing spineless dance music like Gang of four.

Rape me
treatment

Black & white film

Hi steve

IN the simplest terms, here it is: . . .

Go to one or more penitentiarys and shoot [redacted] movie film portraits of the most ugly, hardened criminals available. preferrably bald, big, hairy and tatooed. film at least 20 or more of these fine young bucks sitting in their cells and at the visiting booths and tables. from the skinny chest up. we need at least 5 to 10 male Bitches with thick eyeshadow [redacted] and their denim jail shirts sleeves rolled up to [redacted] the bottom half of their shirt tied up exposing thir stomachs

during the lines "my favorite inside source ill kiss your open sores appreciate your concern you gonna stink and burn" we need footage of a chaotic press scene with lots of reporters with movie cameras and photo flashes [redacted] outside on the steps of a court house. then a inside the courtroom a [redacted]

Rape me treatment Kurdt

Black and White Portrait-footage of the men who did the crime and are now doing time. Big, Bald, sweaty, tattooed love boys cast from the waist up in their cold, concrete tanks. lounging on their bunks. striped and branded with the shadows of prison bars across their chest, face and walls. We need about ten to fifteen different characters. all 200lbs plus and also about 5 to 8 more of whom we call the bitches: skinny, feminine, tight pants wearin, rolled up prison shirts showing their soft, vulnerable ~~frames~~. stomaches. 150lbs and less.

There are many "Behind prison Walls," books for refference. whites, blacks, Italians.

Close ups of female hands lathering up soap. violent-scrubbing hands. soapy wash cloth. begging to be clean. starting in Black & white fading to color as the hands get cleaner. Close ups of:

Stock footage of flowers blooming in time lapsed motion. } **Color** Prefferably lillies, orchids. ya know vaginal flowers. and now they wither and shrink up.

Sea horses footage carousing about. floating slowly. loving life and one another. } color michael Meisel has found some of this footage already.

A man lying in a gynecological chair with legs up in sturrops.

Pierre Cardin

Hi fellow Advocatees,

1993 Came and went without notice.

Besides finishing a record in which we are quite proud of, yet getting shit from people claiming "commercial suicide" before it's release. I must say yes, 1993 has been a most fruitful year. Frances is a sprouting, cherubic joy and has helped in more ways than she will ever know.

She has helped us become more relaxed and less concerned with those wacky Right wing ~~conservative~~ terrorists failed attempts at

Scott

I

I made about 5 million dollars last year.
and I'm not giving a red cent to that elitist
little fuck Calvin Johnson. NO WAY!
I've collaborated with one of my only Idols William S
Burroughs and I couldn't feel cooler.
I moved away to L.A for a year and came back
to find that 3 of my best friends have become
full blown heroine addicts. I've learned to hate
Riot Girl. a movement in which I was a witness
to its very initial inception because I fucked the
girl who put out the first Grrl style fanzine and
now she is exploiting the fact that she fucked
me. not in a huge way but enough to feel
exploited. but thats ok because I chose to
let corporate white men exploit me a few years
ago and I love it. it feels good. and I'm
not gonna donate a single dollar to the fucking
needy indie fascist regime. they can starve.
let them eat vinyl. every crumb for himself.
I'll be able to sell my untalented, very un-genius
ass for years based on my cult status.

1993 came and went without realizing it. ~~had happened~~

Besides recording a record in which we are quite proud of
and getting shit for it from people who havent heard it
I must say, yes it was a fruitful year. frances is a sprouting
cherubic joy and has helped in more ways than she'll ever know by
helping us become more relaxed and less concerned with the foiled
attempts by the right wing conspiriators and terrorists to cut off our
rightful supply of fame fortune and the american way God bless this
mess and thank god for the right to chose USA today and
uh, kill a queer for God bumper stickers. (thanks william, for the
last remark.) yeah I got to meet and do a record with one of the
only people I admire. that was a plus. and equally so was
the pleasure of doing the Advocate interview. of all the gut spilling
Ive done Ive never felt so relaxed than with ______
He was very encouraging and sympathetic. what can I say?
thank you Ill always be an Advocate for you fags. I love you.
and appreciate the gracious compliments.
Hey you should interview Bruce la Bruce from Canada he's made
some fantastic films. Hope noone felt Ive been too patronizing
Love kurdt. stay Gay all the way and ~~the others~~ wipe your Ass with USA today.

Kevin Allman

Scott

In movies the filmmaker tries to depict true life instances. the most interesting occurances during the subjects time frame are picked out of a span of time. Time is much longer than a movie can show and a viewer will have the patience for. therefore we don't realize how time plays such a gigantic part in the leading up to events. two people may have dinner for 2 hours but only 30 seconds of the most interesting parts of the conversation will be used. I feel time and a persons ability to understand time is very important its the only way I can relate to you the very real way a person becomes addicted to substances If we realize and remember things happen over a period of time. then we may understand how ~~we become a drug addict~~ almost everyone who tries hard drugs ie: heroine and cocaine will eventually become literally, a slave to these substances.

I remember someone saying If you try heroine once you'll become hooked. of course I laughed and scoffed at the idea but I now believe this to be very true. not literally. I mean If you do dope once you don't instantly become addicted it usually takes about one month of every day use to physically become addicted. but after the first time your mind say ahh that was very pleasant as long as I don't do it every day I won't have a problem. the problem is it happens over time. lets start with January 1st lets do dope for the first time. concisusly you wont do it again for maybe a month. february you'll do it twice. march 3 days in a row. february. 3 days in a row and once more at the end of the month. march. maybe not at all. april 5 days in a row skip 3 once more. may 10 days in a row. during those ten days its very easy to lose track of time it may seem like 3 days but two weeks can go by. The effects are still as pleasant and you can still chouse

what days you do it so naturally there must not be a problem.
with everyone sometime at least once a year some sort of crisis
happens to everyone, the loss of a friend or mate or relative
this is when the drug tells you to say fuck it.
every drug addict has said fuck it more times than they
can count. This example has only taken one page but
within a year of casual heroine use the person has had
more days off dope than on. It can slowly and
gradually consume you because there are 24 hrs in a day
and no one wants to be hooked. It doesn't happen as
fast as it does in a movie because a movie quickly
has to show all the juicy stuff within 2 hrs.
2 hrs out of 2 years worth of casual drug use is
nothing. by the time youve said fuck it the
long process of trying to stay off begins.
The first kick is usually easy if you have pills.
you basically sleep. which is bad in my opinion
because you think if its that easy I could get
hooked and kick for the rest of my life.
by the second and third time it becomes
very different. It takes sometimes 5 times
longer. the psychological factors have set in
and are as damaging as the physical effects.
every time you kick as time goes by it gets
more uncomfortable. even the most needle phobic person can
crave the relief of putting a syringe in their arm. people have
been known to shoot water, booze, mouthwash etc...
drug use is escapism whether you want to admit it or not.
a person may have spent months, years trying to get help.. but
the amount of time one spends trying to get help and the years it
takes to become completely drug free is nothing in comparison.
every junkie ive ever met has fought with it at least 5 years and
most end up fighting for about 15 25 years, until finally
they have to resort to becoming a slave to another drug the 12 step
program which is in itself another drug / religion. If it works for
you do it. If your ego is too big start at square one and
go the psychological rehabilitative way. either way youve got
at least 5 to 10 years of battle ahead of you.

HOTEL EXCELSIOR
Roma

He said, yes Larry as in Larry King
when we were shooting the film we
found the indigenous people of ALASKA
to be some of the most warm friendly,
blah blah blah etc. Anotter retarded
action Adventure side of beef longing to
portray himself as a distinguished actor.
His P.R man transcribed a basic English
101 course on A piece of paper and
Jean Clod Goddammne actor
man must have studied the Answers
to the hallowing questions that Larry
will be asking for at least a week.
Now thats Entertainment: watching
Sylvester Stallone fumble his way through
An interview with that yo duh

Fred Flintstone accent while spewing out
sentences that maybe uh A really smart
guy might say ya know with a lot of
~~as~~ as well as 'pertaining to. etc. blah.
The indigenous people of ALASKA?
what are you fucking talking about?
the ESKIMOS? or the drunken
Redneck settlers who never see sunshine
who are up to their ball sacks with
raw dead fish guts on A boat
for 9 months out of the year.

NOTES

A note about the letters: Kurt often wrote a draft before completing the final version of a letter. Some of the letters included in this book represent those drafts, while others are letters that were never sent.

Page 1:
Letter to Dale Crover, the drummer for the Melvins, an Aberdeen rock band that heavily influenced early Nirvana.

Page 15:
Letter to Dave Foster, Nirvana's second drummer, who was fired shortly before the recording sessions for "Love Buzz."

Page 19:
Letter to Mark Lanegan, lead singer of the Seattle band Screaming Trees.

Page 32:
Letter to Jesse Reed, Kurt's best friend from high school.

Page 39:
NIRVANA
Kenichewa
Dear ____________________.
NIRVANA is a three piece from the outskirts of Seattle WA.
Kurdt-Guitar/Voice and Chris-bass have struggled with too many undedicated drummers for the past 3 years, performing under such names as: Bliss, throat Oyster, Pen Cap Ch[ew] Ted ed Fred etc . . . for the last 9 months we have had the pleasure to take Chad-drums under our wings and develop what we are now and always will be NIRVANA.
3 regularly broadcasted carts on K.C.M.U. (Seattle College Radio also KAOS Olympia)
Played with: Leaving Trains, Whipping Boy, Hells Kitchen, Trecherous Jaywalkers & countless local acts.
Looking for: EP or LP We have about 15 songs Recorded on 8 Tracks at Reciprocal Studios in Seattle.
Willing to compromise on material (some of this shit is pretty old.) Tour Any-time forever hopefully the music will speak for itself
Please Reply Thank You Area Code (206) N PEAR Olympia WA. 98506

Page 64:
Kurt's questions for a fanzine interview with the Melvins.

Page 102:
Letter to Eugene Kelly from the Vaselines, a Scottish band that was one of Kurt's favorites. Kelly later became a member of Captain America and Eugenius.

Page 144:
A list of possible producers for "Nevermind."

Pages 166-169:
Draft of record company bio of the band for "Nevermind." This bio was never used.

Page 170:
List of elements needed for "Smells Like Teen Spirit" video.

Pages 177-182:
Letter to Tobi Vail, drummer for the Olympia band Bikini Kill, written a few days after the completion of the "Nevermind" recording sessions in spring 1991.

Page 187:
Concept for "Come as You Are" video.

Pages 225-226:
Letter to Donald Cobain, Kurt's father.

Page 227:
Fax from recording engineer Steve Albini on which Kurt made notes about the recording gear to be used for "In Utero."

Page 228:
Notes for the recording of "In Utero."

Pages 231-232:
Letter to Simon Timony of the Stinky Puffs.

Page 240:
Proposed marketing plan for "In Utero."

Page 243:
Concept for "Heart-Shaped Box" video.

Page 252:
I have been forced to become a reclusive Rock Star
IE: No interviews, no radio appearances, etc. due to the legions of self appointed authorities on music who are not musicians, who have not contributed anything artistic to Rock and Roll besides maybe a few second rate long winded, books on Rock and Roll and most importantly who are the highest group of mysogynists in all forms of expression.
I have since the beginning of my first revelation in alternative thought through the introduction of New Wave—then, Punk rock, then alternative soundtracks of Contemporary Classic Rock. Never in years of my awareness of sexism have I seen a more radically venomous display of sexism in my life than in the past two years. for years I've observed and waited like a vulture for any hint of sexism and I've found it in relatively small doses compared to the present state of Rock and Roll, from critics darlings to Samantha fox simply because one of the mem-

bers of what used to be thought of as a band with members Has married an established, musical, success determined by the establishment of non musical music writers. Something smells fishy!

Page 253:
by this time, All conspiracy theories are very very real. With more proof than needed to be bothered with describing. Beaurocracy exists as cancer in the simplest, most naive, grass roots business of pencil vendors, panhandling, fanzine distribution, home baked, hippie cookie sales agents up through the yawn; medical profession, Government related protection agencies, Janitorial positions, and erm, entertainment industries. Journalists will now break their own fingers after engaging in each individuals display of fingerprints on their left breast in the form of a button and they will bow down to let the artists critique themselves and other artists. This is a fanzine written by music fans. We know this to be true because they are musicians. Can they write as well as they play? better. What about Genres. A heavy metal musician cannot review, a dance RnB soul group. It's that easy.
Elitism = Punk Rock
Capitalism =

Page 254:
If you were a music fan than you would contribute to a fanzine.
You have no right to ask the question: do you have artistic control now that you've signed to a major. for all Journalists are at the mercy of their editors.
Second rate 3rd degree burns

Page 255:
If we ever win any more awards we will have 3 impersonators come up and accept the award 3 people who look fairly familiar to us.
Video Concept. Milk it or scentless apprentice drunken fucked up me, man in a room full of people at a party man has gun and is stumbling around falling down threatening to shoot.
man has wild glossy stare.
play unplugged soon.
release a compilation tape of favorite punk songs with vinyl version of album

Page 256:
❤ Shaped box video
William and I sitting across from one another at a table (Black and White) lots of Blinding Sun from the windows behind us holding hands staring into each others eyes. He gropes me from behind and falls dead on top of me. medical footage of sperm flowing through penis. A ghost vapor comes out of his chest and groin area and enters me Body.
during solo. Violin shots. Chris as New Wave keyboardist and very quick edits of strobe light.
image of little 3 year old white, arian, blonde girl in KKK outfit being led by the hand of a KKK parent
Same violet colors as in the New order video
Animation Doll footage. Close up of lillies lying on lighted draft Board. footage of Anatomy models from Kurts collection

Pages 278-279:
Concepts for "Rape Me" video that was never made.

Page 283-284:
Hotel Villa Magna
Madrid
In movies the filmmaker tries to depict true life instances, the most interesting occurances during the subjects time frame are picked out of a span of time. Time is much longer than a movie can show and a viewer will have

the patience for. therefore we don't realize how time plays such a gigantic part in the leading up to events. two people may have dinner for 2 hours but only 30 seconds of the most interesting parts of the conversation will be used. I feel time and a persons ability to understand time is very important. its the only way I can relate to you the very real way a person becomes addicted to substances If we realize and remember things happen over a period of time, then we may understand how almost everyone who tries hard drugs ie: heroine and cocaine will eventually become literally, a slave to these substances.
I remember someone saying if you try heroine once you'll become hooked. Of course I laughed and scoffed at the idea but I now believe this to be very true. Not literally, I mean if you do dope once you don't instantly become addicted it usually takes about one month of every day use to physically become addicted. but after the first time your mind say ahh that was very pleasant as long as I don't do it every day I won't have a problem. the problem is it happens over time. lets start with January 1st lets do dope for the first time. Conciously you won't do it again for maybe a month. febuary youll do it twice. march 3 days in a row. february, 3 days in a row and once more at the end of the month. march, maybe not at all. april 5 days in a row Skip 3 once more. May 10 days in a row. during those ten days it's very easy to lose track of time it may seem like 3 days but two weeks can go by. The effects are still as pleasant and you can still choose what days you do it so naturally there must not be a problem. with everyone some time at least once a year some sort of crisis happens to everyone, the loss of a friend or mate or relative this is when the drug tells you to say fuck it. every drug addict has said fuck it more times than they can count. This example has only taken one page but within a year of casual heroine use the person has had more days off dope than on. It can slowly and gradually consume you because there are 24 hrs in a day and no one wants to be hooked. It doesn't happen as fast as it does in a movie because a movie quickly has to show all the juicy stuff within 2 hrs. 2 hrs out of a years worth of casual drug use is nothing. by the time you've said fuck it the long process of trying to stay off begins. The first kick is usually easy if you have pills. You basically sleep. which is bad in my opinion because you think if its that easy I could get hooked and kick for the rest of my life. by the second and third time it becomes very different. It takes sometimes 5 times longer. the psychological factors have set in and are as damaging as the physical effects. every time you kick as time goes by it gets more uncomfortable. even the most needle phobic person can crave the relief of putting a syringe in their arm. people have been known to shoot water, booze, mouthwash etc . . . drug use is escapism whether you want to admit it or not. a person may have spent months, years trying to get help, but the amount of time one spends trying to get help and the years it takes to become completely drug free is nothing in comparison. every junkie i've ever met has fought with it at least 5 years and most end up fighting for about 15 25 years, until finally they have to resort to becoming a slave to another drug the 12 step program which is in itself another drug/religion. If it works for you do it. If your ego is too big start at square one and go the psychological rehabilitative way. either way you've got at least 5 to 10 years of battle ahead of you.

Page 285-286:
Hotel Excelsior
Roma
He said, yes Larry as in Larry King when we were shooting the film we found the indigenous people of Alaska to be some of the most warm friendly, blah blah blah etc. Another retarded action adventure side of beef longing to portray himself as a distinguished actor. His P.R. man transcribed a basic English 101 course on a piece of paper and Jean Clod goddammne actor man must have studied the Answers to the hallowing questions that Larry will be asking for at least a week. Now thats Entertainment: watching Sylvester Stallone fumble his way through an interview with that yo duh Fred Flintstone accent while spewing out sentences that may be uh a really smart guy might say ya know with a lot of as well as, pertaining to, etc. blah. The indigenous people of Alaska? What are you fucking talking about? the Eskimos? or the drunken Redneck settlers who never see sunshine who are up to their ball sacks with raw dead fish guts on a boat for 9 months out of the year.

Grateful acknowledgment is made to EMI and The End of Music, LLC for the right to reprint lyrics from the following songs: